Innovation and Entrepreneurship in Japan

Japan's innovators and entrepreneurs are a real success story against the odds, surviving recession in the 1990s to prosper in today's competitive business environment. *Innovation and Entrepreneurship in Japan* explores the struggles of entrepreneurs and civic-minded local leaders in fostering innovative activity, and identifies key business lessons for an economy in need of dynamic change.

Ibata-Arens offers an in-depth analysis of strategy in firms, communities, and in local government. *Innovation and Entrepreneurship in Japan* examines detailed case studies of high technology manufacturers in Kyoto, Osaka, and Tokyo, as well as bio-tech clusters in America – demonstrating far-reaching innovation and competition effects in national institutions, and firms embedded within local and regional institutions.

The book is essential reading for academics and students of business, economics, political economy, political science, and sociology. It will also appeal to investors, entrepreneurs, and community development organizations seeking new perspectives on global competition and entrepreneurship in high technology enterprises.

KATHRYN IBATA-ARENS is Assistant Professor in the Department of Political Science, DePaul University, and Abe Fellow in the Faculty of Commerce, Doshisha University.

Innovation and Entrepreneurship in Japan

Politics, Organizations, and High Technology Firms

KATHRYN IBATA-ARENS

CAMBRIDGE UNIVERSITY PRESS
Cambridge, New York, Melbourne, Madrid, Cape Town, Singapore,
São Paulo, Delhi, Dubai, Tokyo

Cambridge University Press
The Edinburgh Building, Cambridge CB2 8RU, UK

Published in the United States of America by Cambridge University Press, New York

www.cambridge.org
Information on this title: www.cambridge.org/9780521125390

First published 2005
This digitally printed version 2009

A catalogue record for this publication is available from the British Library

ISBN 978-0-521-85644-7 Hardback
ISBN 978-0-521-12539-0 Paperback

To Thomas Takishi Ibata and Agnes Kazuko Ibata

Contents

Figures

Tables

Acknowledgments

I thank the entrepreneurs of this book who took the time to be interviewed a number of times over the course of the years 1997–2004. Without their forthright and telling stories, this book would not have been possible. Any errors in interpretation remain my own.

Ben Ross Schneider guided me throughout this endeavor as dissertation chair, advisor, and mentor with his expertise and patient critiquing, greatly aiding my intellectual development. Bernard Silberman offered a depth of knowledge and insight about Japan and prepared me for my fieldwork while I was a visiting CIC scholar at the University of Chicago from 1995 to 1996. Peter Swenson pushed me to refine my arguments and make this research relevant in comparative terms.

I am indebted to Chalmers Johnson, who inspired me with his erudite feedback and encouragement. T. J. Pempel helped me in Japan in making the transition from neophyte to researcher. John Campbell offered me practical advice through the SSRC Japan Dissertation Workshop and afterwards. Ron Morse provided extensive feedback on my penultimate draft. Ron Dore kindly commented on my work at the Northwestern-Princeton Junior Scholars' Workshop on the Embedded Enterprise (2002) and has since been a frequent inspiration in the way he has passionately engaged me in a "critical dialectic" regarding our observations of Japan's economy and society.

I am grateful for the generous financial support provided by a Fulbright Dissertation Fellowship, allowing me to complete the initial fieldwork in 1997 and 1998. A JSPS post-doctoral fellowship in 2002 allowed me to update the research. Earlier financial support from a Hosei University Foreign Fellowship and the Stanford University Inter-University Center (IUC) helped me to prepare my survey and begin the research in Japan in 1996 and 1997. At the IUC, Kikuko Tatematsu was a major force in this regard, in innumerable ways.

This book would not have been possible without the assistance of many people during the course of my stay in Japan. Professor

Fumio Kodama and members of his research lab provided provocative feedback during my residence at the Research Center for Advanced Science and Technology, Tokyo University. Yasunori Baba kindly took me under his supervision upon my return to "Sentanken" in 2002. Seiritsu Ogura, Department of Economics, Hosei University, offered his feedback and inspiration at all stages of this research. Masatsugu Tsuji, Osaka School of International Public Policy, Osaka University, provided me with a much-needed affiliation and office space, greatly facilitating my access to the Kansai region. Kenichi Imai provided helpful criticisms while I was formulating my arguments. Hugh Whittaker inspired me to write more interesting entrepreneurial narratives. A number of other scholars offered critical insights at various stages, including Toshio Aida, Tomohiro Koseki, Hiromichi Obayashi, Shoro Okudaira, Yoshiaki Taniguchi, Koji Wada, and Minoru Yoshii. My research assistant Victor Lang helped tremendously in putting this book together. Lively discussions with my husband, Cris Arens, founder owner-manager of a vibrant small firm, have helped me make this book a bit more pithy and readable for entrepreneurs like him. He also assisted by dealing with all of the "heavy lifting" involving "the kids, the dog, and the house" greatly enabling me to focus. Maximillian and Elizabeth could be counted on to keep everything in its proper perspective along the way. Earlier versions and/or excerpts in chapters 3, 4, and 5 have appeared in *Review of International Political Economy*, *Japan Policy Research Institute Working Paper Series*, and *Asian Business and Management*.

Kathryn Ibata-Arens
Chicago 2004

Abbreviations

APEC	Asia-Pacific Economic Cooperation
ATI	Arizona Technology Incubator
BTI	Boulder Technology Incubator
CAD	Computer-aided design
CAM	Computer-aided manufacture
CEO	Chief executive officer
CET	Center for Emerging Technologies (St. Louis, MO)
DI	Diffusion index
DOD	Department of Defense
DRAM	Dynamic radom-access memory
DYK	Doyukai (SME)
EC	European Commission
EPO	European Patent Office
FDA	Food and Drug Administration
FDI	Foreign direct investment
FRAM	Ferroelectric random-access memory
HR	Human relations
IC	Integrated circuit
IPO	Initial product offering
IPR	Intellectual property rights
IRC	Industrial Revitalization Corporation (Japan)
IRL	Industrial Revitalization Law (Japan)
IT	Information technology
JETRO	Japan External Trade Organization
JIT	Just-in-time
JV	Joint venture
LDP	Liberal Democratic Party (Japan)
LED	Light-emitting diode
MD	McDonnell Douglas

METI	Ministry of Economy, Trade, and Industry (Japan, formerly MITI)
MEXT	Ministry of Education, Science, Culture, Sports, and Technology (Japan)
MITI	Ministry of International Trade and Industry (Japan)
MOF	Ministry of Finance (Japan)
MOST	Ministry of Science and Technology (China)
MOT	Management of Technology
MRI	Mitsubishi Research Institute
NIH	National Institute of Health
NIS	National innovation systems
OEM	Original equipment manufacturing
OSBIC	Osaka Small and Medium Sized Enterprise Information Center
PRDEZ	Pearl River Delta Economic Zone (China)
QC	Quality control
R&D	Research and development
RCGA	Regional Commerce and Growth Association (St. Louis, MO)
RFP	Request for proposals
RIS	Regional innovation systems
ROI	Return on investment
SEZ	Special Economic Zone (China)
SME	Small to medium-sized enterprise
TLO	Technology licensing organization
TPP	Technological product and process innovation
USTR	US Trade Representative
VC	Venture capital
VLSI	Very large-scale integrated circuits
WIPO	World Intellectual Property Organization

1 Introduction

1.1 Introduction

JAPAN is often described as a society of loyal company men and bureaucrats in blue suits, working for a single organization for a lifetime. In this picture of the Japanese system, incremental innovations are rewarded with incremental seniority-based wages eked out over decades of service.[1] This is indeed the story for about 1% of the biggest firms and about 25% of its workforce – at least until the economic collapse of the 1990s.

Japan is also chock full of stories of entrepreneurial struggles. These struggles are not limited to market competition. In fact, the fiercest battles are often waged against the institutional hierarchies of the Japanese national system of production and innovation. The entrepreneurial mavericks at the helm of small and medium-sized enterprises (SMEs) that populate the base of the Japanese production pyramid are the narrators of this struggle.[2] This book explores the way the Japanese system is experienced by those entrepreneurs and workers comprising the 99% of firms and 75% of its working people – a critical source of new business and employment.

Until now, the story about high technology industry Japan has been told from the perspective of the top of the production pyramid (see figures 1.1 and 1.2). That is, most research about the Japanese political economy is conducted in and around the corporate headquarters of Japanese conglomerates (keiretsu groups). These headquarters are in turn situated often a stone's throw from powerful key Japanese ministries in Tokyo charged with industrial policy: the Ministry of Finance (MOF) and the Ministry of Economy, Trade, and Industry (METI). In these circles company men interact with like-minded bureaucrats. At the same time, the foundation of the Japanese economy abounds with the stories of entrepreneurial mavericks.

This book explores the entrepreneurial stories at the base of the pyramid – of those enterprises that are the foundation of the Japanese

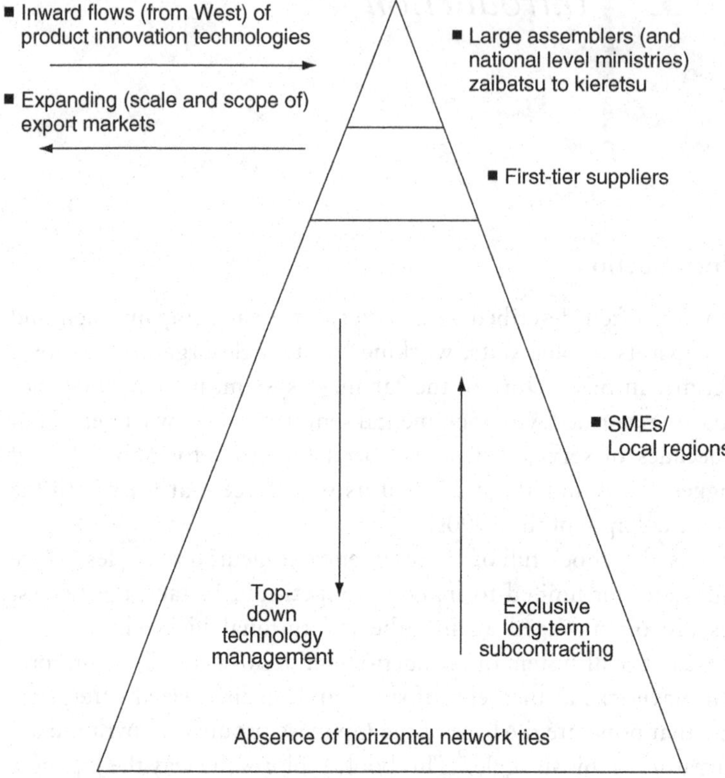

Figure 1.1. Rise of Japan as a model economy, 1946–1970s

political economy – and how these firms have struggled to survive and prosper, particularly since the collapse of the "bubble economy" in the early 1990s. This focus can shed light not only on the sources of the collapse of the Japanese system – but also on the sources of innovation and opportunity that persist.[3] The stories of Samco and Ikeda offer several insights.

1.2 Two stories: Samco and Ikeda

Samco in Kyoto

In the early 1970s Osamu Tsuji, a young Japanese chemist, worked at Kyoto University as a plasma chemistry researcher. He considered

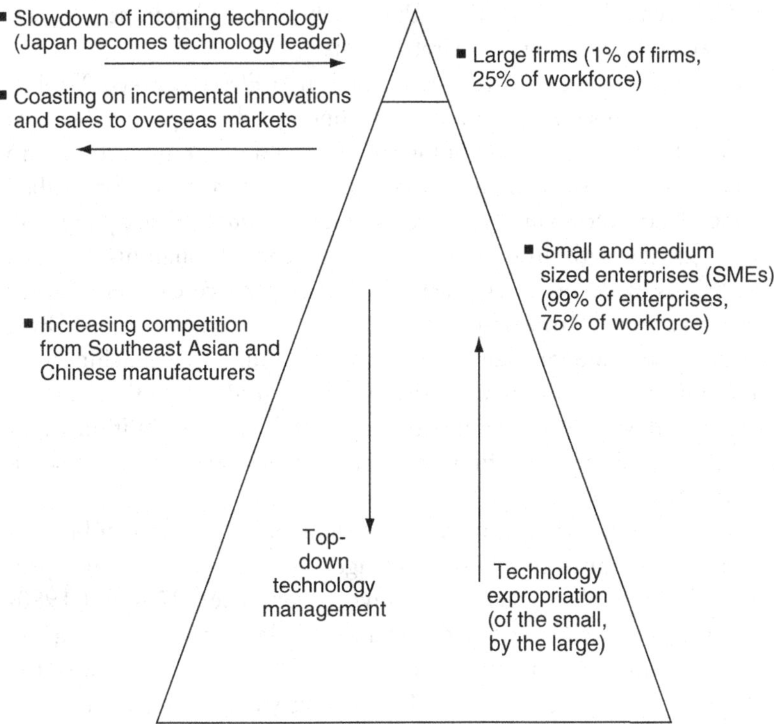
■ Slowdown of incoming technology (Japan becomes technology leader)
■ Coasting on incremental innovations and sales to overseas markets
■ Large firms (1% of firms, 25% of workforce)
■ Small and medium sized enterprises (SMEs) (99% of enterprises, 75% of workforce)
■ Increasing competition from Southeast Asian and Chinese manufacturers
Top-down technology management
Technology expropriation (of the small, by the large)

Figure 1.2. Japan's model matures, 1980s

pursuing his doctorate at Kyoto University for a while, but after a few years became bored with the stuffy "ivory tower" atmosphere and left.

By leaving this prestigious national university Tsuji eschewed the accepted career path of the best and brightest scientists and engineers in Japan. The "best and brightest" generally obtain graduate degrees from national universities and go on to work for a lifetime in a single keiretsu conglomerate. Tsuji chose the path less traveled by his Japanese compatriots. Instead, in 1976 Tsuji began work in the United States for NASA and was soon asked to join its Ames Research Center in Silicon Valley.

In 1978, a homesick Tsuji returned to Kyoto. At first, he could not find work. Hiring managers at big Japanese firms were cautious about taking on such an unproven commodity – in other words, Tsuji lacked the pedigree of a graduate degree from a prestigious Japanese national university. Fortunately, Tsuji had kept in touch with a number of graduate school buddies – those that stuck with the Japanese program and were now working for keiretsu firms.

A friend of Tsuji's – a researcher at Sanyo Electric, asked Tsuji to help him with his ideas for thin-film technology development. The two decided that this new technology could be a great opportunity to branch out on their own. Soon they started a firm they called "Samco" (an acronym for "semiconductor materials company") in Tsuji's garage with little by way of equipment. Through his personal friendships with other engineering and science researchers Samco forged strong relationships with several universities (in Tokyo, Kyoto, and Nagoya). Samco was able to utilize the machinery at these universities and obtain assistance from students so that initially little capital was needed get his company off the ground. Within a year they had developed thin film application machinery for use in semiconductor production.

Tsuji had hoped that Sanyo would be Samco's first customer but was disappointed. Sanyo purchasing managers were wary of buying a product from a vendor outside the Sanyo group. The 1970s and 1980s were the heyday of so-called "exclusive relational contracting" in Japan. In this system, buying from unaffiliated suppliers was too risky for purchasing managers. If anything went wrong with a purchase, blame would be leveled squarely on the purchasing manager's shoulders (rather than spread between the in-group buyer and suppliers).

Tsuji decided that he had to look outside Japan for customers. In 1980 he left Japan on a $300 air ticket to Los Angeles and came back a few weeks later with a purchase order and a down payment of 50% in his pocket from Arco (a US petrochemical producer). Tsuji was elated. Samco was soon selling products to US firms such as IBM and National Semiconductor. Samco was finally able, years later, to sell to Japanese firms. These firms, however, rarely pay on time. Instead large Japanese firms "pay" with promissory notes (*tegata*), effectively putting off cash payment for 60–120 days *after* delivery. Cash flow problems caused by chronic late payments from Japanese buyers as well as his early experience with their conservative purchasing managers have put Tsuji off the idea of ever becoming an exclusive subcontractor to Japanese conglomerates.

By 2003, twenty-four years after its foundation, Samco under Tsuji's stewardship had grown into an internationally renowned thin-film technology producer with its own research institutes in Silicon Valley, Cambridge UK, and Japan. A recent joint venture (JV) formalized in 2003 with Kirin Beer to provide protective coating for the inside of plastic bottles was forecast to surpass the core business in terms of revenue by 2006.[4]

Ikeda in Tokyo

Koichi Ikeda's experiences provide another insight into Japan's struggling entrepreneurs. Ikeda was a talented young engineer in the late 1960s. After graduating from a national university he decided to try his luck at starting a firm that would apply protective thin films to machinery components. He started Ikeda Manufacturing in 1969 in Ota Ward in South Eastern Tokyo and soon found himself an exclusive contractor for the NEC group. Exclusive subcontracting ("relational subcontracting") subjected Ikeda to two downsides of the Japanese production system: cash flow problems (caused by chronic late payments by buyers) and monopsony exploitation (for example, "cost down" of supplier prices (see below) and so called just-in-time (JIT) production deadlines).[5]

Things went well for a number of years, though Ikeda often had cash flow problems because of slow payment from his top two buyers. Nevertheless, he was able to obtain a patent on his ion plating machinery and this helped to stabilize the business in the 1970s. He had a number of other ideas for developing more advanced machinery, but could never quite muster enough funds to put serious effort into research and development (R&D).

Cash flow problems were exacerbated by "cost-down" measures by his top customer. In cost down, large Japanese firms use their monopsony leverage over suppliers by unilaterally reducing supplier prices usually once a year. Since the economic decline in the early 1990s, cost-down demands on exclusive subcontractors have accelerated to even a quarterly basis. Another Tokyo entrepreneur echoes Ikeda's sentiment:

> I have learned from the mistakes made by other firms around me. Large assemblers come in and make an order for a few thousand pieces. Several months later, they ask for more and more, paying on time at first. Then, before you know it, their orders take up most of your production time. That is when they stop paying [on time], when they know you have no choice. Then they start with "cost down," and again you have no choice, because

they know that they have become your primary customer. [A large assembler] tried it with me, but I wouldn't let them put me in that position. It was difficult at first, but we have survived and done well (H 1998)

Cost down is often used in tandem with JIT by large firms to squeeze their suppliers. JIT involves the placement of orders by large assemblers to their suppliers, with 24–48-hour lead time to expected delivery.

Like most of the other entrepreneurs in this study from Ota, Ikeda laughs with derision when asked about how JIT (much-lauded in international circles) has helped increase efficiency in Japan's relational contracting. He recounted how in reality, JIT was all about exporting the cost of holding inventories out of large firms into small firms. In a typical JIT scenario, suppliers employ delivery trucks – full of products they have already produced in anticipation of an order – to park near the docking bays of buyer warehouses. When the order finally comes, the truck delivers the product "just-in-time" for assembly by the buyer. Payment for these goods inevitably arrives months later – limiting the chances that already slim profits can be re-invested in a timely fashion.

Ikeda has tried over the years to get local manufacturers together, but fierce competition over dwindling orders from keiretsu giants exacerbated the barriers already imposed by vertically integrated and insular keiretsu-led production networks. Ikeda was able to establish a collaborative manufacturing network with other local producers. Unfortunately, the seemingly unending wave of local bankruptcies since the 1990s took out several members of the network leaving remaining members in trouble.

Ikeda also tried his luck at drawing on government funds. Though the position has changed since the revision to the SME Basic Law in 1999, Ikeda has found that the supposed "windows" to SME finance are really only windows for the largest of the medium-sized firms – not really small manufacturers. He has seen small manufacturers such as his own firm – led by hardworking folk with solid technology and good management – go under because the banks are not lending to the firms that really need it. Instead, the banks continue avoid risk by lending to medium-sized firms that do not have cash flow problems. Ikeda has tried several times to talk with representatives of various SME finance and other agencies but finds the relationship unchanged at the local level, despite the new laws: "They just give us lip service and in the end nothing is done."

Ikeda also anticipates that lack of coordination among local firms in the face of stiff price competition from Chinese small manufacturers will soon turn to price *and* competition pressure based on higher technology. For Ikeda, this likely scenario will be the death knell for Ota as a manufacturing centre.

In 1998 Ikeda was struggling, with the help of his eldest son, to make new production deadlines while cutting costs – imposed by the second "cost down" in as many quarters. By 2000 company profits had dropped by nearly 50%. In 2003 Ikeda was barely surviving, and his son had taken a job cleaning up after hours (and after working a full day at his father's plant) at a local pachinko parlor to help offset the firm's growing debt. His son is not alone; Ikeda estimates that 90% of the small manufacturers in Ota have at least one family member working on two jobs in this way.

1.3 Regional variations in Japan's national innovation system

These two stories – Samco in Kyoto and Ikeda in the Ota Ward of Tokyo – are illustrative not because they are so different, but because they are representative of the regional differences within Japan's national innovation system. Tsuji and Ikeda's experiences are just two examples of the forty-three firm-level cases in this book that shed light on the reality of the Japanese national innovation system as it is experienced by entrepreneurial start-ups over time.

I followed these firms struggling to become innovative, stay innovative and expand over the course of seven years – and witnessed some succeed. Others, though they started out with seemingly similar technological strengths, failed. I came to realize that the local political economy surrounding these struggling entrepreneurs – and how these entrepreneurs connected with it – has a much greater impact on the firm's ability to innovate than the national-level system that I had been trained as a graduate student to view as the most important.

This book is not, however, an exposé of national-level policy failures and institutional barriers to innovation in Japan.[6] Instead, this book aims to elucidate the puzzle about why, despite widespread national-level failures, clusters of new product and new business innovation persist. Why is it that new clusters emerge irrespective of national-level targeting? In answering this question, this book provides insights into the people and institutions that provide the critical support system for struggling new businesses. These dynamics or synergies somehow turn the raw materials of a region's economy into innovative communities of firms. Unfortunately, few studies attempt to draw inferences about the national- and local-level dynamics through in-depth local case studies.[7] This book also corrects a number of failings in existing interpretations of national innovation systems, in Japan and elsewhere.

Standard explanations in innovation theory, based on structural and institutional factors such as the presence of research universities, large corporations and the like (i.e. the basic ingredients for innovation), for example, would predict that Tokyo would provide Japan with its success stories in the 2000s. Instead, Kyoto is the star. Kyoto city and its environs has emerged since 1990 to become a vibrant high technology cluster of small start-up firms with creative links to area universities that are plugged into the long-term development interests of the community as a whole. What, if any comparative lessons can be drawn from this region in the centre of Japan? These issues will be explored in chapters 6 and 7. At this point, it might be useful to situate the seemingly anecdotal stories of Samco and Ikeda in a broader context. In short, what do these stories, and the others in this book, tell us about the nature of innovation at the firm and local community level?

In today's global political economy, local communities are at once more exposed to international market fluctuations than ever before, and concomitantly challenged to keep pace with rapid transformations in communications and other technology. Current debates about innovation among policy analysts and in the field of political economy are dominated by national-level approaches to studying the challenges of fostering innovation at the local level (Berger and Dore 1996; OECD 1999; Streeck and Yamamura 2001). Characterizations of national innovation systems (NIS) (Nelson 1993) provide broad, aggregate descriptions of innovative trends across national contexts, but lack specific, tangible and proven local-level policy prescriptions.

Consequently, while local-level community and industry leaders are best positioned (spatially) to be potential sources of innovative community building, they are (in contrast to their national-level counterparts) often the least experienced in the policy design capacity that facilitates new business creation, retention and innovation in general (Pages *et al.* 2003). The civic engagement of entrepreneurs and other community leaders in linking the strategic interests of firms to larger issues of community-wide development is an important factor in explaining the sustainability of innovative communities in the long term (Ayuzawa 1995; Mitsubishi Research Institute (MRI) 1996; Storper 1997; Edgington 1999; Sellers 2002).

1.4 Innovative communities: basic ingredients and sufficient conditions

Much has been said about the so-called "supportive socio-political milieu," or "habitat" around innovative firms, but not much has been analyzed in-depth *vis-à-vis* what it is about community-level organizations and networks that make them such critical supports for sustained economic development (Grabher 1993; Omae 1995; Simmie 1997; Storper 1997; Pages *et al.* 2003). Basic ingredients, or necessary conditions, for product innovation and new business creation include: infrastructure (transportation, communications, utilities); research universities, undergraduate colleges and technical schools; the presence of large corporations (with R&D operations); stable and strong local governments; established service industries (legal, financial, consulting); venture capital infrastructure; and amenities (e.g. cultural) attractive to potential (educated, high-skill) residents (Nelson 1993; Porter 1998; Hertog, *et al.* 2001; *The Global Competitiveness Report 2001–2002* 2002). Having these basic ingredients is often insufficient, however, in fostering innovation in a critical mass of local firms (Florida 2002; Takeda 2002; Takeda 2003a, 2003b).[8]

Standard works, while effective at developing a snapshot of institutions and network structures, are at the same time weak in explaining how people forge ties, translate vision into practice and maintain cohesion within developmental coalitions (cross-cutting groups of people with a shared goal of improving the economic situation of their communities) (Berger and Dore 1996; Porter 1998; Dore 2000; Porter *et al.* 2000; Culpepper 2001; Hall and Soskice 2001). But how do you measure these informal, intangible assets of a region? I and others have found that in successful regions a large part of the observed economic process (new product and business creation) is in fact, socially and politically driven (Imai 1998c, 2004; Saxenian 1998b; Ibata-Arens 2004). This book aims to provide practical policy prescriptions as well as advance theory through examining how informal networks, civic leadership, and political "savvy" relate to innovative developmental outcomes. Innovative outcomes at the community level are measured by sales generated by new (tradable) products and new business creation. "Tradable products" are those sold outside the region, with the bulk of product revenue returning to the region.

This regional perspective is useful in identifying certain patterns of social and political "embeddedness" (how enterprise is situated within complex socio-political institutions) that might transcend national–cultural environments (Granovetter 1985; Kumon 1992; Grabher 1993; Uzzi 1996, 1997; Oguri 1998). In other words, understanding enterprise embeddedness can help explain how complex political, social, and cultural contingencies affect economic outcomes that may in turn yield practical policy prescriptions.

1.5 The book's argument: local political economy of innovative communities

The most innovative communities identified in this book comprise particular synergies of *institutions and people.* These communities are more than merely a spatial cluster (agglomeration) of competitive enterprises. Rather, these communities are a geographic concentration (city, region) of like-minded stakeholders (e.g. enterprise mavericks) in the economic outcomes of local enterprises (entrepreneurs, workers, residents, government officials). Community members identify with the shared goals of creating new products in growth sectors. Innovative communities also appear to be infused with a certain civic consciousness. The fact that these communities are populated by entrepreneurial mavericks enhances competition between community members, further stimulating innovation. These communities over time become *sustainable innovative communities* – or innovative communities that adapt over time to externalities (e.g. international market competition) to exit maturing sectors and enter new ones. Kyoto's transition from a traditional silk and pottery center to high (nano, ceramic, thin-film) technology goods is a primary example of this sustained community-level innovation.

"Enterprise mavericks" are entrepreneurs who stake out new business territory on their own (usually through a new product that they have invented, designed, and created themselves). These entrepreneurs identify and capitalize on the interstices of opportunity in creating new products, accessing inter-firm networks, and utilizing policy at a number of levels. These interstices have been alluded to in other terms such as "structural holes" in inter-industry or "human networks," or the meeting of "process need" in product or managerial applications (Burt 1992; Drucker 1993).[9] An example of this kind of synergy is how Kyoto's Murata used his ceramics background in developing advanced condenser technology.

These mavericks are driven and have a particular vision, personality traits that tend to clash with managerial types in large corporations and academic institutions. Once they succeed in business, however, it is their success stories (*monogotarisei*) (Imai 1998a), that lead to emulators within their regions and also attract newcomers (skilled technicians and next-generation entrepreneurs) to the region. One example is Inamori, the founder of Kyocera, who left his former employer after his idea for a cathode-ray tube was rejected by his boss in the 1950s. These individuals tend to avoid hierarchy imposed on themselves or imposed by themselves on their employees. These enterprise mavericks are also an important part of their local communities.

Sustainable innovative communities share three main characteristics:

- First, numerous enterprise mavericks act as *civic entrepreneurs* in pursuing community-wide goals. "Civic entrepreneurs" are defined as politically savvy enterprise mavericks having a keen sense of "giving back" firm and individual wealth and expertise to the larger community, for mutual long-term gain. These individuals have amassed ample stores of (positive) social capital, enabling them to galvanize other firm owner-managers behind collective efforts. Social capital indicates the existence of informal norms that promote cooperation between two or more individuals.
- Second, certain kinds of inter-firm networks provide *critical information and creative ideas*, facilitating innovation in member firms. These loose, locally embedded networks, generally unfettered by hierarchy, have proven better at new product innovation, while their vertically integrated counterparts have admittedly excelled (at least until Japan became a technology leader in its own right and no longer able to benefit from unilateral technology transfer from the West) at producing incremental process innovations in existing (Western) technologies.

  Innovative networks often overlap with broader groups of community stakeholders in the context of "developmental coalitions." Developmental ideas (or visions) shared by (resonate with the interests of) cross-cutting groups of community stakeholders keep stakeholders "on task" in facilitating innovative activity. Community stakeholders include entrepreneurs, business executives, workers, community activists, residents, and local government officials – that is, those with a vested interest in positive socio-economic outcomes. Certain civic leaders and entrepreneurs of a similar ilk provide a certain kind of vision that plugs into nascent civic pride to advance the interests of broad groups of community stakeholders: firms, workers, and residents.

- Third, local governments act as *advocates at the national level* for local firms. This advocacy is secured by politically savvy firm founder owner-managers. Political savvy is the common sense ability to identify and "read" or comprehend the powers-that-be (e.g. government resource and permissions' gatekeepers). This involves knowing which to avoid, which to pay at least lip service to. In Japan, this means that firms that are approached by METI for a survey generally comply, but most are averse to taking METI funds – unless they have a go-between – as they are aware of the bureaucratic hassles that inevitably follow.

  Political savvy is not limited to dealing with government. It also includes the strategies that firms use to circumvent hierarchies while managing to avoid becoming exploited by exclusive contracting arrangements of keiretsu giants. These arrangements lock small firms into the weak end of asymmetrical power relations.

  In essence, innovative market success often depends on political savvy by entrepreneurs and local stakeholders. Political savvy is found in the way in which firms navigate spaces between institutions and networks, exploiting the interstices of opportunity while avoiding the negative affects of hierarchy. In other words, the politics of innovation affect market outcomes.

My findings, supported by other recent research into what can be called the "local political economy of innovation" indicate that certain communities of innovation are often similar across national boundaries, while often dissimilar from other regions in their own national economies. Consequently, in-depth local case study research into innovative communities in domestic and international comparative context may yield powerful insights into the kinds of institutions and people that foster the development of sustainable communities of innovation. Japan's lagging start-up rate since the mid-1980s is an indication of the failure of its national innovation system to produce results in this regard. For example, the enterprise start-up/closure rates for all establishments, including new public, private, and additional offices of existing firms, over the period 1996–1999 was 3.5 (open) v. 5.7 (closure). Over the period 1999–2001, the start-up rate remained paltry: 3.2, while the closure rate remained high, 4.8 (see figure 1.5, p. 15).

This book is fundamentally a firm-level case study analysis of innovation in high technology industry. Its narrative is from the perspective of entrepreneurs, as they navigate local-, regional-, and national-level institutions in their pursuit of innovation and growth. The chapters explore the sources of innovation found in firm-level strategies, interfirm networks, regional characters, and national-level policy. The regional variation of Japan's national innovation system is illustrated

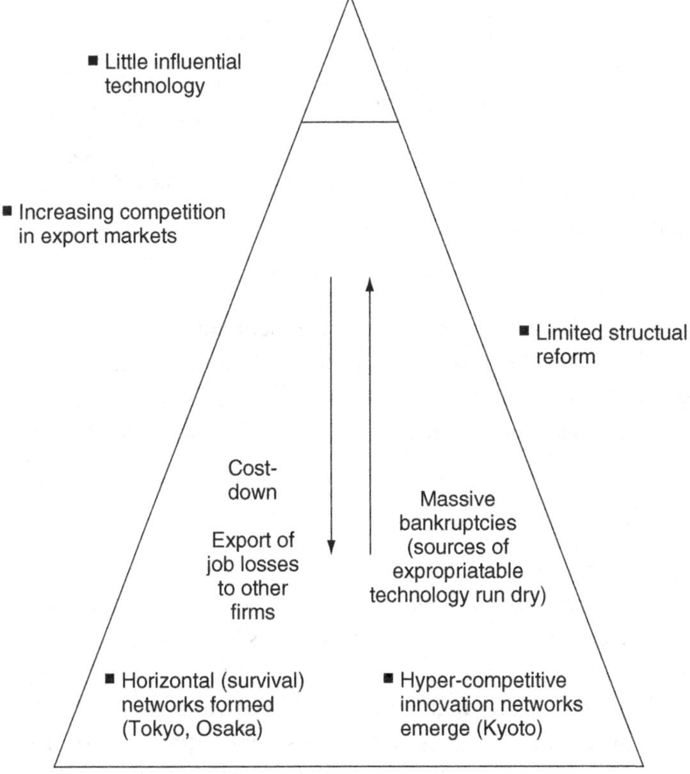

Figure 1.3. Japan's model collapses, 1990s

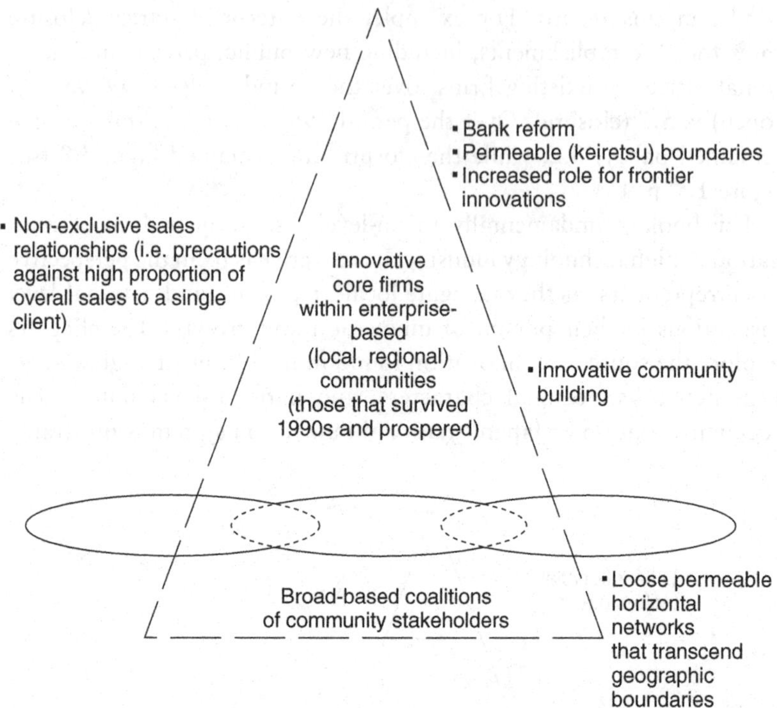

Figure 1.4. Rise of the Kyoto Model, 2000s

by the emerging "Kyoto Model" of entrepreneurship in comparative context. The book concludes with lessons for entrepreneurs and governments. Figures 1.1–1.4 illustrate the rise and fall of the Japanese national innovation system and the subsequent emergence of the Kyoto Model.

1.6 Outline of the book

In chapter 2, I introduce the firm-level case studies. I analyzed the experiences of forty-three high technology manufacturing firms, from the mid-1990s to the early 2000s. These firms are located in three industrial clusters across regions in Japan: the Ota Ward in Tokyo, Eastern (or "Higashi") Osaka, and the southern corridor of Kyoto. The forty-three firms are divided into four groups: innovative leaders (15), moderately successful (15), mixed successes (9), and innovative failures (4). Firms in the 1990s employed from ten to several hundred people and

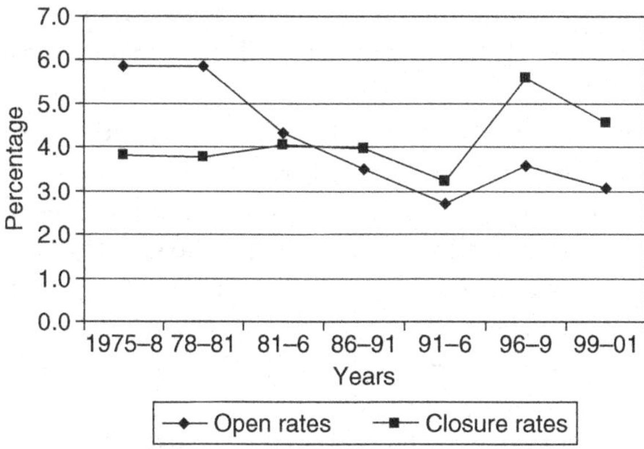

Figure 1.5. Japan open/closure rates, 1975–2001
Source: SME White Paper (2004).

were capitalized at from 1 million to hundreds of millions of yen. Some firms have grown exponentially since, while others have faltered.[10]

Innovative leaders

Firms considered innovative leaders were active in developing and manufacturing new products in growth sectors such as fiber optics and medical machinery. The value-added level of these products was high, and firms were currently engaged in R&D for additional products. A standard definition of "value-added" defines it as the value of a firm's output minus the value of inputs bought from other firms. These innovative leaders found it easier in the late 1990s, despite the recession-plagued Japanese economy, to do one or more of the following: engage in new product R&D, obtain skilled workers, and seek new clients. The most innovative firms were the least likely to have any kind of keiretsu link. Firms falling into less innovative rankings were struggling on one or more of the measures mentioned.

Firm-level strategies

After introducing the entrepreneurs and their firms, I examine their struggles for independence, innovation, and competitiveness within the Japanese political economy. As a number of works have shown, the Japanese political economy has been dominated since the 1950s by a set of interlocking (insular and hierarchical) institutions that have undermined innovation in aggregate and at the local level (Ibata-Arens 2000a).

Firm-level strategies in the face of these barriers involve two activities. First, these firms have been successful at *de-linking from production hierarchies*. Second, firms have managed to *circumvent state-sanctioned and big business-sponsored* associations and networks – no small task in Japan – in favour of forming and joining loose, horizontal, inter-regional and international inter-firm networks. Successful de-linking and network building has depended in part on the leadership of local civic entrepreneurs and other community stakeholders.

While many Japanese firms struggled throughout the 1990s, the innovative position of the leaders improved (some rising to world renown) while those at the lowest levels of the innovative ladder fell further behind – a few resulting in bankruptcy. This reflects the growing gap between hyper innovators and losing businesses in Japan and elsewhere.

Fostering innovative activity

Chapter 3 evaluates explanations of how innovative activity is fostered at the firm, region and national level in Japan in comparative perspective. I begin with a clarification of definitions and measures of innovation, particularly technological product innovation, the focus of this study of innovation in high technology industry. I then situate current debates about innovation and innovation policy within the context of standard explanations of the Japanese economy. I find that the bulk of the research on Japan's innovation system is based on faulty empirical foundations. This empirical weakness has resulted in a number of recurring misperceptions of Japan (for example, about the true nature and impact of relational contracting on innovation) in the international literature – particularly in the field of political economy – that has compared Japan to other major economies. A re-evaluation of major works in the light of firm- and regional-level practice in Japan is in order.

National-level policy

In chapter 4, I explore how in the late 1990s national-level policy in Japan, for the first time, tried to incorporate local-level initiatives and enterprise-based policy (the latter initiated by or in response to the expressed needs of firms) into efforts to jump start the national economy. These policies include the *Innovative cluster plan* and *Industrial revitalization corporation.* This chapter shows that despite noble efforts, existing institutional biases (top-down governance and administrative guidance) as well as elitism in national (central) ministries have interfered with local-level successes. For example, national-level ministries are often criticized by locals for their practice of seeking out proven local-level initiatives, then coming in, throwing money at and subsequently taking credit (in national and international circles) for local success. As a result, truly local-level initiatives are often hidden in reports on the results of "national" policy. This has resulted in further undermining trust between the national government and local-level leaders. Understanding the local-level dynamics of so-called "national policy" in Japan offers a cautionary tale for policymakers and practitioners charged with supporting innovative firms and building sustainable innovative communities.

Inter-firm networks

In chapter 5, I analyze the relationship between particular kinds of inter-firm networks and innovative outcomes in individual member firms. I highlight the experiences of a number of successful inter-firm networks that I have followed since the mid-1990s. These networks have spurred innovation and growth in local communities – particularly in Kyoto but also, albeit to a lesser extent, in Osaka and Tokyo. These networks are led by entrepreneurial mavericks acting as civic entrepreneurs (having a keen sense of giving back to local communities for mutual long-term gain). This provides further insights into why the *Innovative Cluster* and other "network creation" policies initiated by national-level bureaucrats in Japan have largely failed.

On the other hand, my findings offer clues in identifying interstices (between networks and people) of opportunity for local firms, entrepreneurs, and other community stakeholders seeking sustainable community development in Japan and elsewhere. In fact, by 2003, seven years after I began my case study research in Kyoto, Ota, and Higashi Osaka – a number of my cases have gained national and international fame. For example, METI has brought the successes of several Kyoto area firms to national attention in their hope of finding a new model for Japan's still-struggling economy.

The Kyoto Model

In chapter 6, I follow up on the discussion of regional variations in chapter 5. In doing so, I focus on the vibrant innovative community of firms that has emerged in and around Kyoto. An emerging Japanese literature examines the "Kyoto Model" of entrepreneurship and the lessons that can be drawn for new start-ups. Cases were drawn from my original forty-three firms for their representation of Kyoto-style entrepreneurship and innovative strategies. I also include entrepreneurial stories of older, more established Kyoto firms. The chapter concludes by considering whether Kyoto can be a model for other places (see figure 1.4).

Comparative strategies

Chapter 7 compares the local political economy of firm-level innovative strategies and inter-firm innovative networks in Japan with varying experiences in the American Midwest, based on case study research that I conducted in 2003 and 2004. This chapter also – by way of a brief comparison – draws from the findings of other recent research in local political economy in China and Germany that illustrate the important similarities across national boundaries of these local innovative communities. At the same time, these comparisons show the significant differences between these communities and other struggling communities within their own national contexts. This implies the futility of trying to construct national innovation systems from the top down, while at the same time providing lessons on locally informed, enterprise-based sustainable community development. In this regard, I reintroduce the constructs presented in the book's Introduction (civic entrepreneurs, developmental coalitions) in the context of a set of hypotheses for further cross-national testing.

Sustainable community development

Chapter 8 summarizes the findings of the preceding chapters. I conclude with a discussion of the relevance of this enterprise-based local political economy approach to innovative and sustainable community development for local, regional, and national policymakers and entrepreneurs.

Notes

1. Innovation is of two types: *incremental* (process) and *product*. Process innovation is making improvements to the appearance and/or functionality of existing technology. Product innovation is measured in this book by patents and new product R&D that result in new products that increase firm sales. (See appendix 1.)
2. In Japan, SMEs are defined (by METI) as establishments employing 4–299 employees and Large Enterprises as those employing 300 or more. SMEs are defined as establishments capitalized at less than ¥100 million, and Large Enterprises as those capitalized at ¥100 million or over. The European Union defines SMEs as having 250 employees or fewer with a turnover of 40 million Euros or less or a balance sheet evaluation of 27 million Euros or less. In the European Union, "small firms" have 50 or fewer employees, while micro enterprises have five or fewer. In the United States, SMEs are categorized as those firms employing 500 persons or fewer. Some countries consider SMEs to be firms with up to 200 employees.

   The original data set of forty-three randomly selected case study firms forms the basis of this book (see appendix 1). A few cases (i.e. Kyoto Model main cases) were subsequently included. In some instances, in order to protect the anonymity of a source, pseudonyms such as "E firm" are used. Due to space constraints, representative cases (of innovative level and region) are discussed in the greatest detail while others are mentioned briefly, if at all.
3. For an overview of the study of innovation, see Hauknes (2003).
4. Osamu Tsuji, Interviews 1998, 2003.
5. Technically, a monopsony is the situation whereby there is only one buyer for a particular commodity or service. In Japan, exclusive subcontracting arrangements mean that small firms have faced *de facto* monopsonies.
6. For a discussion of how Japanese entrepreneurs have struggled against the MOF-controlled financial system, "keiretsification" of the economy, and the patent system, see Ibata-Arens (2000).
7. For a notable exception, see Culpepper (2001).
8. Shuzaburo Takeda, Interview 2004.
9. Others have noted the role of inter-organizational discontinuity in inducing innovation. See Ritchev and Cole (1999).
10. See appendix 1.

2 *Regions and firms*

2.1 Introduction

FROM the mid-1990s to the early 2000s I followed the experiences of forty-three high technology manufacturing firms located in three industrial clusters across regions in Japan: Ota Ward in Tokyo, Higashi (or "East") Osaka, and the southern corridor of Kyoto. In this chapter I focus on firm-level case studies.[1] Through the personal narratives of the entrepreneurs themselves, I identify a number of successful (and also failing) strategies of innovation and competitiveness. These entrepreneurial case studies are also illustrative of the regional variations in Japan's national innovation system. Before the case studies, I provide an overview of the nature of high technology industrial production in the regions of study.

First, I provide a snapshot of the industrial structure of each region. I review trends in products and markets in the 1990s and 2000s. Second, I review how (new product) innovation is measured in this study, and how firms rank relative to one another and generally in today's global high technology industry. The rationale for focusing on SMEs stems from the fact that the bulk of new product innovation, particularly in engineering and high technology industry is found in smaller firms – in Japan and the USA alike (Japan Small and Medium Size Enterprise Agency 2003).

Finally, I introduce the entrepreneurs and case study firms. I examine their struggles for independence, innovation, and competitiveness within the Japanese political economy. As a number of works including my own have shown, the Japanese political economy has been dominated since the 1950s by a set of interlocking (insular and hierarchical) institutions that have undermined innovation. Interlocking institutions in Japan comprise mainly elite ministries and bureaucrats (e.g. METI, MOF) and Japanese conglomerates (keiretsu) controlled and managed from the apex of political and economic power in Tokyo (supported by legislators and a factionalized – that is, either uncompetitive and rent-seeking or competitive but politically weak – SME sector).

These interlocking institutions working in tandem within Japan's pyramid production structure have had three main effects on entrepreneurs: first, they have created a patent system built on technology expropriation (initially from foreign competitors). Second, Japan's system of industrial finance is both biased towards large (and in post-1990s reform years, medium-sized) established firms and lacks the expertise in evaluating good business ideas. Third, part and parcel of the smooth functioning of the production pyramid has been vertically integrated relational "exclusive" contracting, that begets inter-firm networks (and monopsony abuses) of similar ilk (Ibata-Arens 2000).

Entrepreneurial firms that have survived and prospered in Japan have managed to circumvent these barriers to innovation in a number of ways, and inter-regional patterns in aggregate success have emerged. Firm-level strategies for innovation and competitiveness (in the light of these barriers) have involved two activities. First, firms have de-linked from (pyramid-like) production hierarchies. Second, firms have circumvented state-sanctioned and big business-sponsored associations and networks, in favor of loose, horizontal, inter-regional and international inter-firm networks.

De-linking from hierarchy will be discussed here and inter-firm networks will be examined in chapter 5. In addition to showing the extent of regional variation in Japan's national innovation system, the competitive and innovative strategies employed by these firms can provide lessons for entrepreneurs (and regions) elsewhere. For example, understanding how Japan's central state-driven national innovation policies play out at the local level may be relevant in the number of countries (particularly in Asia) in which Japanese conglomerates, backed by the Japanese state, are attempting to re-create the production pyramid abroad.

A number of works have dealt with the ramifications at national and local levels of industrial "hollowing out" and thus will not be addressed here (Katz 1998, 2003; Porter *et al.* 2000; Gao 2001; Lincoln 2001; Yamamura and Streeck 2003). This chapter focuses – from the perspective of high technology firms – on firm-level strategies for success. At the same time, firm-level strategies have not been pursued in an institutional vacuum. That is, successful strategies seem to represent certain regional patterns of innovation. The case study firms in this book are located in three distinct regional innovation systems: Tokyo,

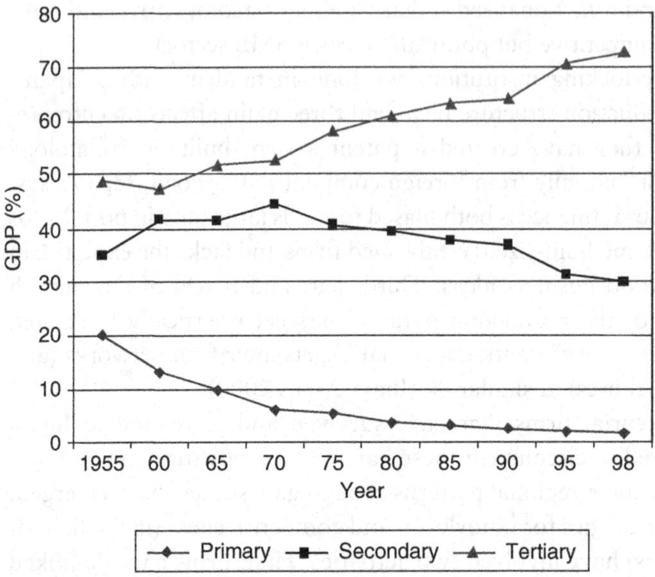

Figure 2.1. GDP share change, by sector, 1955–1998
Source: METI White Paper (2002a).

Osaka, and Kyoto. These regions share a number of similarities while exhibiting important (firm-level) differences, making for an informative comparative study.

2.2 Regions: industries, products, and trends

In the post-war period, the regions of Tokyo, Osaka, and Kyoto (together with Saitama) have produced much of the nation's general, electric and precision machinery. These capital goods producers supply global high technology industries including semiconductors and information technology (IT). Each has been hit by the move of operations and product sourcing of Japan's big electronics producers offshore – mainly to Southeast Asia and China.

Since the 1960s, the proportion of service sector output to total GDP has been steadily increasing nation-wide, while the percentage of manufacturing contribution to GDP has been slowly declining (see figure 2.1) (METI 2002a). Tokyo has maintained its dominance in manufacturing overall, home to the corporate headquarters of the

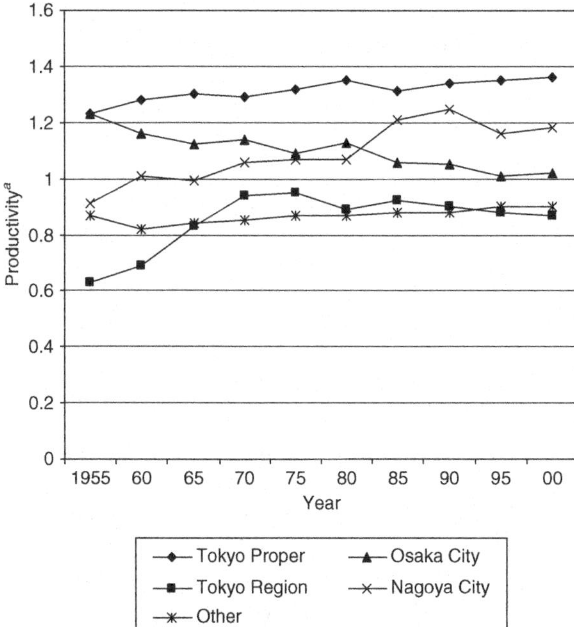

Figure 2.2. Manufacturing, by region, 1955–1998.
Source: METI White Paper (2002a).
Note: [a] Productivity is measured by the value of goods and services produced in a given period, divided by the hours of labor used to produce them in the same period.

biggest of the big "keiretsu" conglomerates. Manufacturing has declined in Osaka. Nagoya, on the other hand, home to major automobile producers such as Toyota, has steadily increased its share of manufacturing productivity (see figure 2.2) (METI 2002a).

In 1999 among firms considered "successful" in terms of yearly sales, in southern Kanto (the area encompassing Ota), average sales per firm totaled 12.1 billion yen, while successful firms on average outside this area were in Tokai (4.9 billion yen) and Northern Kanto (4.8 billion yen). Kinki (Kansai) was in fourth place (4.2 billion yen). Though Kinki firms had lower average sales per firm than Tokai or Northern Kanto, they contributed overall to 9.1% of total national sales in 1999. Tokai and Northern Kanto represented 5.8% and 3.9% of the national total, respectively. Southern Kanto was again by far the leader in

Table 2.1 Sales, by region: regional totals and firm-level averages, 1998–1999

Region	*Number of firms* [a]	*% of national sales 1998–9 (%)*		*Regional total sales million yen (1999)*	*Average sales per firm, million yen*
Hokkaido	468	2.1	1.8	1,551,560	3,315
Tohoku	743	3.2	2.8	2,397,529	3,227
Northern Kanto	686	3.8	3.9	3,310,205	4,825
Southern Kanto	4,648	60.2	66.6	56,670,693	12,192
Tokai	1,003	7.2	5.8	4,929,318	4,915
Kinki	1,821	11.8	9.1	7,747,216	4,254
Shikoku	297	1.5	1.4	1,195,899	4,027
Kyushu	980	5.2	4.4	3,753,273	3,830
Other	894	4.8	4.2	3,501,109	3,785
National total	**11,540**	**100.0**	**100.0**	**85,056,812**	**7,371**

Note:

[a] Private firms employing 1 or more persons with annual sales ≧ ¥5 million and total yearly sales up ≧ 10% for two consecutive years.

Source: *Chiiki Economic Report 2001.*

percentage of total national sales (66.6%) (see table 2.1) ("Chiiki Keizai Repoto" 2001; Naikakucho 2001).

Over the period 1995–2001, the negative impact of industrial "hollowing out" across industrial regions in Japan is reflected in the bankruptcy rates over time (see figure 2.3). The bankruptcy rate across regions continued to accelerate in the latter half of the 1990s. Comparing bankruptcy rates in 1995 and 2001, rates rose from 0.44–0.50 in Kanto and 0.50–0.75 in Kinki (SME 2002). New enterprise start-ups continue to lag behind closures, as shown in the Introduction. The ratio of new business start-ups to closures across industries is as discouraging (see figure 2.4). The diffusion index (DI), a measure of economic vitality and production outlook among firms, experienced a precipitous decline between 1996 and 1998 and again

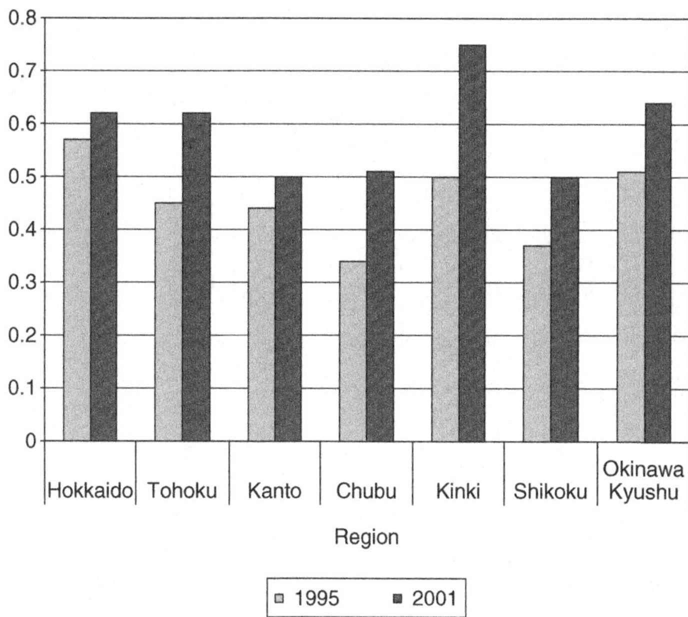

Figure 2.3. Bankruptcy trends, by region, 1995 and 2001[a]
Source: SME White Paper (2002).
[a] Firms with capitalization of ¥10 million or more. The rate was determined by comparing a given region's bankruptcy rate with the national decline in total number of firms.

between 2000 and 2001. It remained stagnant across regions in the first quarter of 2002 −51.2 nationally and stagnated at−53.9 in Kinki and−55.2 in Kanto (see figure 2.5) (SME 2002).

Within the context of these aggregate trends, case study firms fell into four groups: innovative leaders (15), moderately successful (15), mixed successes (9), and innovative failures (4). I outline measures of innovation, and the difference between innovative leaders and failures, below.

2.3 Innovative levels of high technology firms

Leaders

Firms considered innovative leaders were active in producing new products in growth sectors such as fiber optics and medical machinery.

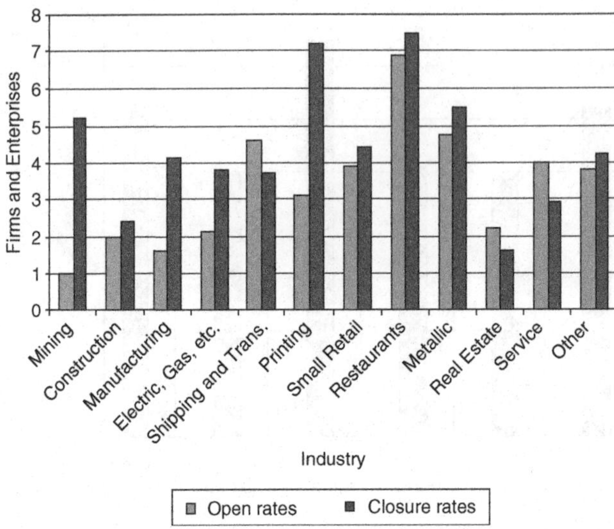

Figure 2.4. Open/closure rates, by industry, 1999–2001
Source: METI White Paper (2003c).
Note: Open (closure) rate = Average yearly number of firm openings (closures)/1999 number of firms × 100%.

The value-added level of these products was high, and firms were currently engaged in R&D for additional products. As previously mentioned, a standard definition of "value-added" defines it as the value of a firm's output minus the value of inputs bought from other firms. These innovative leaders found it easier in 1998, despite the recession-plagued Japanese economy, to do one or more of the following: engage in new product R&D, obtain skilled workers, and seek new clients. The most innovative firms were the least likely to have any kind of keiretsu link (defined by subcontracting, stockholding, and sales proportions).

By 2000, a number of the innovative leaders had excelled in terms of their success in marketing self-patented new products, increasing global sales share, and expanding into other (niche) markets. A new product is a previously non-existing good or service. For example, a novel application of an existing technology in one industry to another industry might be considered a "new" product while a product resulting from mere surface engineering of an existing one would not.

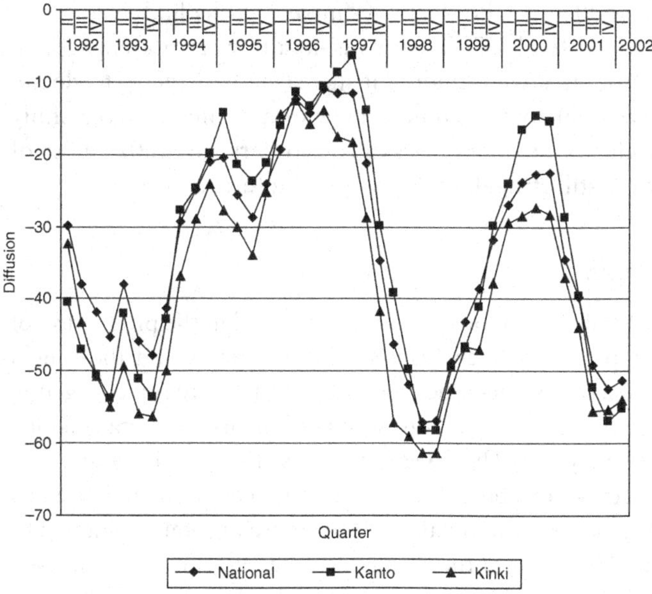

Figure 2.5. Diffusion index, by region, 1992–2002[a]
Source: SME White Paper (2002g).
Note: [a] The diffusion index (DI) is a composite measure of economic vitality.

Moderately innovative

Firms considered moderately successful at innovating were less likely than "lead" firms to be producing final products in growth sectors. The products of these moderately successful firms had an average value-added level. These firms may not have been currently conducting new product R&D, and they found it neither easier nor more difficult to seek new clients, engage in R&D, or obtain skilled workers. By 2002, some moderately successful firms had become leaders, while some stayed at their original levels.

Mixed success

Firms having a mixed experience with innovation were unlikely to be currently engaged in the production of goods for growth industries (although these firms may have been active in earlier growth sectors, such as semiconductors). Products of "mixed" firms had average-to-lower value-added levels. These firms generally were not engaged in current R&D or they were finding it increasingly difficult to do so. Mixed firms were likely to find no change or a decline in successfully seeking new clients or obtaining skilled workers. By 2002, most of these firms were still struggling, a few slipping further behind.

Innovative failures

Firms that had failed to innovate were not engaged in the production of growth sector products. Such firms held few patents and those held tended to be of a low value-added level. The firms were not engaged in R&D and found it more difficult to seek new clients and obtain skilled workers in recent years. They were also most likely to have a strong keiretsu link across the board (i.e. have a parent, be a fully-owned subsidiary of that parent, and have 70% or more of total sales going to one client). By 2002, half of the failing firms had gone out of business.

By 2002, the innovative position of the leaders improved (some rising to world renown) while those at the lowest levels of the innovative ladder fell further behind – a few resulting in bankruptcy, as just mentioned. This reflects the growing gap between hyper innovators and losing businesses in Japan and elsewhere. How hyper innovators got to be that way is a function of a number of strategies.

2.4 Firm-level strategies

In all aspects of doing business, innovating firms have sought to avoid any significant link with keiretsu big business. In terms of how these firms went about avoiding "keiretsification" (i.e. the assimilation into the vertically integrated production pyramid), there are six main strategies of independence: niche market targeting, balancing sales ratios, avoiding technological expropriation, collaborative R&D and manufacturing, forging international connections, and relying on social networks.

- First, top firms produce goods in *niche markets*. Niche markets are focused segments of (mass) markets and are therefore large enough for a small firm to profit, but generally not lucrative for big firms to enter. In high technology, a semiconductor has a mass market, while the machinery that applies a protective/conductive coating onto a component targets a more focused segment – or niche – of the broad semiconductor-related market.

- Second, firms sought to maintain a *balance in sales ratios* among their clients. In managing the sales ratios among their customers, few of the firms interviewed allowed the proportion of total sales to a single buyer to be more than 40%. Most stated that, if possible, they tried to reduce ratios for large customers to around 15%. In some cases, firms have achieved these sales ratios by selling directly abroad to foreign, often US, firms, thereby circumventing traditional mediating agents, such as Japanese trading firms.
- Third, firms *avoided technology expropriation*, which was often attempted against them under the guise of "long-term, trust-based" relational contracting. The history of the Japanese economy – or at least as it has presented to foreigners – has been told by the powerful. Japan's firms hold vast untold stories of technological exploitation of small firms by large. Stories abound of keiretsu group representatives toting hidden cameras on client site visits and/or paying corporate spies to pose as students or researchers as a way of gaining access to proprietary information and technology. A few of these experiences are recounted by the entrepreneurs in this book.
- Fourth, firms engaged in *joint R&D* and *collaborative manufacturing* with other SMEs. A major catalyst for this interaction has been the fact that the lion's share of value-added profits, government subsidies, and main bank finance has been siphoned off by their larger corporate competitors. Consequently, small firms have banded together to develop and manufacture products jointly.
- Fifth, firms make *international connections* via JVs and by employing foreign technologists in-house. Many an entrepreneurial firm reports that they have found that dealing with firms from the USA, Europe and other parts of Asia, despite the language barriers, far easier than trying to do business within the insular corporate hierarchies of Japan. Once these maverick entrepreneurial start-ups tasted freedom from Japanese hierarchies, they never again allowed themselves to be pulled in.
- Sixth, they relied on (often Internet-based) *social networks* as sources of ideas and technology. These strategies helped firms to subvert traditional mediating structures (i.e, situated between the SMEs at the base of the pyramid and the large assemblers at the top). Other strategies having mixed success included participating in

independent national-level (SME) organizations. This last strategy is explored in chapter 5.

In 1998, about three-quarters of the firms I interviewed were engaged in R&D of new products. To survive and prosper in high technology industries, firms are under pressure to keep moving into new technologies.[2] Although many were engaged in new product R&D, a much smaller proportion had significant success in terms of holding high-value-added patents and moving into new technologies. Of the firms engaged in new product R&D, 60% maintained external links supporting in-house R&D with other SMEs, including foreign firms. The firms were generally satisfied with the results of these collaborations.

Other relationships included government research institutes (43%), university faculties (41%), and private research institutes (25%). Few firms expressed satisfaction with these relationships, citing a lack of market expertise on the part of government institutes and universities, and the high cost of private research institutes relative to output. Firms were least likely to forge a relationship with a parent firm (a main buyer) for R&D purposes. (Of the forty-three firms, eight considered themselves to have a parent, while a total of nineteen, or 44%, had a degree of keiretsu linkage – for example, as a subcontractor or in terms of sales. The latter would often consider its main buyer a "parent" of sorts.) In addition to technological ties with foreign firms via joint R&D, innovating Japanese firms have forged joint business ties with SMEs in other countries.

In the next section, I introduce the case study firms, highlighting the entrepreneurial struggles of the most successful (in terms of new product innovations resulting in increased sales) and the lessons that can be drawn. Firms having less success in innovating also provide insights into institutional pitfalls and firm-level mistakes. These lessons also illustrate the conflict between Japan's central state, big business-driven national innovation system and the entrepreneurial firms and regions in which they are located.

2.5 Firms in Ota

Leaving a sinking ship: Shinkoh

Shinkoh Electronics, founded in 1974 by Tetsuo Kinoshita, manufactures precision fiber optic devices for computer applications. Kinoshita was working his way through college in 1960 at a canning factory when the firm suddenly went bankrupt. Unable to finish school, Kinoshita took up work at a nearby opto-electronics firm in Yokohama and worked for the next thirteen years, saving his money and learning a lot about photoconductive cells. By the early 1970s, Kinoshita decided to move on.

Soon after starting his firm in 1974, Kinoshita tried to make contact with other Ota firms for possible collaboration, but found that most small firms were firmly situated within keiretsu hierarchies and subsequently reluctant to share information. At the same time, Shinkoh was unable to get assistance from any government agency or private financial institution in Japan for its early product ideas. It seemed to Kinoshita that while the Japanese government ignored small start-ups with solid technological R&D blueprints, innovatively weak corporate giants got the bulk of government funds. Kinoshita knew that his ideas had promise. Using 1 million yen (about $10,000) of his savings, he began producing lighting equipment in the 1970s. By 1978, Shinkoh was producing a unique light sensor with applications for cameras and copiers. He planned to get around to completing the voluminous patent paperwork but a large manufacturer, Ricoh, swept in, obtained a patent on his sensor and soon gutted his fledgling sales. Kinoshita knew he would have to get connected to someone with resources in order to compete with Japanese giants.

Kinoshita forged ties with SMEs in other countries such as Taiwan and the USA. For example, collaboration with an American NASA-backed LED prototype engineering firm, Quantum Devices, produced devices with clinically proven results in cancer-curing "photodynamic therapy." R&D in full-spectrum photo-semiconductor devices has taken Shinkoh from a parts maker for traffic lights in the 1970s to a global market player in opto-electronics.

Establishing sales ties with firms in the USA, and a producer of lighting equipment in Taiwan, Shinkoh has grown based on sales made through these firms. Paradoxically, as Shinkoh's financial position in Japan has strengthened for the first time Japanese banks have approached the firm to offer loans – precisely at the point that his firm no longer needs the funds.

In the late 1990s Shinkoh was located in the southernmost point of Ota Ward. By 2003 Shinkoh had been relocated to Kanagawa, the prefecture immediately to the south of Ota. Kinoshita explained that the air in Ota was getting unbearable, and most of his employees had been commuting from the cheaper housing in Kanagawa into Tokyo anyway. Even Kinoshita's own home is in Kanagawa. He sees other high-tech firms like his moving out of Ota in droves. Kinoshita says "with Internet connectivity, a telephone and fax, we no longer need to be in Tokyo." The only worry for Kinoshita is attracting young talent away from the congested yet social beehive of Tokyo to the clean, wide-open spaces of Kanagawa. As for firms remaining in Ota, Kinoshita is not so optimistic: "the community's high-tech leaders continue to expand and move out of Ota, soon Ota as a community of firms will be no more".[3] Seiken, another firm whose technology has risen exponentially since the mid-1990s, agrees.

No thanks to METI: Seiken

Nobuo Shiratori, the founder of Seiken, an Ota producer of precision electronics for the semiconductor industry, tried a number of times in the 1990s to obtain (then referred to as) MITI finance. Though he was confident about the global market potential of his products under development, MITI was not interested. Instead he saw the funds inevitably go to large firms with "new" products in the works that really weren't so fundamentally different than their tried-and-true product lines. He tried local banks but, lacking the backing of a major keiretsu group, he was unable to obtain funds.

Instead, Shiratori made alliances with other SMEs in Taiwan, South Korea, and Singapore, exchanging technologists and technology in joint development projects. By 2003, Seiken had a number of new product patents as well as more in the application pipeline. Situated in the low-end market within the semiconductor industry in the mid-1990s, Seiken had reached the high end by the early 2000s, proudly exhibiting his array of new products at the Holy Grail of international high-tech trade fairs, SEMICON. Shiratori adds that this achievement has been no thanks to government assistance. He is not naïve though; when Ota Ward representatives came around last year to ask if his firm was interested in obtaining METI-backed R&D grants (*joseikin*), he did not refuse. Though his firm had become a medium-sized firm by that time and had plenty of money, he took the Ota/METI funds. "We don't have to pay it back, so why not," he says. Commenting on how participating in the local government sponsored networks helped his firm, Shiratori said "being on their lists has not helped one bit, Ota-Net for example seems to lump all sorts of firms together with no rhyme or reason – its meaningless. We, and other high technology firms like us, have done it completely on our own".[4] Other Ota producers managed to survive the 1990s by making more local connections.

Surviving through merger: Kyodo Electric

Keijiro Shono (Kyodo Manufacturing) and Shizaburo Kuniyasu (formerly of Kuniyasu Wire) often did business together over the years. Kuniyasu Special Electric Wire Co. Wire (KW) was founded by Shizaburo in 1960. KW produced cable and wire harnesses for computer mother boards and peripherals. Kyodo was a manufacturer of large-scale electrical machinery systems as well as electrical relays and counting devices for use in manufacturing. Kyodo often purchased KW wires for its systems. Kuniyasu reflected on a tumultuous time at his former firm:

> Years ago, a large firm came in [on the pretense of being a potential client] and copied a cable product after examining it. They made a few minor changes and produced it themselves. We did not have a patent yet for the product, so we had no recourse.

The large firm's sales of the stolen product severely undercut Kuniyasu's profits. Kuniyasu was in a serious bind. Meanwhile, Keijiro Shono's company Kyodo was doing well. In 1995, as Keijiro Shono was preparing to retire, Kyodo merged with Kuniyasu. After the merger, Shono stayed on as chairman and Kuniyasu took over as president. With the merger, however, 39% of their product went to one keiretsu firm.

From the start of the merger, both Shono and Kuniyasu agreed that too much sales dependence on a single keiretsu group buyer was dangerous. The two devised three strategies to help the newly merged firm to survive the recessionary 1990s. First, of their 100 employees in 1998, forty had been let go by 2003. Second, in order to compete with growing competition from small manufacturers in China and South East Asia, they upgraded their sales, customer service, and product maintenance with a "we provide it all" motto. Third, they tried to enter the growing market for medical devices and machinery by collaborating with other SMEs in Japan and abroad in new product R&D. To date, no new patents have come out of these efforts, however.

The struggles of Kyodo Electric (and Kuniyasu Wire prior to the merger) to be innovative and competitive provide three main lessons: first, avoid dependence on a single client and second, protect your intellectual property at all costs. Finally, if you can't go it alone, collaborate with someone you really trust.[5] Another Ota firm, Kasasaku has not been so fortunate.

The cost of sticking with the system: Kasasaku

In 1998, Misuo Kasasaku, founder of his eponymous firm had a positive outlook. He had just obtained patent approval for his IC-related burn-in board and connectors. His products were sold to PC, mainframe, and aerospace makers. He was able to keep his largest sales to a single client at under 10%. At the same time, however, a few of his earlier product patents had been made useless by a large firm making slight modifications on the surface technology (*shuuhen*) and obtaining a "new" patent.

Nevertheless, Kasasaku was positive he would pull through. His clients included Fujitsu, Panasonic, and Matsushita, and he had been a loyal supplier to each, always complying with delivery demands and cost down. Though he could not get any government or bank finance, he had a decent nest egg. In 1998, he was approached by a South Korean firm to jointly develop products and sell them in the Korean market, but he demurred. Better stick with his trusted Japanese keiretsu groups, he thought: "what if they [the Koreans] were just interested in taking-off with my technology?" Kasasaku also stuck with the local government's network, but never obtained any orders from this route.

In 2003, Kasasaku's outlook was decidedly different. His personal savings had been devastated. Sales had dropped from 15 million yen in first quarter 1999 to nearly zero in the same quarter in 2003 ("Tokyo Manufacturing 2001 Summer Report of Comprehensive Survey Results 2001). He managed to remain in business through three drastic measures. First, he moved out of the second floor of the building he owned, subletting the freed space and cramming his office, R&D, and production into the first floor space. Second, in 2002–3 he did not take a salary, taking just enough out of the company to subsist (*taberu gurai seikatsu suru*). Finally, he had let seven of his ten employees go. One of his most talented technologists, forty-two years old in 2003, had been unable to find another job and was reduced to selling rice snacks (*o-nigiri*) out of the back of his car.

It should be noted that innovators such as Shinkoh and Seiken are far from the norm in Ota. These innovators have been subject to the same institutional barriers as not-as-successful local firms but were "savvy" enough to get away from them. For most Ota small manufacturers, exclusive subcontracting has integrated entrepreneurial firms over time into the production pyramid (i.e. keiretsified them). The production pyramid as a set of (insular, closed-to-exit, top-down technology management) institutions excels at process innovation, sometimes through technology expropriation. At the same time, the 1990s have shown that these hierarchies fail to produce product innovation and new business creation. Further, external shocks (increasing competition, currency rate fluctuation) have been absorbed within the pyramid through the exporting of costs from the top (large firms, less likely to be the source of truly new products and new business) to the bottom (small firms which are more likely to produce innovations). The bulk of Ota firms have thus been the worst hit nationally, as their main buyers have shifted production abroad. The fact that a handful of Ota firms have survived (Kyodo) and prospered (Shinkoh, Seiken) attests to the entrepreneurial and strategic capacity of certain firms, rather than reflecting regional trends. The experiences of Kasasaku and Ikeda, the innovative failure in Ota with which this book began represent the typical Ota small manufacturer.[6] Firms in Higashi Osaka have been somewhat more savvy in dealing with the powers-that-be.

2.6 Firms in Higashi Osaka

The economic value in social networks: Namitei

In 1965, after earning his engineering degree from Kinki University, twenty-three-year-old Masatsugu Murao began working for his father's nail, clip, and wire making company. Masatsugu's father Kazuaki, started Namitei (then called Naniwa Seitei which was changed to "Namitei" in 1991) in 1947. Masatsugu reflects upon his father's reign over the firm: "He had a way of reading market trends from the very beginning. For example, he says that his father thought to himself in 1946 – as he looked around at the war-torn expanses of cities in Japan – "this country is going to need a lot of nails to rebuild." From this idea emerged the firm that still exists today.

Kazuaki's son Masatsugu joined the firm during the heyday of Japan's "high growth period" that had started a decade earlier in the early 1950s. At the time, like many Japanese small manufacturers Namitei had profited from the surge in barbed wire orders for the Korean War. As a result, Namitei had been able to amass enough funds by 1963 to begin developing the cutting technology to make contoured wire (*ikeisen*), helping the company to start moving into a niche market (most customers want the standard round shape) within the wire industry.

Namitei prospered throughout the 1960s, until the rapid rise of the yen in the early 1970s, resulting from the devaluation of the US dollar after the Nixon administration announced in 1971 that the American currency would no longer be backed by gold. The impact on the Japanese economy came to be known as the "Nixon dollar shock." Japanese manufacturers were hard hit by the rapid appreciation of the yen. Unfortunately Namitei had just started selling large volumes of product to US automobile producers. The dollar shocks devastated Namitei's sales, and by the 1980s they had dropped by 50%. Many of its competitors were going under: of Namitei's nail and bolt maker competitors, half had gone under by the end of the 1980s. The ones that survived did so on the basis of proprietary technology ("Finding a Way out through Upgrading Technology" 1996). Namitei was at a crossroads – should they continue as a component and parts producer – and remain vulnerable to currency rate fluctuations and other external shocks – or try to develop final products?

In 1985, in the midst of deliberations about the strategic direction of Namitei, Masatsugu Murao's father suddenly died. Masatsugu took over as president. Like many entrepreneurial start-ups, his father had run the business with much charisma and personal style. The family had depended on his leadership over the years. Masatsugu was honest with himself; he and his three brothers knew that they could make things but also knew that they lacked the market expertise in creating new sellable products. The firms' survival depended on them figuring something out – right away. What could three young brothers with fifty employees and a company to keep in business do?

They decided to try flooding trade magazines and newspapers with advertisements about their expertise and calling on potential clients to propose products: it worked. The same year, a Tokyo firm saw a newspaper article plugging Namitei and called Murao up, asking if the company would produce hollow cable with special specifications, such as underwater pressure resistance.

Murao's initial reaction was "probably not" but thinking of his workers who he was about to lay off, instead he said "send us the specs and we can make it, no problem." Three days later the specs arrived. The potential buyer wanted a 1 km long cable, which wasn't unusual. They also wanted internal dimensions of 0.005 mm. This was highly unusual. As far as Murao was aware, no one had yet produced cable with an internal dimension of less than 0.1 mm.

Murao realized that there simply did not currently exist cutting machinery that could cut that small. He would have to develop it himself – and fast. The next call from the potential buyer asked for delivery within two weeks. At one time, Murao would have refused the order, but he thought of his father's commitment to their workers and his legacy. Murao said "OK, we can do it." He hung up and made a call to a long-time family friend, Hiroshi Saito, then president of Nippon Steel. Namitei had purchased all of its steel from Nippon, and Saito had developed a relationship with Murao's father back in the days when Saito was Nippon's Osaka Branch Manager. The latter had officiated at two of Masatsugu's brothers' weddings. Saito immediately dispatched two of his top engineers to Namitei and together they figured out how to cut the cable to the required specifications.

Namitei made the delivery date, and soon after got a call from the purchasing manager of the Tokyo firm. The man demanded: "send a blueprint of your cutting specs." Murao laughed to himself, and replied "Well, that would be like handing over our trade secrets – your credit doesn't pay for that." The manager said with some derision, "You're a unique company. If you're that confident, we may ask you for your services again." A few days later, the order came in for a cable of the same specs in dimension, but this time for 3 km in length. After Namitei delivered, an order came in for 6 km, then 10 km. By that time, Murao says they had figured out through his informal channels in local government that this must be for that Japan–United States "Pacific Ocean Cable Project" (to lay transcontinental fiber optic cable between the two countries) – what other underwater project would require cable this long and internal dimensions this small?

Murao also learned from his informal contacts that the pressure was on at the highest levels to get the cable in the ground. The buyer hadn't had the courtesy to inform Murao of this from the get-go – though he was not surprised, large Japanese firms, especially in Tokyo, tend to be very closed-mouthed about things. By protecting the intellectual property of Namitei's precision cutting process, Namitei has since been able to command 100% of Japan's world market share for underwater fiber optic cable.

At the time, Namitei developed, serendipitously, another soon-to-be lucrative product. In 1985, as Namitei was producing the first round of multiple km cable lengths, Murao saw that his workers were having trouble putting the cable through the standard end-of-production cleaning process. Cleaning involved dipping cable into and out of an open vat of solvents. At these long cable lengths, it took too much time to clean the cable, and Murao's workers complained of the solvents' fumes. Namitei's production team created a device to save time and prevent fume exposure – dubbed "Namijet." Namijet consisted of an air-tight box within which a high-pressure hose was placed, connected to a dispenser of cleaning solvents. The hose would spray the cable as it passed through the box. The contraption sped up the cleaning process significantly and was fume-free. Namitei soon saw the market potential, patented Namijet and sold it to capital goods producers, including semiconductor producers.

Namitei's experience provides several lessons: first, in 1985, after the sudden death of their father, Masutsugu Murao and his brothers used potential clients to come up with new product ideas as well as tapping into information channels in local government. Second, after deciding on a new product idea, Namitei relied on its long-established social network with Nippon Steel to obtain the initial technological expertise to develop the products. Third, when pressed by its customer to share its "know how" by providing production specs, Murao refused, thereby protecting the firms' intellectual property from expropriation.[7] Finally, Namitei saw the inter-industry market opportunity of its Namijet cleaning device.

Maverick spirit and a little political savvy: Soda

As Yasaku Soda was completing his degree in engineering in Osaka, he was recruited by Hitachi. Having earned high marks on their entrance exam, Soda was soon designing temperature regulation systems for air conditioning products. His main focus was in developing machinery that could help clean the air of automobile plants. In collaboration with Horiba, Soda developed testing chambers to measure the kinds of gases in auto exhaust. Soda worked in design for seven years and then as product management for another seven.[8]

In the process of developing these systems, Soda realized that if you did not control the temperature, wind, and humidity around the testing system, the results would vary widely. Through trial and error, he designed a system that could control and regulate the air that circulated within the testing chambers. He proposed to his bosses the idea of making the Hitachi testing units more efficient and accurate. Soda says, "my idea just did not fly at Hitachi. I was told that such a specialized system could not be produced in large lots and was therefore not viable."

Soda had other ideas. He rented a small plant and with two friends had produced his first air cleaning/testing system by September 1974. By December, he took the plunge and went independent. He left Hitachi, but maintained ties to its technologists, who he had befriended over the years. Soda had hoped that his former bosses at Hitachi would kick-in some support, but in the end his parents were the only ones to invest.

In 1978, Soda visited the newly opened regional offices of the SME Finance Corporation in Higashi Osaka. He applied for funds to help him purchase land to build his own factory and was surprised when they approved his application. "I think that mine was the smallest firm that they had ever lent to." In the same year, he entered into a JV with Horiba to develop testing system rooms for auto makers. These systems hit the market just as auto makers were becoming more sensitive to the need to reduce emissions and Soda sales increased steadily in the 1980s. Soda continued to plow as much as possible into R&D and Soda currently holds 85% of the world market for these systems. In 1979, Soda hired one of his juniors at Hitachi and still maintains loose ties with their technologists, occasionaly hiring a talented technologist chafing under the corporate hierarchy. For example, Soda recently hired an engineer from the Osaka University graduate school who had quit Hitachi after only a year, citing the anti-creative atmosphere. Another former Hitachi employee consults for Soda when the latter applies for METI programs. Soda says that this person's time at Hitachi has made him quite adept at METI paperwork.

In the early 1990s, Soda sensed that the auto industry might not always be such a lucrative market. In 1990 he started to think about air cleaning systems for operating rooms and labs that would clean the air in specific areas of a room, rather than having to clean the entire room. Within five years he had created a system that could be installed above the operating table (standard air cleaning systems require a full-room assembly) like a light fixture. This product is cheaper to produce than the full-room system and saves valuable room space. He has in the last few years put a lot of effort into clean air systems for the medical field and has sold systems to Kobe University and other teaching hospitals in the area.

Soda has relied on his loose ties through friends and former co-workers at Hitachi and Osaka area universities to attract talented young technologists as well as those who can navigate governmental hierarchies. He has also prioritized R&D into new products, even when the market potential for such ideas was uncharted. Finally, Soda was savvy- enough to employ someone adept at completing government paperwork in order to successfully gain funds from government programs.

Kyoto firms, like their counterparts in Higashi Osaka, have shown business acumen and political savvy – perhaps on a grander scale. Kyoto offers a number of entrepreneurial stories in cutting-edge high technology industry, including Kyocera, Murata, and Horiba, among others. These stories are explored in detail in chapter 6. For now, I return briefly to Kyoto's Samco – the entrepreneurial machinery maker with which this book began.

2.7 Firms in Kyoto

Core technology and niche markets: Samco

Samco is among the most successful of the independent SMEs I interviewed, having mastered its core technology with two strategies: international ties and collaborative R&D.

International ties

Over the years, Samco established international ties in two ways. First, Samco actively sought out foreign technologists to employ in-house. Currently, more than 10% of Samco firm's workforce is foreign, the bulk of them technologists. Samco also employs foreign legal and management staff from the USA, Southeast Asia, and Eastern Europe. In the start-up phase of the firm in the 1980s, these technologists worked in Kyoto. Over time, Samco established R&D centers in other countries – nanotech (USA), silicon (Japan), ceramics (Cambridge) – which also participate in the international exchange of technologists.

R&D focus

On start-up, Samco's first inclination was to try to establish ties with the research labs of large, established firms. Samco quickly learned, however, that these firms had no interest in collaboration without exclusive subcontracting ties. Instead, Samco cooperates with about ten other (mostly Japanese) SMEs on joint R&D, and also several American firms. In the early stages of Samco's development the firm faced the dilemma between forging potentially stable long-term exclusive ties with large firms (with deep pockets for R&D expenditures) and risky, loosely organized relations with small firms like his own. Tsuji chose the high-risk route. A number of products have emerged from close collaboration with other small firms as well as university students.

Samco has been able over the years to obtain numerous patents in the USA and Japan. Tsuji says that from the beginning his firm sought to avoid an exclusive sales relationship with any keiretsu group. Currently less than 10% of sales go to its top client. In 2003, Samco held more than fifty original patents on various products.

Commenting on the state of Japanese government support for R&D, Tsuji says that the Kyoto regional governments' SME Center has been helpful over the years in allowing his firm to benefit from MITI (now METI)-sponsored research programs. Samco has found, however, that the most creative product plans arise out of the interplay among firms and ideas, not from government support. At the same time, Tsuji has been savvy enough to use the regional SME Center as a go-between in obtaining R&D funds from the government. Samco technologists have also participated in various networks and study groups sponsored by local government.

Tsuji explains that in large firms such as Hitachi, with vast cadres of researchers, one problem is that a lot of money is spent on not very much innovation. The fact that giants like Hitachi have enormous political clout means that big firms can always depend on the government for favorable policies and special funds. The challenge for Tsuji – recently selected as a national role model for would-be entrepreneurs – is maintaining the right balance. This means being savvy at utilizing government channels for information and funds – but not getting too comfortable in the relationship. Instead, Samco has observed that the most promising new products come out of the collaboration of smaller firms working together in dynamic collaboration. Unfortunately, according to Samco, because of the informal nature of most SME to SME links, these innovations don't show up in government reported statistics.

In fact, Samco participates in and has established local area networks and study groups – for example, Tsuji co-founded the Kyoto Venture Forum, in which the presidents of 100 leading firms such as Samco, Omron, Kyocera, and Horiba get together to evaluate the business plans of new ventures. The Forum has its origins in the Samco-initiated Venture Study group of fifty local firms. These kinds of initiatives are discussed in chapter 6.

Not surprisingly, then, Samco has established collaborative R&D programs in recent years with research centers in Silicon Valley, Singapore, and Taiwan. This international collaboration complements the research relations Samco has with Japanese universities. For example, Samco has established ties with the engineering program at Cambridge University, whereby Cambridge engineering graduate students conduct internships at Samco. Entering the 1990s from a solid financial and technological position has meant that Samco had capitalized on the fallout from the decade's failures.

Surviving the collapse of the "bubble" in the 1990s

Asked what strategies were employed to help the firm weather the storms of the recessionary 1990s, Tsuji outlined four programs. First, Tsuji made it a point to stay at the forefront of new product development. Second, Samco reduced production costs by setting a numerical goal of 15%. By 2003, costs had already been reduced by 9.8%. Third, Samco took on the top people let go from other tech firms, especially research technicians. Fourth, the firm acquired new plants, which were relatively inexpensive after the collapse of the real estate "bubble." Each of these was achieved on the basis of Samco's long-time policy of maintaining financial strength – i.e. capital liquidity – which Tsuji adds has not been a major focus for his Japanese competitors.

Nevertheless, Samco has not been able to escape all of the negatives of operating in Japan, such as the delayed payment system:

> If I sell to IBM, the money comes right away. If I sell to Hitachi, 150 days later a draft [*tegata*] comes – not cash. In fact, about half of the firms we sell to pay in drafts. We pay out cash to all of our suppliers, so we often have cash flow problems.

Samco's experience shows that even firms that are able to surmount the barriers posed by the vertically integrated production and patent systems must still deal with the biases in the financial system. Tsuji's long-time focus on cutting-edge technology research really began to pay off in the 2000s.

Expansion in the 2000s

In 1995, Samco was approached by Kirin Brewery about developing coating technology and over the course of seven years the two collaboratively developed this technology. As a result, in 2003 Samco and Kirin obtained a joint patent on carbon thin-film coating technology for "PET" (recyclable) bottles. This technology makes it possible to produce beer in plastic bottles without worries about leaching and also facilitates the recycling process. This JV is likely to generate such revenue that it is expected to overtake Samco's core business revenue by 2006. Tsuji decided to farm out the production of these bottles to another manufacturer, choosing instead to stick to Samco's core competence in developing cutting-edge thin-film technology.

Over time, Japan's METI has come to recognize the success of Samco and similar firms and often asks Tsuji to advise the ministry on various technology policy projects – so much so that he is now a METI employee (*yakuin*). Tsuji, however, cautions start-up firms from depending on government programs, as they are notoriously weak at assisting real start-ups. Tsuji argues that METI should focus on these entrepreneurial mavericks (particularly for technology upgrading, *gijutsu kaizen*) rather than the relatively established medium-sized firms (*chukenkigyo*) that seem to be METI's bias in its innovation cluster and other technology programs. The policy implications of this bias are addressed in chapter 4.

Samco's experiences offer three main lessons. First, you should start out by going it alone. In the start-up stages, do it on your own and do not depend on government programs. The important thing is to establish a vision or goal and strive to meet that goal with specific, quantifiable targets (sales, R&D expenditure). Second, forge international ties (have openness). Circumvent exclusive (e.g. subcontracting) relationships in favor of loose, international networks of R&D and sales ties. Third, strive for capital strength (liquidity) and build in specific targets for (a) healthy profit margins and (b) cost reduction. Another measure of Samco's overall success is that, in May 2002, the firm successfully fielded its first initial product offering (IPO).[9]

In its third decade, Samco has come to be viewed as an archetypical "Kyoto Model" firm and its founder and president Osamu Tsuji is the consummate first-generation Kyoto entrepreneur. Other Kyoto entrepreneurs of similar ilk include Koji Akita.

Mastering the art of (Internet-based) collaborative manufacturing: Akita

In 1982, twenty-eight-year-old Koji Akita, with a degree in management, began working for his parents at their small mom-and-pop sheet metal processing workshop in Kyoto, Akita Works. In 1965, Koji Akita's father had taken over the family business, which had been established in 1946 by his own father. In the early post-war years, Akita Works produced barber and beauty shop equipment, and later in the early 1960s began to produce their own brand of dryers and steamers. That business did well for a while, but by the time the young Koji Akita had joined the firm, Akita Works had just started (in 1981) sheet metal processing, while the earlier final goods business had fallen away.

Like many other subcontractors of Koji Akita's parents' generation, Akita Works' livelihood was dependent on a small number of clients. Akita Works' customers routinely demanded delivery within twenty-four hours after placing their orders. This kind of production turn-around time was back-breaking while at the same time profits were slim and inconsistent. Akita Works was going nowhere fast, stuck at the lowest levels of the production ladder in the manufacturing industry.

Akita knew that he had to do something to get his family out of this no-win situation. Having an interest in computers, and confident in his family's past success in producing final goods in earlier generations, Akita decided to take what little cash his family business had and risk making a change. He spent it all on computer hardware and software. With a room full of brand new computer equipment, Akita now had the basis for his entrance into software design. With some hard work and a little luck, by 1985 Akita Works had developed software to be used in product design and process management. These developments allowed Akita Works to get into the production of software-driven automated equipment and also to start thinking seriously about getting into the software business for the long term. The Akita Works Software Design Department (of two people) kept plugging along. By 1988 they had developed a software package that could easily monitor and control a variety of manufacturing processes without complex inputting requirements on the part of the end-user.

The software, called "AMS," attracted the attention of some large Japanese manufacturers and Akita had soon generated enough business to spin off the software design department into its own subsidiary: "Act".[10] In the same year both parent and subsidiary moved to a newly constructed building. By 1990 Akita Works had its own computer-aided design (CAD) system and by 1991 was able to establish an in-house processing technology center.

In 1991, at the age of thirty-seven, Akita Koji officially took over his parents' business as president of Akita Works. Soon thereafter, Akita came up with a plan – under the auspices of a local business network, Kiseiren (discussed in chapter 5), to improve his own and others' expertise in innovative approaches to marketing. Having read the Japanese translation of Peter Drucker's classic (1954/1996) text, *The Practice of Management* (*Gendai no Keiei*) but never having met Drucker, he initiated the "Peter Drucker Study Group" to focus on jointly dealing with challenges in marketing and innovation. Each month, member firms would contribute about ¥20,000 ($200) for materials, speakers and to facilitate the development of an Internet-based method of communicating among members. Meeting regularly with other ambitious young managers, Akita began to contemplate other collaborative opportunities with study group partners.

Both subsidiary and parent grew throughout the 1990s, with Akita Works getting into the production of semiconductor production equipment and sensor and testing equipment (the latter with applications in over 2,000 types of products). Akita Works also started – with other Kyoto SMEs – collaboratively producing final goods such as birthing capsules and medical sensors. Some of these collaborative manufacturers had been introduced to Akita via Kiseiren and his own Peter Drucker Study Group. In 1988, Akita Works began collaborating with a faculty research lab at the Tokyo University (Higuchi Lab) for the joint research and development of electrostatic devices, which continues today. By 1995, Akita Works' capitalization reached ¥20 million, while the number of employees held steady at twenty-five into the 2000s. In the 1990s, the subsidiary Act continued to develop custom-made software with applications in a number of areas, including CAD/computer-aided manufacture (CAM) and education.

Asked how Akita Works is different from the many small manufacturers in Japan that have gone under in recent years, Koji Akita observes:

> The suppression of individuality, especially in large firms [*kosei o osaete-shiyo*] has exacerbated the tendency of Japanese people to lack strength of expression and to allow themselves to be caged-in by organizational structures [*tojikomeru*].

In essence, Akita described the stultifying effects on entrepreneurs of the production pyramid – most pernicious in Ota Ward of Tokyo. Akita also says that the tendency for firms, especially large ones, to erect walls around themselves, within which employees are expected to make the firm the number one priority in their lives – over family, friends, and other social networks – discourages the free flow of information and ideas among all sizes of firms. Akita, through these networks has, like Tsuji at Samco, used the local and regional government as a buffer between his own firm and national resources.

Nevertheless, though Akita Works was finding it easier to attract skilled workers, the continuing credit crunch made purchasing new equipment more difficult. Akita Works often uses the Internet to access new customers, and its own web page helped as well. This strategy is discussed in detail in chapter 6. Akita notes that "until recently, it was very difficult to access information, as large assemblers have had privileged access to information from government programs and industry organizations."

Koji Akita took his parents' ailing sheet metal workshop and created a state-of-the-art software development firm. He didn't do it alone. He reached out to local business networks such as Kiseiren. Where a network niche was missing, he created one. With the help of these networks, discussed in chapter 5, Akita mastered the art of collaborative manufacturing.[11] Kyoto firms have not all been as fortunate as Akita and Samco, and Japan's keiretsu way of doing business challenges the most talented Japanese businessmen.

Top-down management of a spin-off: Seiwa Information Systems

Seiwa Electric, started in 1949, produces control panels, clean room lighting systems, and other large scale light-emitting diode (LED)-based systems. At Seiwa Electric in the 1980s, Takehiko Araki was running the mechatronics and electronics R&D in these products. In 1989, Seiwa decided to develop the IT capability of the production management, using UNIX systems. Araki was hand-picked by Tomita, Seiwa's founder, to run the new effort.

By 1994, his development team's success in creating proprietary software to run real-time production of the various manufacturing systems at Seiwa Electric prompted Tomita to suggest creating a "Seiwa group" of independent firms, each firm having its own core business. Seiwa Electric would continue producing large-scale lighting systems and other firms would spin off from the parent and produce specialized niche products, such as the UNIX-based production management software that Araki's team had developed. Tomita said to Araki: "Well, I can't give you much money, and all that you can take with you in terms of company assets is your own know how. Other than that, I will support you" (Yano 2001).

Araki had always wanted to strike out on his own, so he took the risk. Five members of his product development team joined him in the new venture. Araki was told by Tomita that the new subsidiary, Seiwa Information Systems (SEIS) would eventually become completely independent. At first, the parent would own the majority of stocks (60%). Later on, as SEIS revenue stream became more independent from Seiwa Electric, the parent would step back from its subsidiary. Araki and his team moved out of the corporate office and into a venture business incubator in Kyoto (Kyoto Research Park) in 1995. SEIS soon had developed an Oracle®-based relational database program used in product management and process diagnostics for manufacturers. In the first year after start-up, Seiwa Electric remained SEIS' largest client (70% of sales).

In 1998, three years after its foundation, Araki described his relationship with the SEIS parent as cooperative and that the parent was keeping its promise of staying out of the day-to-day operations of SEIS. Soon thereafter, SEIS began to increase its outside sales and hire new software engineers.

By 2003, SEIS had twenty employees and its sales were no longer dependent on its parent. SEIS customers included a number of well-known Japanese firms including Omron, Hitachi, and Japan Electric as well as international firms such as Sun Micro Systems. In the meantime, Tomita's son Yasuhiro had risen to the presidency of Seiwa Electric. The parent still owned 53% of SEIS shares.

The parent began demanding more "administrative guidance" and "management strategy" meetings with subsidiary. Araki was shocked, it was not as though SEIS was failing and the parent had to come in and shake things up. On the contrary, SEIS' sales had climbed steadily and a number of new products were in the pipeline. Araki was baffled by this change in management strategy – from cooperative to one-sided, particularly considering the experience that Tomita's father and Seiwa Electric had with one of its main buyers when it was still a small, struggling entrepreneurial start-up:

> The customer, a large firm, said they wanted to rent part of our manufacturing plant that at the time was producing an electrical wiring product that we were developing. They paid top dollar, so we agreed. After a year, the firm suddenly pulled out. Within months it was producing *our* wiring product under its own brand name. Somehow they had managed to make copies of every minute detail of our product specs – "their" product was identical.

At the time, Seiwa Electric was still a small firm, with neither-the legal expertise nor the funds to retain a lawyer. Even if they had found a lawyer to take their case, Araki noted that the Japanese courts, and the government in general, had a heavy bias toward big firms. According to Araki, their rationale was that if there was money to be made, particularly in foreign markets, it made sense that larger firms were better equipped to get a given product to market faster and in greater quantity than small firms. In other words, the end-goal of obtaining a greater slice of the global market pie justified the means of starving the little guy at home.[12] Little did Japanese bureaucrats and their minions in the courts know that by squeezing the little guy over time the sources of (and incentive for) innovation would dry up.

Yoichi Ishikawa, founder of another leading small manufacturer in Ota notes that the biggest keiretsu groups even exploit their own (in-group) suppliers:

It's a problem with patent rights. Parent firms come in and ask for product specs, you know, on the ruse that they are just checking to make sure things are running smoothly or something. They take [the specs] and produce the product themselves, or sometimes farm out production to another small manufacturer in Japan, China or Southeast Asia. The worst offenders are the big name brand keiretsu groups – they know they can do it with impunity. We know who they are and we know not to deal with them. (Yoichi Ishikawa, Interview 1998).

In 2003 at SEIS, what had started out seven years earlier as a cooperative arrangement between parent and spin-off had deteriorated into counter-productive top-down management, monitoring and annoyance. Tomita's son, the new president at Seiwa Electric, had himself inserted as "chairman" (a position equal to president, though usually created in small firms as the founding president is ready to retire and turn over the management reins to his son) at SEIS. The relationship had soured to such an extent that Araki decided it was time to get out. By the end of 2003, at the age of fifty-seven, he took early retirement. He pondered about trying his hand at starting his own firm, or perhaps focusing on reducing his golf handicap.[13]

How Samco and Akita have come to embody the Kyoto Model of entrepreneurship – and how Seiwa represents an anomaly in Kyoto though reflecting patterns in aggregate in Japan – will be explored in chapter 6. The analysis takes on the next level, namely international comparisons, in chapter 7. Using comparative case studies in the American Midwest with reference to Germany and China, I examine how the patterns observed in Kyoto might be unique to innovative small business in other places; what, if anything, might be Japan-specific; and what is more widely distributed in terms of best practice.

Conclusion: Japan's "entrepreneurial gems" and the regional variation in its national innovation system

A good question to ask at this point is whether technological independence came as a result of eschewing exclusive keiretsu (vertically integrated) ties, or whether, through a firm's original technological independence, it was able to avoid being assimilated. While this is to some degree a "chicken-or-egg" question, several interviewees stated that in many a case of bankruptcy the firm that went under had in the past been a technological leader, but had eventually been put out of business by its parent's (primary buyer's) cost-down measures, as well as falling prey to abuses in the patent system. Firms that were savvy enough to avoid these hierarchies altogether, while obtaining government finance through semi-arm's length arrangements survived and prospered.

These innovators have also utilized local and foreign business networks for information and market access. This has possible implications for would-be emulators in other countries (discussed in chapter 7), as the successful firms in this research represent the exception to the rule of doing business in Japan. SMEs that have survived and prospered have generally done so despite the structures that dominate the Japanese political economy. In sum, hidden within the vertically integrated production pyramid (i.e, within Japan's national innovation system) lie ample stories of success, or "entrepreneurial gems."

These successes (and failures) also reflect interesting patterns of regional innovation. These socio-politically embedded regional innovation systems (RIS) succeed because entrepreneurialism is fostered while reliance on government policy is not. Supportive local governments act as advocates at the national level and are themselves prompted into action by politically savvy local entrepreneurs. Embedded within a complex system of social capital that generates overlapping networks and coalitions, entrepreneurs and local government officials can be confident that a favor given today will be returned in some manner in the future.

In many ways, firms in Higashi Osaka have greater affinities with Kyoto firms than their counterparts in Ota. For example, the Kansai (or "Kinki") region encompassing both Higashi Osaka and Kyoto (and Kobe and Nara) has two major characteristics. First, it is located far from the monitoring and oversight of the apex of bureaucratic and political power in Japan. Second, the Kansai region as a whole has few keiretsu conglomerates, save for home-grown Matsushita.

At the same time, Higashi Osaka, lying just south west of Kyoto, has struggled to increase value-added levels. Kyoto, on the other hand, as a cluster of firm-level successes and as a region of institutions and people, outpaces other regions in terms of egalitarian distribution of wealth between firms, number of entrepreneurial start-ups, globally competitive niche market producers, and other measures of innovation.

This success has garnered the attention of the central state in the latter's attempts to find a model of entrepreneurship and new business creation to save Japan's floundering economy. Japan's national approach to innovation has taken on a regional perspective in recent years – due in large part to the undeniable success of regions like Kyoto. National bureaucrats would be deluding themselves, however, if they attributed the rise of Kyoto to national policy. One size does not fit all. The "Kyoto Model" is worthy of closer examination and is the subject of chapter 6.

Until now, firm-level success in Kansai has been hidden in national-level reports on innovation in Japan. This is in part a consequence of the smaller (per firm) contribution to GDP (in turn in part a result of top-down credit taking within the pyramid). The lack of attention is also a result of the tendency of central state ministries to concentrate their (research and policy) efforts on the Kanto Plain (Tokyo and environs). Consequently, outsiders have never been privy to an accurate depiction of how the system really worked for the bulk of participants – SMEs and the entrepreneurs at their helm.

I would argue, however, that it is in the firm- and regional-level successes of these hidden entrepreneurial innovators that the prosperity of the Japanese economy lies. The personal narratives of entrepreneurial struggles inform us what the institutional barriers to innovation and new business creation in Japan are. The institutional interlock (e.g. between big business biased state economic ministries, patent systems, and courts) within the production pyramid works in negative ways for entrepreneurs and undermines innovation in general. In aggregate, weak intellectual property rights and the use of monopsony leverage, particularly in technology expropriation of the small by the large, undermine innovation. For example, it might seem obvious to an outsider that if a small firm were asked to share its proprietary technology with a client it would refuse out of hand. It should be noted in this context that in Japan, the monopsony leverage of keiretsu-dominated (pyramid) production hierarchies is embedded within a rule-of-the-powerful legal system. Small firms can seldom afford the legal fees or count on precedents for winning cases against the government's big business darlings, which remain the primary homes for retiring elite ministry bureaucrats. The reality is that in aggregate these institutions have created a climate rife with disincentives against the creation of new products and new market entry.

So, the social and the political matter a lot – at the national and local levels alike. Further, fundamental change in Japan has been precipitated only by a decade of crisis. Even so, it remains to be seen if reforms currently on the books will stick. One major hurdle is to change the way of thinking about the Japanese political economy – from inside and out. First and foremost is the reality of how so-called "relational contracting" (and its concomitant socio-political pyramids) has stifled innovation and new business creation at the ground level. If observers of Japan's pyramid organization or *soshiki* (so-called "trust-based relational contracting" with big firms in the lead position) had examined the system's underside they might have anticipated the dilatory impact on innovation in the long term. Perhaps these persons would then not have been so quick and confident to suggest Japan as a worthy model for other places. No entrepreneur worth his (or her) mettle (and forthright keiretsu insiders) on the ground in Japan ever bought into this trust-based relational contracting rhetoric – though it may have rung true in the upper echelons of corporate hierarchies in Tokyo and the most naïve of their subcontractors. The latter, by the way, have largely gone under since the 1990s.

Chapter 3 situates current firm- and region-level practice within broader theoretical debates about innovation and innovation policy. How policy (informed by theory) relates to practice is the subject of chapter 4. Chapter 4 also assesses what the Japanese government is doing (and not doing) to fix the problem of innovation management through its national innovation policy.

Notes

1. Case studies written based on two firm-level surveys (implemented in 1997–8 and 2002–3), interviews with firm founder-owner-presidents, internal company documents, and secondary materials.
2. Development capacity is critical for small firms to engage in innovation in final goods production across industries. See for example Gary Herrigel, "Emerging Strategies and Forms of Governance in High-Wage Component Manufacturing Regions," *Industry and Innovation* 11, no. 1/2 (2004).
3. Tetsuo Kinoshita, Interviews 1998, 2003.
4. Nobuo Shiratori, Interviews 1998, 2003.

5. Shizaburo Kuniyasu, Interviews 1998, 2003.
6. Shizaburo Kasasaku, Interviews 1998, 2003.
7. Matutsugu Murao, Interviews 1998, 2003.
8. Yasuku Soda, Interview 29 July 2004.
9. Osama Tsuji, Interviews 1998, 2002.
10. While building his subsidiary, Akita remained active on the local PTA. Through this volunteer work, he began to see the long term need of getting future generations of Kyoto skilled with computers. As a result, Act branched out into multimedia teaching and learning software. One of the packages about which Koji Akita is most proud is Act's "Time Travel in Kyoto with GPS" program enabling the user to explore Kyoto's history in an easy to use multimedia format supported by navigation technology. This product is for use by primary school children.
11. Koji Akita, Interviews 1998, 2003.
12. A 2004 court case in the US offers an apt comparison: "A federal jury in Los Angeles awarded $134.5 million in damages to Masimo, a small medical device company ... after finding that a unit of Tyco International willfully infringed four patents held by the company." Mary Williams Walsh, "Tyco Unit Loses Patent-Infringement Case," *The New York Times*, 27 March 2004.
13. Takehiko Araki, Interviews 1998, 2003.

3 Innovation theory: firms, regions, and the Japanese state

3.1 Innovation: definition, measures, and theories

Definitions

INNOVATIVE activity, sustained over time, is what keeps firms in business and provides resources (tax, employment) for the communities within which they are embedded. Not surprisingly, how innovation is (and should be) fostered within firms, local communities, and nations has been of interest to scholars and policymakers for a long time. For Schumpeter, the innovative impulse, driven by individual inventors and entrepreneurs – including that for new goods, new methods of production, and new markets – sets the capitalist engine in motion (Schumpeter 1934).

The OECD has compiled a comprehensive set of definitions and measures of various kinds of innovations with the goal of facilitating cross-national comparisons of "innovation policy." This new field is an amalgam of industrial policy and science and technology policy (OECD 1997). In general, innovations:

> comprise new products and processes and significant technological changes in products and processes. An innovation has been implemented if it has been introduced on the market (product innovation) or used within a production process (process innovation) (OECD 1994)

This book is concerned with innovation in high technology manufacturers in particular. As such, it is focused on determining factors supporting (and undermining) technological product innovation at the firm level:

> A *technological product innovation* is the implementation/commercialisation of a product with improved performance characteristics such as to deliver objectively new or improved services to the consumer. A *technological process innovation* is the implementation/adoption of new or significantly improved production or delivery methods. It may involve changes in

equipment, human resources, working methods or a combination of these (OECD 1997, emphasis added)

Measures

Patent data is often used as a measure of innovation, despite being not terribly effective in capturing the actual source of innovation (OECD 1996). In Japan, the holder of a patent is often not the original innovator, because of the practices of outsourcing product development to subcontractors, absorbing the subcontractor firm (or merely the technology), and then reporting it as an "in-house" development. A growing amount of research indicates that large corporations have engaged in systematic expropriation of the innovative design work of small firms.[1] With this caveat, innovation in this study is measured by a composite measuring firm-level innovative output that does include patent data.

Evaluating the Japanese political economy based upon whether or not "innovation" exists often leads to the mistaken conclusion that large keiretsu assemblers are the primary source of innovation. This misperception is understandable, given that many high-value-added products are produced under keiretsu group names.

It should also be noted that what is considered "high technology" in the 1990s may have become comparatively "low-tech" or even obsolete by the early twenty-first century. Take for example, the advent of transistors, and later semiconductor technology, which replaced the use of vacuum tubes in computers in the twentieth century. Currently in the development stage in the computer industry, for example, are bio-gels and laser-crystalline technologies that seem likely to take over as standards in memory storage.

Further, there are cases where relatively high technology (computerized) equipment and production machinery make products that can be called "low-tech" relative to other parts in the final product (e.g. fasteners holding a computer's drive reading device, which are suspended over the disk drive). In this research, "high technology" products consist of those included in the production of high-value-added manufacturing products. This includes a cross-section of firms in the manufacturing industry including electronics, electrical machinery, general machinery, and precision machinery.

At the lowest levels of innovation and value-added, a firm is engaged in the operation of technology, maintenance, and quality control.

A firm reaching higher levels of production becomes involved in production management, improvements in technology and molding. At the highest levels, the firm is engaged in product design, new product development, and equipment development.[2]

While the measurement of innovation has been a firm-level exercise, the presence or absence of innovative output by firms has implications for the international competitiveness of the national economies within which firms are embedded. With such high stakes, analyzing the sources of innovation has varied widely. This is in part a consequence of the fact that innovation is driven by a number of factors. These include the behavior of individual entrepreneurs (Schumpeter 1934; Drucker 1993), local support institutions (associations and networks), and the national-level policies of states (Nelson 1993).

The comparative advantage that certain states – such as Japan, Germany, and the USA – have developed in high technology manufacturing has given rise to analyses that have sought to determine whether there might be something about the national-level system of innovation that produces innovative activity over time. This body of research is loosely organized around the notion of a "national innovation system" (NIS). An NIS has been defined as "the network of institutions in the public and private sectors whose activities and interactions initiate, import, modify and diffuse new technologies" (Freeman 1991; Freeman and Soete 1997).

At the same time, between entrepreneurs and firms and the national context are various agglomerations of people and institutions, or "clusters," supporting firm-level innovation. Roelandt and den Hertog define clusters as:

> economic networks of strongly interdependent firms (including specialised suppliers), knowledge producing agents (universities, research institutes, engineering companies), bridging institutions (brokers, consultants) and customers, linked to each other in a value-adding production chain (Roelandt and den Hertog 1998)

Clusters are of three main types: *regions* (Marshall 1890; Krugman 1991), *sectors* (Porter 1990), and *value chains* (Verbeek 1999). It may be that the most successful regions are a combination of these types: spatial agglomerations of firms in inter-related sectors within value chains in which they hold a competitive advantage for the highest levels of value-added. For example, Marshall (preceding Porter's cluster analysis by nearly a century) observed that industrial districts benefited from innovative exchanges between spatially concentrated people, enterprises, suppliers, and skilled labor (Marshall 1890). Todtling and Kauffman outline a number of features within the regional innovation systems in Europe, including high-skilled local labor, networks rich in "untraded [informational] interdependencies," abundance of knowledge providers (e.g. university–industry links), activist regional governments, and the prevalence of collective learning (Todtling and Kaufmann 1999).

In the 1980s, prompted by the perennial economic success of certain regions, in contrast to domestic competitors, in Germany, Italy, and the USA, studies emerged that examined the institutional context within which certain agglomerations of firms (e.g. clusters) seemed to surpass their domestic and international rivals in terms of their ability to become innovative, adapt to changes in the global market, and remain innovative over time (Piore and Sabel 1984; Saxenian 1990, 1994a, 1994b; Sengenberger *et al.* 1990; Locke 1995). Much of the innovative activity in these regions takes place within inter-firm (supplier–customer) networks. That, is product and process innovation tends to take place interactively along the value chain, as opposed to within major firms, universities, or research institutes (Todtling and Kaufmann 1999). Research on Japan's regional innovation systems lags behind studies in the USA and Europe.[3]

In the 1990s, aiming at generating effective innovation policy, the OECD generated a number of innovation indicators. These indicators, outlined in its "Oslo Manual" (1997) laid the foundations for systematic cross-national studies of innovative activity in OECD countries, particularly European cases. A major concern in these studies is how to get from the measurement of pockets of (atomized) firm-level innovation to the diffusion of innovation across firms. "Diffusion" is the way in which technological product innovations spread from their initial market introduction to other firms, regions, countries, and industries (OECD 1997). One problem in diffusion, however, is that once technological knowledge reaches the community level, it becomes a public good (and therefore accessible by all) and the profit incentive of individual entrepreneurs and firms is undermined (OECD 1997).[4]

This research assesses high technology firm-level innovation within regions in Japan. Reflection on the contributions of existing works in explaining the conditions under which innovation is fostered (or undermined) at the regional level – in Japan and in a comparative context are a useful starting point for examining the attempts by the Japanese state to jump-start innovation at the firm level through an array of policies (the subject of chapter 4) and their impact, if any, on firm-level practice (the subject of chapters 5–6).

It seems that states, particularly Japan, have struggled to produce useful national innovation policy. For example, rapid developments in communications technology (e.g. the Internet) in the twentieth century have undermined the capacity of national governments to regulate, monitor, and control the activities of domestic firms. At the same time, the rise of the knowledge-based (and high technology) economy has led to the realization that firm-level innovation is inextricably linked to the people and institutions in a firm's environment (e.g. government policies, suppliers, competitors, socio-political and cultural practices).

The systems within which firms are embedded can be either *enabling* or *constraining* (and sometimes both) of a firm's innovative activity. How and under what conditions these people and institutions (or "framework conditions," see OECD 1997) serve enabling functions for firm-level innovation is an important area of study (Lundvall 1992; Nelson 1993; Freeman 1995).

This has also become a major source of debate (and consternation) among national policymakers charged with innovation and entrepreneurship policy. Chapter 4, on Japan's cluster initiative, illustrates the difficulties national governments have in getting from theory to practice in fostering innovation at the firm level. For example, post-war METI policy is often credited with creating the national conditions under which Japan's keiretsu giants emerged. A nimble MITI in the 1950s and 1960s evolved into an out-of-touch bureaucracy in the 2000s, unable to get a handle on the needs at the base of the production pyramid and in SME development.

Recent works have chronicled the failure of Japan to produce radical innovations (Porter *et al.* 2000; Lincoln 2001; Grimes 2001). While these works provide important insights regarding the role of the central state in facilitating or hindering economic activity, analyses limited to national-level differences do not identify important nuances in the effects of local and regional institutional environments (both constraining and enabling) on innovative outcomes at the firm level.[5]

A decade of economic crisis and inadequate policy response in Japan in the 1990s has shown a system unable to cope, particularly in supporting innovation in small firms on the technological frontier. What, then, is the optimal industrial policy for enterprises to support innovation and growth? This question has several parts:

- First, what role, if any, should governments play at the central, regional and local levels?
- Second, should the state play an interventionist role ("picking winners") or merely a supporting role (providing information and other enabling infrastructures)?
- Third, what should the policy relationship be with new entrepreneurial enterprises?[6]

Successful economies – those able to adapt at certain junctures to and navigate changes in the international technology environment – including Germany, Italy, Taiwan and the USA, have succeeded by having not one but several innovation systems.[7]

Various theories – including flexible production (relational contracting), flexible specialization (nimble agglomerations of SMEs), and industrial districts – have tried to explain why certain regions within national economies survived and prospered while others failed to adapt to post-Fordist production after the 1970s. A number of works have laid an important groundwork by outlining the new parameters of competition between big and small firms, and the changing role of the state.

Unfortunately, the theories that have been used to compare Japan with other advanced industrialized economies – such as arguments about the benefits of relational contracting (the *locus classicus* being the work of Ron Dore) – are empirically dubious. These works have painted a fallacious picture of the way in which the Japanese political economy works. Misperceptions rife in this literature are part of the reason why "Japan's lost decade" has confounded scholars and practitioners, particularly in terms of the critical question of how to foster innovation and entrepreneurship. What follows is a re-evaluation of major works in flexible production (relational contracting), flexible specialization, industrial district- and local network-based explanations of Japan's post-war competitive success in terms of what these works explain – and fail to explain – about firm-level innovation (and the lack thereof) in Japan.

3.2 Firm-level innovation in Japan

Odagiri and Goto (1993) provide an historical overview of the Japanese system of innovation, from its origins in the Tokugawa

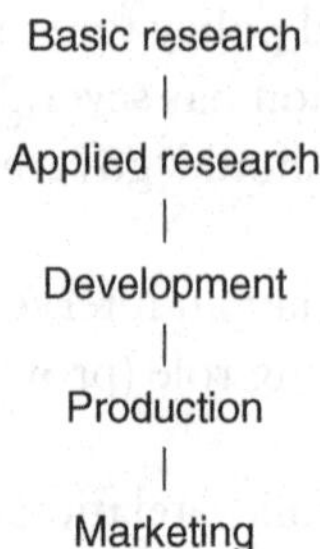

Figure 3.1. Linear model of innovation

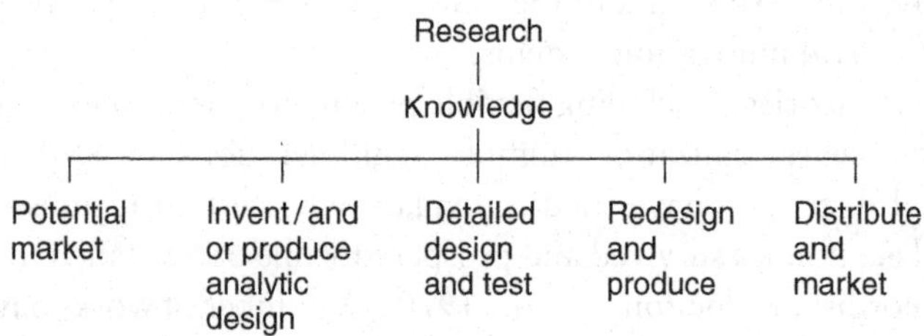

Figure 3.2. Chain-linked model of innovation

shogunate (1603–1868) and the Meiji Restoration (1868–1912). In these periods Japan borrowed technology from abroad on a large-scale, combining foreign technology with indigenous skill. This process laid the foundations for the structure of innovation in Japan that exists today. From the Meiji period into the pre-war era, Odagiri and Goto confirm that Japan's basic strategy was to transfer technologies from Western countries, especially in automobiles and electrical equipment sectors. Part of this strategy was a state-sponsored policy of reverse engineering and technology import through licensing and/or joint ventures (Odagiri and Goto 1993).

Imai and Yamazaki find that the core firm in an industrial network plays a crucial role in knowledge creation. In Japan, these core firms are large, keiretsu companies. It is within these keiretsu-controlled networks that the bulk of interactions – among firms and their subcontractors – takes place within and across industries.[8]

Aoki and Rosenberg posit a "chain-linked model" of innovation in Japan, in contrast to earlier, linear models (Figures 3.1, 3.2). Aoki and Rosenberg argue that scientific research capability does not sit at the apex of a hierarchical, linear process of innovation. Rather, basic research sits alongside other sources of technological improvement. In their "chain-linked" model, feedback occurs among the constituent parts in the process of innovation. They choose to downplay the fact that innovation remains dependent on an original "upstream" innovation. Without original, frontier innovation, the process of innovation becomes less truly "interactive," even in their model (Aoki and Rosenberg 1989).

Lagging start-up rates in Japan compared to other industrialized economies reflect the difficulties of moving from dependence on foreign technology to the basic innovation critical to fostering overall innovative capacity. Callon (1994), for example, examines the sources of breakdown in MITI-led technology consortia. This breakdown is discussed in terms of high technology R&D consortia (between MITI and select computer producers), particularly VLSI (very large-scale integrated circuits). He argues that MITI's industrial policy mechanisms are much better suited for exploiting existing (US) technologies than for facilitating innovation at the technology frontier. This is because frontier research is more speculative, and no longer in the area of "catch-up." Like earlier studies, Callon also focuses on large firms such as NEC and Fujita and their R&D links to the Japanese state (Callon 1994). This bias to big business and the central state in theory and practice in Japan has been a major source of misperceptions in the standard works on the Japanese economy. The following re-evaluation of major works on flexible production, flexible specialization, industrial district and networks shows how on-the-ground practice in Japan has never been reflected in standard explanations of Japan.

3.3 Flexible production

"Flexible production" is often described as the structuring of production and markets through the joint actions of governments (particularly central governments) and private enterprise in order to encourage innovation and minimize risk (Morales 1994). The system is said to be "flexible" because it can be adapted rapidly, particularly through state interventions, to exogenous changes. The Japanese flexible production system – i.e. the flexible way in which firms and society are linked in the development, manufacture and distribution of goods – was, at least until the 1990s, upheld as the ideal. Central state interventions targeting and sheltering infant industries, coupled with corporate strategies, supposedly demonstrated the successes of flexible production; examples include the successes in Japan in nurturing the development of the automobile and electronics industries. In the flexible production model, the central state plays a role in structuring the market through industrial policies (e.g. tax incentives). Large firms are at the core of this model, taking the lead technologically and in markets.[9] Small firms, in response to the changing needs of big firms, are expected to follow, and must do so nimbly (Abdul-Nour *et al.* 1999).

Flexible production is a system that supposedly operates somewhere between markets and hierarchies (Gerlach and University of California Berkeley 1992). Works on flexible production attribute the success of these production relations in part to long-term, obligational, "trust-based" relations. Interestingly, the existence (and meaning) of "trust" is never examined: trust exists because big firms and their state representatives say it exists.[10] Imai *et al.* (1985), for example, argue that supplier production networks work in Japan because of long-term reciprocity. They admit that big firms often "make unreasonable demands for production times, prices" and the like on their subcontractors. They defend these practices because in the long term subcontractors are paid handsomely.[11] Imai *et al.* admit, however, that there is "no guarantee the lead manufacturer will return the favor in the future" (Imai *et al.* 1985). These misperceptions of the Japanese economy, oft-cited in international comparisons, are illustrated in the work of Ron Dore.

Institutional interlock

For Dore, the foundations for successful state policy are threefold. Dore argues for a Confucian perspective as the basis for industrial success in Japan where good policy rests on a national collective identity, the high prestige of bureaucrats, and strong industry associations. Overall, Dore sees concerns for fairness and community as underpinning the Japanese system, and believes that a sense of common purpose and social solidarity make the rigidities in the Japanese system such as long-term relational contracting, flexible (Dore 1986). In sum, Japan has a community model of capitalism.[12]

An aspect of this community model that gives it systemic quality is its "institutional interlock" – that is, the way the institutions of lifelong employment in large firms, long-term obligated supplier relations, and so forth are interlinked. Yet, this institutional interlock, I would add, depended on the inter-firm hierarchies – keiretsu dominated vertical assembler–supplier production and favorable macroeconomic environment (growing export markets) – for its pre-1990s survival. The former stability of the Japanese system also depended on the support and cooperation, mandated by controls on exit and voice, at the base of the production pyramid, namely smaller firms and local communities.

Elsewhere, Dore has argued that other countries, specifically Britain, can find functionally alternative institutions to certain Japanese characteristics that encourage the creation of a system that provides for or enhances national identity, cooperation, and consultation between managers and workers, bureaucratic hierarchies, lifetime employment, financing for industry (through long-term planning and investment), and inflation control (Dore 1987). Yet, these are aspects of Japan as it was, not as it is now. The Japanese system worked effectively in the period when Japan was riding high on its export of incrementally innovated electronics and automobile products. Faults in the system became more obvious in the 1980s and 1990s when Japan's economy failed to adapt to new crises, such as industrial "hollowing out" and bank failure. Dore cautions that the "natural immunity of Japan cannot last forever" and acknowledges that MITI (now METI) policy has become less effective over time (Dore 2000). Picking winners, it seems, is more difficult at the frontier.

Role of the state

Like earlier developmentalist works, Dore emphasizes the central state's role in creating effective industrial policies (Johnson 1986, 1995; Amsden 1992). In doing so, Dore and others have identified important institutional features of the central state and key private sector institutions that have made certain structural rigidities, such as lifetime employment and keiretsu assembler–supplier relations, flexible in the past (Dore 1986). These "flexible rigidities" were indeed able, for example, to withstand the oil and dollar shocks of the 1970s. In more recent years, however, a growing body of evidence raises doubts as to the effectiveness and positive impact of state policies in structuring production.

Sakai (1990), for example, finds that many vibrant businesses were forced under as a result of state policies, precisely because these firms lacked established connections to the top levels of the policymaking pyramid.[13] Johnstone (1999) argues that the central state often gets technology policy wrong, and provides a number of examples of Japanese inventor–entrepreneurs who saw the commercial possibilities of US technologies and succeeded, despite MITI policy and interference. Admitting that the system may be in decline, Dore evaluates changes in the economic environment such as the end of high growth rates, shrinking export markets, falling asset prices, the recession, and the renewed authority of the American model.[14]

Technology and innovation

Dore points out that the incremental innovation on which Japan's postwar high growth was based depended on long-term capital, stable corporate governance, and consensus-driven decisions. At the same time, he acknowledges that paradigmatic changes in innovation require rapid decisions. Dore argues that as the pace of innovation changes as technology enters the maturing phase, the Japanese (and German) model will be resilient.

Dore provocatively argues that any distinction between fundamental and incremental innovations and their attendant impact on setting the parameters of competition is "protean" (2000 p. 233). In the conclusion of *Stock Market Capitalism: Welfare Capitalism*, Dore comments on innovation. For example, on the critical question on how growth can be rejuvenated, Dore acknowledges that the capacity for innovation is of the greatest importance. Yet despite doing so, Dore admonishes Japanese who have argued that Japan's system is suited for catch-up but no good for the new stage of innovation at the frontier – that is, for trying to emulate the hyper-capitalism of Silicon Valley.[15]

Japanese scholars have drawn parallels between the Department of Defense (DOD)/Route 128 nexus and the role of MITI in the private sector in Japan, arguing that the DOD–defense industry relationship is organized similarly to MITI–keiretsu ties (Ueda 1997). However, it can be argued that the elements of bureaucracy and hierarchy inherent in these structures are precisely the reason why the Route 128 community lagged behind Silicon Valley in the 1990s.[16] Dore states that a "careful account would most certainly show that in the US too, it is ... the corporate recipe [the community model] which produces the overwhelming bulk of [incremental] innovative activity." It would be interesting to read an analysis by Dore of the institutions he finds key in *radical* product innovation – a critical source of emerging sectors.[17]

Signs of decline

While Dore has remained steadfastly committed to the Japanese flexible production model, others have observed that aspects of the Japanese system that supported the model may be irrevocably changing. For example, Smitka (1991) chronicles the success of Japanese auto makers like Toyota – and the sources of their decline in recent years. Japanese auto giants have been very effective in their use of relational contracting with suppliers in making incremental innovations on US technologies, but in recent years capital and labor costs have risen dramatically and led to a decline in the industry. Smitka does not, however, adequately recognize the decreasing ability of large assemblers to transfer these rising costs to suppliers – which has also led to a decline in the power of auto assemblers. Poor performance and unprecedented layoffs in major Japanese auto makers in the 1990s is illustrative of the decline of the model. The period of Smitka's study ends in the 1980s, and this may explain why he does not address the difference in the institutional mix required for radical v. incremental innovations.

For Smitka, two factors behind the success of Japanese auto manufacturers are "trust-based contracting" and "competitive incentives." Trust is created through several mechanisms including: a long period of "courtship" before interdependence is solidified and the establishment of clear norms (on pricing, quality, etc.); supplier "cooperation associations," created by assemblers; and competitive incentives, including regular unilateral target supplier price reductions, which are said to encourage innovation (though this innovation has been an unintended consequence of transferring assembler costs to suppliers).

Trust?

Smitka compares the subcontracting relations prevalent in the auto industry to other manufacturing sectors in Japan (watches, consumer electronics, machine tools, printing, and steel). He found that a decentralized design process, in which capital goods tended to be specialized, forced assemblers to cooperate with suppliers and the latter with each other. For Smitka, these comprehensive supplier associations played the greatest role in the success of the automobile industry. Labor was homogeneous across sectors (with high-wage union in-house and lower-wage non-union and temporary workers in their suppliers' firms). These two aspects – supplier associations and homogeneous labor –[18] contributed significantly to the high vertical integration of the industry. In Smitka's later work examining the decline of the automobile industry, an analysis of a breakdown of trust between assemblers and suppliers is missing. This is unfortunate, since one would expect Smitka's model – based as it was on trust – to be truly tested in this period (Smitka 1991, 1996). In fact, my findings suggest that trust (in contrast to power asymmetries) was never an important basis for relational contracting agreements.

Inter-corporate alliances

Later works have continued this focus on the benefits of relational contracting for large firms. Gerlach's "intercorporate alliances," for example, are relationships based on localized networks of long-term, mutual obligation. These alliances comprise complex and often overlapping networks of vertical, horizontal, and diversified relationships. These intercorporate alliances, taken together, provide the basis for what Gerlach sees as the successful Japanese model of "alliance capitalism." Alliance capitalism has four manifestations in Japan: intermarket keiretsu, vertical keiretsu, small business groups (e.g. technoparks), and strategic alliances including JVs and project consortia.[19] He acknowledges that small business groups get short shrift in the literature, despite accounting for over half of all sales and assets of the Japanese economy. Nevertheless, he focuses exclusively on intercorporate alliances among six top keiretsu groups (Dai-ichi Kangyo, Fuyo, Mitsubishi, Mitsui, Sanwa, and Sumitomo).

Gerlach cites some negative effects of keiretsu organization and speculates that the truly innovative firms are actually entrepreneurial independents such as Honda or Sony (Gerlach and Lincoln 1992). He surmises, however, that:

> Viewed as a whole, Japan has done remarkably well at creating the virtues of a small-firm economy: spawning high rates of new venture formation,

instilling a sense of entrepreneurialism among the managers of those ventures, and nesting this in the context of strong patterns of competition (Gerlach and Lincoln 1992)

Gerlach supports this claim with one case, that of NTT. However, data on the paltry number of new business start-ups and the problems with spin-offs in Japan in the course of the 1990s undermine his claims. Though acknowledging the impact on keiretsu power of moving from technological follower to leader, Gerlach still finds that Japanese keiretsu groups "organize a substantial portion of their innovative activities through long-term relational contracts with their own keiretsu affiliates." For Gerlach, these are convenient pre-existing structures for sharing information, conducting finance activities, and carrying out inter-industry collaboration (Gerlach and University of California Berkeley 1992). He concludes that Japan has succeeded at creating a set of alliance forms in keiretsu that combine the best elements of entrepreneurship and integration. More recent large-scale business failures in Japan's corporate groups and their attempts at keiretsu reorganization belie his interpretation.

Flexible production arguments such as those advanced by Dore, Gerlach, and Smitka focus on the interactions between big business and the central state – namely, the benefits to large firms of encouraging exclusive relational contracting with suppliers. These approaches have not been concerned with the kind of innovation that supports small business communities and new business creation. Flexible specialization arguments, on the other hand, emphasize the role of small firms in local communities in this regard.

3.4 Flexible specialization

"Flexible specialization" is the use of flexible (multi-use) equipment and skilled workers in craft production. In flexible specialization models, local clusters of SMEs are the main engine of innovation in small firms. The notion of flexible specialization is distinct from flexible production. First, regional and local governments play a more important role than the central state in supporting communities of firms. Second, unlike flexible production arguments which focus on large firms and concepts such as "flexible rigidities" and "the community model," flexible specialization focuses on the innovative role of small firms. Innovative communities of machine tool makers in Germany and Japan are often cited as evidence of the successes of flexible specialization. Indeed, the adaptability of these communities in response to the economic crises in the 1970s supports arguments in favor of flexible specialization: that is, communities of small craft-based enterprises have been more flexible than mass production-based large firms in adapting to the technological environment of the late twentieth century.[20] Piore and Sabel (1984), for example, point out that the development of mass production has depended on the coexistence of its "technological counterprinciple" – the small firm sector. They cite Japan's substantial small firm sector favorably and contrast it with the situation found in Britain. According to Piore and Sabel, successful industrial districts in Germany, Japan, and elsewhere share three characteristics:

- First, they produce a wide range of products for highly differentiated regional markets.
- Second, firms in these districts make flexible use of increasingly productive, generally applicable technology – that is, firms produce the specialized machines that make the general goods in an economy.
- Third, these districts become catalysts for the creation of regional institutions that balance cooperation and competition. This flexible specialization is said to encourage permanent innovation.

Political institutions

In the past, political institutions supported this permanent innovation. These political institutions typically displayed municipalism, welfare capitalism, and familialism. Municipalities, or territorial confederations of small shops coordinated by an urban center (such as in the case of Lyonese silk weavers), protected firms against market shocks. They provided wage-stabilization systems and local trademarks for quality control, among other things. Second, industries were stabilized through the collection of taxes for unemployment insurance programs, which kept workers attached to their trade during slack times. These welfare measures also included the creation of vocational schools and health and safety guidelines. The entrepreneurial use of kin relations, or familialism in business dealings, resulted in loose alliances of SMEs specializing in component manufacturing operations.

Painting in broad strokes, Piore and Sabel describe Japan's system of production in terms understandable to those interested in the political economies of Europe and the USA. Japan's inter-firm relations, according to them, are most similar to France's *système motte* (federation of specialized firms and long-term main bank investment) as are Japan's "techniques of control." Japan's system of labor control likewise resembles that of the USA in the 1920s, as is its Keynesian stimulus of domestic demand, and its numerous industrial districts are akin to plant communities in Germany. These broad comparisons need attenuation and clarification, however, in order for informed conclusions to be drawn about the Japanese industrial system.

First, in their description of the history of Japanese firms they surprisingly skip from the 1930s to the post-1945 period. Consequently, they miss the opportunity to point out the relationship between central-state created wartime control associations and the continuities between the pre- and post-war periods, particularly in the institutional hierarchies between firms and the state. Second, Piore and Sabel identify technical assistance programs and later the creation of state-subsidized local research centers as being of help to small firms in developing innovative products. They skimp on supporting evidence, however, instead relying on a single source throughout.[21] To make matters worse, the source is a 1982 appeal for "presidential discretion" by an American firm via the US Trade Representative (USTR). In its appeal this firm cites its own research on the threat of Japanese competition – hardly an objective source. As a consequence, Piore and Sabel offer no evidence or evaluation of the success of these state-sponsored centers, and seem merely to be satisfied that they exist.[22] Research documenting how many centers sit unused, their high technology testing equipment and other machinery gathering dust (though providing nice revenue for large capital goods producers) contradicts their conclusions (Callon 1994). Third, Piore and Sabel miss the opportunity to make a more explicit comparison between Japan and Germany in their mention of the Japanese system of mass production being built largely on craft principles. Instead, the notion of craft principles in the Japanese context is left undefined and a discussion of the ways in which the Japanese system is built on them is absent. Piore and Sabel's analysis would have benefited from the inclusion of some of the extensive work in Japanese on craft principles in Ota Ward, for example (Matsumoto 1996; Tomohiro Koseki 2002).

Fourth, the authors' use of Nissan to describe rationalization programs and the relationship between large firms' authority and small firms autonomy is likewise superficial. The professionalization (in contrast to a prior familial nature) of inter-firm relations, with big firms at the top and smaller firms below, is characterized, for Piore and Sabel, by an observable shift in Japanese terminology: "subcontractor" (*shitauke*) becomes "outsourcing firm" (*gaichu-kigyo*) and "father" or "old man" in the deferential sense (*oyaji*) becomes "president" (*shacho*). They fail to appreciate how this rationalization also meant the dissolution of a family-like sense of obligation (or at least a pretense of it). As the relationship was rationalized/professionalized, it also lost the obligatory character of those familial ties.

Finally, Piore and Sabel interpret the responses of SMEs to the turbulent 1970s as simply the rationalization of production, "as they had many times before."[23] This rationalization was manifested in the shift to the JIT ("just-in-time") or *kanban* system. However, the interpretation of the dynamics of this new wave of rationalization depends on where one is sitting in the production pyramid. The assemblers' spin was that it was an important step towards a "cooperative industrial structure." A supplier's understanding of what was happening was that it was an attempt to shift inventory costs to them, an attempt that in fact succeeded. This is one illustration of how the system was in reality being pushed to its limits, as the earlier obligatory ("wet") ties were transformed into the opportunistic and often predatory ("dry") ties of today.

Lean production

Others are less optimistic about the global trend away from intra-firm mass production. For example, Harrison's view of current events is that large firms are moving toward "lean" production structures. Though outsourcing of production to small firms has increased, resources have remained firmly within large firms. In fact, Harrison finds that there has been an unprecedented concentration of resources within large firms. Large conglomerates have improved their production methods, allowing them to have global reach in order to control production at the local level. Hierarchy has persisted in these new structures (Harrison 1994).

Also acknowledging the persistence of hierarchies in these inter-firm relations, Sawai (1999) finds that flexible specialization as a production strategy adopted by small firms was realized by virtue of the leadership of SME owners, acting as political agents in the face of hierarchies within the Japanese production pyramid. Small firms were forced to struggle to survive and remain competitive in the face of pre-war and wartime central-state control policies, which protected entrenched interests, and firms unable to maneuver around these state-created barriers were either coopted or perished. Sawai and others view small enterprises not as providers of cheap, low-skill labor, but rather as important sources of leadership and highly skilled and specialized technology.

Like Sawai, Friedman's research on the Japanese machine tools industry finds that small tool makers succeeded through cooperative flexible manufacturing in regional economies. Friedman finds that these relations have evolved out of political struggles aimed at subverting bureaucratic plans for "rationalizing" their enterprises into vertically integrated production hierarchies. Friedman's findings indicate that MITI, instead of creating effective small business policy as often perceived, were in fact out of touch. In fact, Friedman finds not one case of successful implementation of MITI policy in the entire history of the industry (Friedman 1988). He does not discuss particular firm-level examples, opting to examine the Sakaki region (of Nagano prefecture) as a whole. Consequently, he fails to explain what successful firm-level strategies of flexible specialization are, and how they operate. Friedman's argument would benefit if he specified the ways in which firms subverted bureaucratic plans and worked with other firms in cooperative production. The role (or lack thereof) of particular associations, networks, and local government representatives, apart from the Sakaki Chamber of Commerce, is not explored. Despite the absence of thorough empirical analysis, Japan remains the ideal referent for authors examining the industrial potential of Western European countries.

Recent works analyzing successful firm and community strategies in European countries have continued to refer to the perceived Japanese model of flexible specialization. For example, Herrigel (1996) finds that successful adaptations in the 1980s by certain districts of SMEs in Germany to the demands of flexible specialization was characterized by SMEs avoiding rigid vertical subcontracting. Like the SMEs in this study, small producers in Germany avoided exclusive subcontracting relationships.

Decentralization?

Herrigel admits that his earlier predictions that decentralization, cooperation, and trust would triumph over corporate hierarchy may have been off the mark (Herrigel 1997; Herrigel and Sabel 1999). In its heyday in the 1980s, according to Herrigel, the German craft-production-based alternative flourished in competition against Fordist producers. However the entry of even more flexible producers, particularly the Japanese, exposed the rigidities in the German system. Herrigel remains optimistic, however, given that the Japanese are currently experiencing adjustment problems of their own. Other sources of hope for Herrigel are isolated cases of German producers successfully adapting to the new competition.[24] Interestingly, these exemplary German firms' experiences have been quite similar to the successful Japanese innovators analyzed in this book.

Herrigel has revised his argument to account for industrial decline in Germany. His reassessment of his work on flexible production hierarchies in Germany actually points to Japan as being more flexible, because it: (1) has less skill or artisanal attachments to a particular job or craft, which allows for more autonomy of work teams and greater speed in the introduction of new technologies; (2) holds low inventories which enhance production; and (3) lacks the bureaucratic elements of the German system that separate R&D from production (Herrigel 1997; Herrigel and Sabel 1999). In the following paragraphs, I examine how these three interpretations may in fact arise from misperceptions of the Japanese system.

Identification with craft

Herrigel is misinformed when he concludes that the Japanese system of production is less hierarchical and more flexible than that of Germany. This misperception stems from focusing on the closer relationship in Japanese firms between "conception and execution" in R&D and production. That is, Japanese industry is populated by what could be called, based on Herrigel's descriptions: "collective generalists" as compared with "fragmented specialists" in Germany.[25] While it is true that the "learning by doing" relationship between R&D and production has a positive effect on productivity and innovation in Japan, to conclude that this translates into less hierarchy in the system is incorrect.[26] In fact, others have argued that production in work teams is mainly a consequence of central-state–big business-created enterprise unionism, which has thwarted workers' craft identification in large firms (Koike 1995; Aida undated).

Low inventories

Second, there is debate within Japan about the relationship of the JIT or *kanban* system of holding no inventories at the assembler level and productivity, a practice which Herrigel sees as key to Japanese flexibility. While the JIT system does force collaboration between levels of the production hierarchy (e.g. subcontractors must deliver components on twenty-four-hour deadlines to assemblers, so they must always be at the ready), it is rather the scarcity of resources at lower levels of the production pyramid than "eliminating all production buffers" *per se* that forces systematic collaboration among suppliers. Denied capital surpluses from selling inventories, these suppliers are forced to outsource production to other firms. In essence, inventories are eliminated only at the upper levels of the production pyramid. Numerous stories of trucks filled with components and parked waiting on streets near the delivery bays of assemblers in order to meet JIT deadlines illustrate this point.

Bureaucratic elements

Finally, Herrigel's distinctions between the *Berufe/Meister* craftsmen identities and craftsmen identities in Japan are overstated.[27] Japanese craftsmen are arguably less fragmented within firms, but they remain highly fragmented outside the firm, lacking unions and a concomitant political voice. Herrigel does later mention in passing certain limits on flexibility in Japan. For example, he admits that there is indeed an overidentification with the community of the firm while at the same time little institutional infrastructure outside of the firm. In sum, Herrigel's revisions to his argument regarding the limits of German manufacturing flexibility point to precisely the same elements of hierarchy identified in this book.

Like flexible specialization arguments, theories explaining the success of certain industrial districts focus on communities of small firms. In contrast to flexible specialization, industrial district-based arguments emphasize the firm over the community as the primary force behind innovation and growth. At the same time, firm strategy is focused on being responsive to the needs of large firms. In this sense, industrial district models can be said to be the complement of the large-firm flexible production models discussed earlier.

3.5 Industrial districts

A third way of looking at firms and their productive environment is through industrial districts (Marshall 1890).[28] "Industrial districts" are communities of spatially clustered firms. State policies favoring the needs of big business are often at odds with the viability of these small firm-based industrial districts. Best (1990) takes the theory of flexible specialization to task for its emphasis on community as an agglomeration of firms and the environment surrounding them, and instead grounds his notion of the industrial district in the strategic actions of firms as "collective entrepreneurs." The resulting community evolves out of cooperative and competitive strategies at the firm level (Best 1990). Similarly, Whittaker examines industrial districts in Great Britain and Japan, and sees a decline in small firm-based industrial districts, due to the breakdown in subcontractor relations with large firms (Whittaker 1997)

In Best's (1990) analysis, the "new competition" in Japan and Italy between industrial districts of producers wins out over the "old competition" of US-style mass production and managerial hierarchy. Best sees these highly competitive entities as having four dimensions:

- First, the firm is organized like a collective entrepreneur and has a strategic not an hierarchical orientation.
- Second, consultative coordination occurs across phases in the production chain. This coordination is effective due to shared network norms of mutual responsibility within groups of firms.[29]
- Third, extra-firm infrastructure encourages both competition and cooperation.
- Fourth, strategic industrial policy is the dominant pattern in these districts: policies are aimed at shaping markets rather than reacting to them.

The empirical basis of Best's argument is his aggregate descriptions of the industrial systems of Japan and Italy. In his account, however, the Japanese system comes out as not being quite as free-flowing and competitive as his ideal. Japan's industrial structure is described by Best as an institutional complex of large firms, controlling hierarchical and captive value-added networks. Large firms are at the apex of these hierarchies while vast vertical tiers of smaller firms comprise the base. Best regards the industrial policy agencies of the central government as key to the system, which throws doubt on his claim of having a firm-centered theory. Best's inter-firm networks actually look much like the production pyramid presented in chapter 1 of this book.

In contrast to Japan, Italy's industrial structure comprises networked groups of small firms supported by inter-firm service associations. In Italy's system, the industrial policy initiatives of local government are of primary importance. Best notes the similarities between the active governmental support of inter-firm networks and production-type associational activities in Italy and Japan, but unfortunately, his evidence about Japan is sketchy. For example, data showing how the central state supports SMEs through a "whole range of extra-firm institutions," is from a single source – an English version of a MITI published outline of its policies.[30] Citing this outline, Best notes several laws targeting SMEs, including the rationalization laws and association laws in the post-war period. These laws that Best touts as demonstrating the effectiveness of government SME policy were in reality designed primarily to assimilate firms into vertical hierarchies. Like others, Best makes the mistake of assuming that (a) the fact that these institutions exist on paper means that they are actively functioning entities and (b) that this presumed activity is in the best interests of Japanese firms. He says:

> Without such services [provided by said institutions] small and medium-sized firms in Japan would be under more pressure to provide such services for themselves which, in turn would lead to larger firms and hierarchical organizations.[31]

Findings that follow in the chapters in this book on inter-firm networks and the Kyoto Model show that, on the contrary, firms in cooperation with one another in local business networks and associations having zero ties to the central state and only informal links to local government provide an array of self-funded services to improve their competitiveness, including market research and joint new product development. These findings are confirmed by recent research in Japan on successful network forms (Imai 1998). These activities have not, contrary to Best, "led to larger firms and hierarchical organizations." Interestingly, instead of highlighting experiences of SMEs, seemingly a logical move given that they comprise the industrial districts that are key to his argument, Best uses the giant Nissan as exemplar of a leader of the new competition. Nissan's poor performance in subsequent years, however (lagging sales and massive layoffs) contradicts his claims.

While Best's analysis is purportedly grounded in small enterprises, he draws his evidence for the Japanese industrial district model from the experiences of large firms and the policies of the central state. Fields (1995), on the other hand, grounds his analysis both theoretically and empirically in the small enterprise. He notes that Taiwan's system of production has been seen as speedier and more agile than Japan's. Not surprisingly, Taiwanese state attempts to institute vertically integrated subcontractor networks (i.e. the 1984 Center Satellite Plan), explicitly modeled on the Japanese auto and machine tools industries, have failed. Fields offers one of the few analyses that includes a balanced treatment of the role of the state while accounting for the role of small enterprise in development, growth, and innovation.

Fields explains the successes of Taiwan's small enterprise-based economy and contrasts it with Korea's chaebol-dominated economy (chaebol are corporate groups like keiretsu) through an "embedded enterprise framework."[32] He argues that the owners and managers of firms are embedded within institutions which are in turn shaped by state policies, cultural norms, and social and political relations. The economic actions and preferences of firms are consequently shaped by these relations. In this approach, institutions (formal, informal, temporary, and regularized) are an intervening variable between the state and economic outcomes (Fields 1995).

Fields focuses on the organization and behavior of business groups and their ties to the state. He argues that in order to account for the variation in enterprise structure between Korea and Taiwan one must understand the social and political institutions in which the business groups are embedded and how this environment has evolved over time. Success or failure in state challenges to socio-cultural norms – for example, in policies creating general trading companies in Korea and the failure of such policies in Taiwan – is determined by the willingness and ability of the state to influence the preferences and behavior of economic actors. The state's will and wherewithal are in turn determined by its internal coherence and harmony, its ideological constraints, developmental strategies, its institutional compliance mechanisms, and its institutional relationships with key economic actors.

In this scheme, the developmental trajectories of Korea and Taiwan can be summarized as follows. In the 1960s Korea's military and civilian political leaders and technocrats were tightly organized within the state. Ideologically, the Korean state was organized around the well-defined national goal of rapid economic growth. Consequently, the central state overcame socio-cultural obstacles to its polices through massive subsidies and incentives to a handful of industrial combines. With the acquiescence of the state, chaebol thrived at the expense of thousands of smaller enterprises. During the period of industrialization, chaebol generally deferred to the state when their policy goals clashed. In the long-term, social and political costs forced the state to adjust industrial policy, which exacted costs on an increasingly autonomous and less cooperative big business sector.

In Taiwan, however, at the onset of industrialization, a minority nationalist regime adopted industrial policies and created an institutional framework quite different from that in Korea. The paramount concern of the Taiwanese government was the prevention of the concentration of financial power, and the maintenance of price stability. These goals greatly restricted the scale and influence of Taiwan's business groups. At the same time, "traditional socio-cultural norms," including familial enterprise relations affecting the development and organization of business groups, were restrained only when they conflicted with state goals of stability and equitable income distribution. This structure had the effect of limiting the economic possibilities of state policy. In the late twentieth century, the political and social roots of state strength declined, affecting its capacity to check the growth of business groups.

There is no doubt that the concentration of economic resources in large combines allowed the state in Korea to focus industrial policy and permitted big firms to exploit economies of scale. As with the other studies previously discussed, when the goal is industrialization or catching-up to lead economies, efforts to structure society around central-state–big business-dominated institutions are quite effective.[33] Problems arise once this goal has been met, however, and Fields makes a fundamental distinction between the dynamics of state–big business nexuses v. those of state–small (local) business nexuses. When the goal is no longer industrialization but innovation and fostering creativity, institutional structures supportive of small firms, rather than big firms, are most effective at maintaining growth and competitiveness.

In a chapter in a book on the "Four Asian Tigers", Fields further develops his notion of the embedded (within governmental and societal institutions) enterprise in Taiwan (Fields 1998). He sees three factors converging to create an industrial structure conducive to flexible specialization: regime motivations, market opportunities, and cultural proclivities. First, a major political motivation of the Kuomintang (KMT, Nationalist Party of China) regime was to limit the concentration of private capital. Consequently, when state policies to manufacture and export were created they applied to all firms and not to a handful of select firms, as in Japan and Korea. Second, Taiwan's highly educated labor force and experienced merchants enhanced the market's transactional efficiency. Start-up and market entry are easier and more rapid than elsewhere in East Asia. Complementing the KMT regime's desire to avoid capital and power concentration, the relative ease of entry (and exit) act as counter-pressures to hierarchy. Third, "Chinese cultural proclivities" toward connections (*guanxi*), particularly trust-based, familial ties make Taiwanese firms extremely flexible in the areas of labor, savings, and entrepreneurialism (nimble and swift). At the same time, Taiwan's flexibility primarily in labor-intensive industries may not match the new technological environment, which requires increasingly complex and sophisticated technological innovation.

As with the firm-level focus of industrial district models, theories examining local inter-firm networks tend to focus on smaller firms. Network arguments also emphasize the supportive environment around firms that can be provided by local and regional governments.

3.6 Local networks

Discussions of local inter-firm networks appear most often in the literatures of business and economics.[34] Not surprisingly the central agents are the firms that make up the networks.[35] A role remains for national industrial policy, however, in creating a supportive environment for new start-ups. The geographic proximity of firms to each other also plays an important role. DeBresson and Amesse find that geographic proximity is crucial to having a nurturing environment for innovative ventures (DeBresson and Amesse 1991). Saxenian finds, however, that being "clustered" is not enough to ensure innovation. Firms must be embedded in an environment that is non-hierarchical and informal. For example, Boston's Route 128 economy has failed to remain innovative due to its conservative, hierarchical nature, in contrast to the dynamic environment of Silicon Valley. Saxenian argues further that regional policies (i.e. metropolitan or county) must help firms to grasp and respond quickly to changing conditions rather than protect or isolate them from competition or external changes.[36] This is consistent with my findings that local and regional governments in Japan have acted as advocates for local firms in the areas of technological exchange and market information sourcing, for example.

Saxenian examines the phenomena of "collective innovation" found in Silicon Valley and contrasts it with innovative decline in Boston's Route 128. She concludes that innovative regions are decentralized industrial systems organized around regional networks of firms, tied to R&D at local universities and supportive local government. These relations encourage creativity and innovation that is free-flowing and that involves a variety of actors and entities. For Saxenian, a region's industrial system has three parts: local institutions and culture (public and private, formal, and informal), industrial structure (with varying degrees of vertical integration, and a variety of links among parties), and corporate organization (hierarchical or horizontal, centralized or decentralized) (Saxenian 1994b).

Boston's Route 128 comprises mainly a small number of highly self-sufficient corporations. These firms exercise centralized corporate control and are dominated by vertical information flows. They tend to produce products having military applications, with the result that industrial research programs at the Massachusetts Institute of Technology (MIT) have likewise had a military focus. The social context of these Route 128 firms is conservative and based outside the firm and craft (e.g. churches, schools, tennis clubs). This conservative context reinforces stability and company loyalty within firms. Further, operations from design to marketing tend to be internalized within the firm. Consequently, Route 128 firms became isolated from external sources of information and know how. According to Saxenian, these rigid and hermetic hierarchies were to blame for the region's loss to Silicon Valley of the lead first in semiconductor technology and later in PC production.

Silicon Valley, in contrast, is a decentralized network-based system which comprises loosely linked firms employing technologists having greater loyalty to the craft than the firm. These firms and technologists interact within a variety of informal and formal cooperative practices and institutions, especially associations. Stanford University, through its Industrial Park, has fostered dynamic ties with both established firms and new enterprises. Silicon Valley faltered briefly in the 1970s and early 1980s when it adopted mass production and hierarchical management strategies, because these mass production strategies segmented the production process (relocating the fabrication of semiconductor wafers to lower-cost areas) and separated R&D from manufacturing and assembly. In the late 1980s and 1990s the Valley rebounded, thanks to a return to the earlier principle of collective innovation.

Like Saxenian's analysis of the innovative community in Silicon Valley, Locke (1995) argues that dense, egalitarian networks among firms have been the basis for economic vitality in Italy. The reasons for Italy's success rests in "socio-political networks" comprising associationalism, inter-group relations, political representation, and economic governance. Locke identifies three ideal types of networks: hierarchical, polarized, and policentric.[37] Briefly, Locke's hierarchical network type corresponds loosely to the production pyramid and his polarized type is akin to dual-structure theories. Regions comprising dense networks of open and inclusive associations and interest groups having multiple horizontal links (policentric relations) have been the most vibrant in Italy. Policentric networks facilitate information sharing, provide for the pooling of resources, mediate conflict, and generate trust among local economic actors.

In sum, the elements of hierarchy in some regions in Germany, Korea, and around Boston's Route 128 correspond closely to the inimical effects of the Japanese production pyramid on innovation that this study reveals in Japan. My findings, taken together with the recent findings of successful small firms and the innovative communities in which they are embedded in the US, German, Italian, and Taiwanese cases, further undermines arguments about the cultural uniqueness of Japanese hierarchies. On the other hand, the free-flowing yet communal nature of Silicon Valley, for example, should not be seen as a model that Japanese innovative communities have emulated. Rather, the findings of this book show that Japan has endogenous alternatives to hierarchy. One example is the Kyoto Model of entrepreneurship and innovation, discussed in chapter 6.

3.7 Comparing theories of innovation

Scholars have taken a variety of approaches to explaining the factors behind successful communities and economies (e.g. in terms of global market share, new product innovations). These works advocate various types of inter-firm interaction as being best practice for firms and the communities and the economies in which they are embedded. Previous studies have emphasized three different levels of analysis: a given economy as a whole (Dore, Fields, Gerlach), regions or industrial districts within economies (Friedman, Herrigel, Piore and Sabel), or the firm itself (Best, Johnstone, Locke).[38] Some have argued that the central state has played a key role in making domestic firms competitive and can still play a role in innovation at the frontier (Dore, Fields). A few ignore the role of the state altogether or argue that the state does not play a role in innovation or new business development (Best, Friedman, Gerlach, Johnstone, Smitka). Others take a more balanced approach and argue that firms and the economies in which they are embedded can work effectively within local and regional governments in making sound industrial policy (Herrigel, Locke, Piore and Sabel, Saxenian).

Empirically, some have chosen to evaluate industrial competition in aggregate, not focusing on any industry in particular (Best, Fields, Gerlach). Others have supported their arguments with empirical evidence from specific sectors, including the machinery and machine tools industries (Dore, Friedman, Herrigel, Piore and Sabel), consumer electronics (Johnstone) and the automobile industry (Locke, Smitka). In more recent years, research has focused on high technology industries (Saxenian).

Table 3.1 condenses the main findings of each body of literature: flexible production, flexible specialization, industrial districts, and local networks. Reading table 3.1 from left to right, we see a corresponding increase in emphasis on firm-level v. state-level strategies as explanations for innovation, productivity, survival, and so forth (central state approaches have been common in the field of political economy, less so in economic sociology and virtually non-existent in economic and business literatures).

Table 3.1 Comparison of inter-firm interaction types

	Flexible production (Dore, Gerlach, Morales)	*Flexible specialization (Friedman, Piore and Sabel)*	*Industrial districts (Herrigel, Whittaker)*	*Innovative networks (DeBresson and Amesse, Saxenian)*
Level of analysis	Economy	Communities of firms (regional)	Communities of firms (district)	Communities of firms (regional)
Explains	Success of Japan in weathering exogenous market shocks, maintaining global market share	Ability of some countries (Germany, Japan, USA) to adapt production systems from Fordist/mass to flexible/specialized	Resilience/survival of certain agglomerations/ local clusters of firms over others intra and inter nationally	Maintaining innovation and new business creation/innovative communities
Goal	Efficiency in production	Innovation	Community building	Innovation
State role	Structuring of production and markets	Creation of industrial community that favors innovation	Support for inter-firm networks	Regional-local-level policies to support businesses
Central-state role	Key	Background, supportive	Strategic/shaping of market	Negative, drag on innovation (bureaucratized and formal)
Degree of local/ regional government role	None	Key	Key (regional, Herrigel)	Can support more durable (than international alliances) networks

	Flexible production (Dore, Gerlach, Morales)	*Flexible specialization (Friedman, Piore and Sabel)*	*Industrial districts (Herrigel, Whittaker)*	*Innovative networks (DeBresson and Amesse, Saxenian)*
Large-firm role	Lead	Trading partner	Exploitative	Network partner
SME role	Flexible, in adapting to environment created by large firms	Core, innovative	Entrepreneurial	Core
Key concepts	JIT, flexibility in system, decentralization	Trust, embeddedness, reciprocity	Shared network norms, entrepreneurial firm	Innovation clusters (Schumpeter), learning by doing
Locale	Global reach	Local clusters	Local clusters	Regional clusters

An underlying thread in the analysis of the above works has been the identification of misperceptions and misinterpretations in Japan and elsewhere of various works that attempt to determine the sources of and barriers to innovation. My main concerns are as follows:

- First, many scholars have ignored the contributions of small enterprise, leading them to overlook an important element of innovative activity in Japan. This glossing over of the vast SME sector, which is a critical element of the Japanese economy, was perhaps unproblematic before, when rates of growth were high and export markets growing. The formerly invisible contribution of SMEs to overall innovation (as well as the expropriation of innovations from SMEs) has been rendered visible by the 1990s economic crisis.
- Second, the bulk of the literature has focused on the exploitation of economies of scale by large firms, an integral part of the success of which was relational contracting. The assimilation of SMEs into these hierarchies was part and parcel of the supposed flexibility in the system. The global technology environment has entered a new phase, however, and Japan must now compete at the technological frontier. Incremental innovations on existing foreign technology no longer support the economy in this context. We must now accept that the focus on central-state/big business cooperation, in practice and in scholarship – will not yield the sources of best practice for firms and states. Instead the most promising work in the emerging literature includes a more nuanced role for small enterprise and often local governments.
- Finally, recent works have begun to point to the embeddedness of firms within certain institutional frameworks that either encourage or hinder innovation. The least developed, but perhaps most promising finding of the emerging literature is the political role small firms often have in transforming the institutional environment in which they are embedded, such as their efforts to create alternatives to hierarchy. The result of these transformations has been more innovation in newly vibrant enterprise communities.[39]

The firm-level analysis that follows here illustrates the problems the persistence of hierarchies in the Japanese production system have caused for innovation in small firms in particular, and new business creation in general. Further, as a matter of policy, firms (rather than governments) are in the best position to design and implement these de-linking and innovative strategies. Comparisons of the three regions in this study (Kyoto, Osaka, and Tokyo) show that firms in Kyoto have had an easier time of establishing horizontal, inter-firm connections in part due to their low degree of linkage with Japan's traditional hierarchies.

3.8 Conclusion: bringing the local (more fully) back in?

Among the main factors affecting how relevant state policies are for productive and innovative enterprise activity is the quality of information exchange between the state and the firm. Firms assess the quality of information from government sources and parse out the information that is deemed useful. At the same time, firms are loath to provide information to the government that could be used to ratchet up regulation of their daily activity. Governments consequently struggle to obtain accurate information on the state of firm operations. Despite these information problems, states must make policies that matter to local firms in order to foster new business creation and innovation. The many failed national-level policy initiatives in Japan (Grimes 2001, Lincoln 2001), and similar problems in Germany (Herrigel 1997 Herrigel and Sabel 1999) in the 1990s attest to the difficulties in making policy reforms that produce measurable innovative output.

In Japan, major impediments to effective policymaking and implementation stem from two main institutional features of its political economy. First, the central state has relied upon intermediating institutions, such as peak business associations, for information on business conditions at the ground level. Consequently, most firms lack alternative channels to national-level politics and policy. These big business-dominated associations mirror the "keiretsified" production structure of post-war Japan, whereby smaller firms are assimilated into vertically integrated production structures. As a consequence, the bulk of firms in Japan have generally lacked both voice and exit within these production structures and inter-mediating institutions (Japan. Chusho Kigyo Cho 1990; Miyashita and Russell 1994; Ayuzawa 1995; Imai 1998b).

These intermediating institutions have been effective at regulating business activity and at supporting the assimilation of the smaller firms into keiretsified production structures. Yet, intermediating institutions have not done so well at obtaining reliable and accurate information on business conditions and needs at the local level that would foster innovation. As such, the Japanese national government has struggled, and largely failed, to engender new business creation and innovation at the local level. Recent research has shown that national policies aimed at jump-starting innovation at the local level have proven irrelevant or even inimical (MRI 1996; Ibata-Arens 2000b). In Japan and elsewhere, national governments are struggling to make polices that matter at the local level.

At the same time, alternative institutions have emerged in Japan and elsewhere that are attuned to the needs of firms and entrepreneurs and support the growth of innovative and stable communities of firms. These supporting institutions, including certain types of cooperative business associations and dynamic inter-firm networks, have emerged despite (and often in direct opposition to) the dominance of existing hierarchies (Ayuzawa 1995; Culpepper 2001; Ibata-Arens 2006).[40] One factor behind the success of these often informal institutions is that they tend to come into being not by state fiat but instead by the efforts of local and regional government leaders and firm-level entrepreneurial mavericks. Moreover, the ability of certain agglomerations of firms, institutions, associations, and networks to create better products and enhance community-wide innovation has depended on political savvy, involving the effective coupling of resources such as state funds and information with entrepreneurial ideas.

Given this, I would argue that what is needed in the study of Japan and other struggling advanced economies is systematic analysis of the development of *informal* institutions that empower local firms and enhance community-wide innovation. Consequently, we need a research agenda that can examine the national- and local-level policy dynamics in fostering the development of such institutions. Specifically, I would like to see more emphasis on a firm-centered "embedded enterprise" approach that accounts for important firm, local, and regional level factors in engendering the development of enabling institutions that enhance firm performance, particularly *vis-à-vis* innovation.

The nature of enterprise embeddedness structures what strategies of interaction are available to firms and their intermediaries. In non-liberal or coordinated national institutional contexts, successful firms have engaged in political strategies, in navigating the policy environment, and impacting policy outcomes in their pursuit of innovation and competitiveness. These political strategies are most effective because of (and sometimes despite) firms' embeddedness within various institutional configurations of local and regional communities.

The political interplay between two levels of embeddedness – firms *within* national and local institutions – best explains why some regions succeed while others fail at competing and maintaining innovation in the global technology environment. For example, it may be the case that the most effective policies are often those that emerge out of local-level dynamics, while national governments play a background, though supporting role (Piore and Sabel 1984; Saxenian 1994b; Locke 1995; Herrigel 1996). Also key are intermediaries such as local business owners or community leaders savvy at fostering productive links between various governmental bodies and resources and local firms (Inaba 2002). This civic entrepreneurship is discussed in chapters 5–7. This involves what Kenichi Imai has referred to as *monogotari sei*, or the ability to inspire others with entrepreneurial vision (Imai 1998). Further, a local-level focus is more inclusive of SMEs – a primary source of new business and job creation across economies.

The chapters that follow demonstrate three things:

- First, Japan at the national level remains stuck in an outdated way of thinking about innovation. Transformations in the global economy (e.g. communications technology) have rendered national (in the top-down sense) approaches ineffective.
- Second, locally nuanced enterprise-based policy has engendered innovation and growth while the central state has been out of touch with and even inimical to these developments at the local level. Regions such as Kyoto excel in new business creation, entrepreneurship and (globally recognized) innovation while other regions lag behind.
- Third, patterns in regional innovation systems may present a new model of innovation and entrepreneurship, as cross-national comparisons to the American Midwest illustrate. In sum, existing arguments about Japan's national innovation system have been overtaken by actual practice at the firm and regional level.

Chapter 4 examines Japan's national-level quest for entrepreneurialism.

Notes

1. See, for example, Miyashita and Russell (1994); Whittaker (1997).
2. See Yamashita (1995). A few producers, including NEC, have made moves to return a portion of production to Japan, citing lower profits

and lack of skill of the foreign workforce. Another, perhaps more significant, reason has been the inability in some cases to manage (control) technological innovation and the flow of technology in target economies (NHK Special 1997). See also Keisuke (1996) for a discussion of this "extremely strict and detailed" control in the Japanese production system.

3. The work of David Edgington in this regard is a notable exception. See Edgington (1999).
4. This is one reason why "collaborative manufacturing" tends in reality to operate as "sustained contingent collaboration" (Herrigel and Wittke 2004).
5. Also overlooked is the opportunity to explore the narratives of the political struggles of entrepreneurs, small business owners and local leaders in fostering innovative activity.
6. Scholars have begun to recognize the significance of studying industrial change from the perspective of small enterprises. For example, Lamoreaux, Raff, and Temin have found historical evidence that indicates that the explanation for long-term national differences in economic performance reside in either the non-industrial sector or in small business (Lamoreaux *et al.* 1999).
7. Nelson (1993) provides the first systematic comparative study of national innovation systems. The chapters in this edited volume compare three groups of countries: (1) large high-income countries (Britain, France, Italy, Japan, USA), (2) smaller high-income countries (Australia, Canada, Denmark, Sweden), and (3) lower-income countries (Argentina, Brazil, Israel, Korea, Taiwan). National systems of innovations are compared on the basis of how they emphasize the relative role of R&D activity and funding, the characteristics of firms in key industries, the role of universities, and the role of government policy, if any. Innovation systems vary by sector as well as by country. For example, the agriculture sector tends to be similar across economies, and unlike most other sectors within economies. Institutions found key to supporting industrial innovation include national education systems, public infrastructure, laws, sound financial institutions, and fiscal and monetary trade policies. In addition, the literature on convergence in the field of international political economy confirms that institutional configurations between the state and private sector that work well when the economy is a technological recipient may not work at all when a country becomes a technological leader. Different national systems function better at different junctures. For example, the German system was unsuitable for Fordist mass production but was very well suited for flexible manufacturing in the 1980s. Another finding in the convergence literature is about institutional "tightness of fit." Institutions are embedded within a certain national and historical

context and cannot be plucked out and made to work (or even understood) in a different institutional context. (See Berger and Dore 1996.)

8. Imai and Yamazaki, in Shinoya and Perlman (1994). Several of the contributions to this volume address Schumpeter's concerns about sustaining innovation in an economy of large firms that are given to bureaucratization.
9. Wang (1998) observes that the nature of production networks in Japan (in contrast to those in Taiwan) are structured, predictable, and hierarchical, though he does not perceive these as negative aspects of the system. In contrast, Perrow (1992) cautions that the trend toward vertically integrated firms signifies the erosion of civil society.
10. See Smitka (1991, pp. 4–5) for a discussion of trust creation.
11. When I mentioned this to interviewees at SMEs who participated in my study, they found the assertion laughable.
12. For a discussion of these arguments in the context of the "varieties of capitalism" approach, see Ibata-Arens (2003).
13. Friedman (1988) likewise finds state industrial policy irrelevant to the success of machine tool makers in Sakaki, in Nagano prefecture.
14. In doing so, Dore interestingly cites the USA, manifested in US-trained MBAs and PhDs as the main culprit and the root cause of the rapid "financialization and marketization" of the Japanese economy.
15. It should be noted that recent Japanese literature has in fact questioned the utility of transplanting the Silicon Valley Model to the Japanese context (Imai 1992, 1998b and Ueda 1997).
16. "DOD/128" refers to the US Department of Defense's long-time ties to the vertically integrated and insular corporations populating the Boston Route 128 manufacturing corridor.
17. Dore has been critical of the rise of "market individualism" in Japan as represented by financial rewards to individual inventors rather than their firms. (See Dore 2004.)
18. Enterprise unionism in large firms in Japan makes labor homogeneous within sectors, as union identification is with a particular firm, not the craft.
19. See Gerlach, and Lincoln (1992, figure 3.1, p. 68) for a stylized illustration of the "status position" of each of the four alliance forms.
20. A key element of success in these flexible industrial communities is *trust.* For a discussion of trust in industrial communities, see Hirst and Zeitlin (1991); Piore and Sabel (1984).
21. See Piore and Sabel (1984, n. 72, p. 326).
22. Ibid., p. 180.
23. Ibid., p. 254.
24. Ibid., p. 82.
25. See Herrigel (1997, pp. 188–92) for a detailed discussion of the skill and functional hierarchies in Germany that limit local autonomy.

26. See Amsden (1992) for a discussion of how "learning by doing" affords workers opportunities to approach the creation and production of new products in a team atmosphere.
27. In fact, Matsumoto (1996) examines the *Meister* system of craftsmanship in local Ota manufacturing firms.
28. Best (1990) subdivides the notion of flexible specialization into four kinds: industrial districts, federated enterprises, solar firms, and workshop factories.
29. The notion of shared network norms is taken from Kenichi Imai. See Imai *et al.* (1985).
30. Best (1990, pp. 242–50).
31. Best (1990), p. 243.
32. Fields reviews recent works in economic sociology and comparative political economy in the formulation of this framework. The sociocultural approaches of the former (Biggart, Granovetter, and Hamilton) and the statist approaches of the latter (Amsden, Evans, and Stephans) address the interconnectedness and interdependence of market and nonmarket institutions explain developmental paths better than neoclassical arguments.
33. Fields (1995, n. 1, p. 239) cites Amsden (1989) in asserting that in explaining the variation in growth rates in late-industrializing countries, it is essential to examine big business–state reciprocity and the internal and external behavior of diversified business groups. In contrast, my research shows that the agents of focus at the technological frontier should be SMEs and local governments.
34. Freeman (1995) classifies innovative networks into ten types: JVs and research corporations; joint R&D agreements; technology exchange agreements; direct investment (minority holdings) motivated by technology factors; licensing and second-sourcing agreements; subcontracting, production sharing, and supplier networks; research associations; government-sponsored joint research programs; computerized data banks and value-added networks for technical and scientific interchange; and other networks, including informal ones.
35. Others view the individual as the central agent in innovation and growth. For example, Wright (1999) argues that the technological success of the USA in the nineteenth century was based on networks of individuals (professionals and technicians), not firms. See also the Introduction in Lamoreaux *et al.* (1999).
36. Saxenian (1994b) finds that local governments have played a role in providing test equipment, lab space, and business services to small businesses.
37. See Locke (1995, figure 1.2, p. 27) for a stylized diagram of each ideal type.

38. Smitka's analysis is industry-based.
39. Japan, particularly then MITI, has focused since the mid-1970s on identifying the factors facilitating innovative inter-firm network formation and the lack of it in the country. (MRI 1996); Imai (1998a, 1998b).
40. Culpepper (2001) finds that the most effective impact of state policy is not fostering state–firm cooperation but instead engendering *inter-firm* cooperation. He argues that countries lacking the mechanisms to achieve non-market coordination will need to invest in "building up the power of private associations," that they will not be able to control.

4 *Japan's quest for entrepreneurialism*

4.1 The Cluster Plan

In the early 2000s, Japan had still failed to fully recover from the economic doldrums. Unemployment rates had surpassed the US jobless by 1999 (Porter *et al.* 2000). In 2003, new business creation remained paltry. A 2003 study, the *Gem 2003 Executive Report* (2003) indicated that Japan was less entrepreneurial – on a variety of firm and individual level measures – than all of the advanced industrial countries, save Russia.[1] Of the world's forty major economies, most were at three entrepreneurship levels (high, moderate, low) based on measures including new firm start-ups, innovative output, and the like. Highly entrepreneurial countries included Chile, Korea, and New Zealand. Most countries were moderately innovative, such as Canada, Finland, Singapore, the UK, and the USA. The least entrepreneurial countries were France, Japan, and Russia. Japan failed at both individual- and firm-level innovation and entrepreneurship, making it among the least entrepreneurial countries in the world (see figure 4.1 and table 4.1). (See also appendix 1: in the *Gem 2003 Executive Report* 2003; Porter 1990, 1998; Porter *et al.* 2000.)

The Ministry of Economy, Trade and Industry (METI) is spearheading the Japanese government's current efforts to fix its innovative and entrepreneurial problems. In 2001, METI launched its "Cluster Initiative," culminating in 2002 in a package of policies called the "Cluster Plan." The "Plan" has become the most ambitious and comprehensive METI plan since its 1960s bet on heavy industry (Inoue 2003).[2]

The intent of the Plan is threefold: to improve productivity, spur innovation, and foster new business creation. The Plan targets nineteen clusters across nine major regions in Japan, incorporating 5000 SMEs, 200 universities, and a variety of support institutions, all coordinated by the national and regional METI bureaux. Figure 4.2 details each regional project. Having followed METI and MOF policy since the

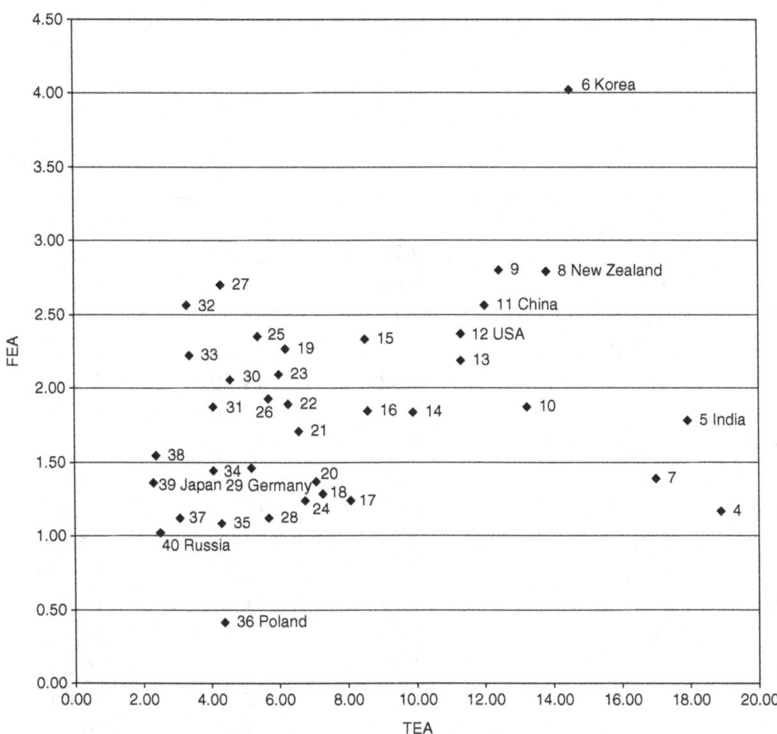

Figure 4.1. Trends in global entrepreneurship 2002–2003[a]
Note: Outliers: Uganda (#1), Venezuela (#2), and Chile (#3), were omitted because they severely skewed the scale of the graph. Massive self-employment arose in these countries primarily due to the lack of alternative forms of viable employment.

mid-1990s, it seemed to me that there was certainly a different kind of buzz around this new "Cluster Plan."

4.2 Executives and (former) bureaucrats

I set out to get the perspective of someone currently in industry who also had an insider's historical memory of METI in its 1960s heyday. I obtained an interview with I-san, Vice Chairman of a major keiretsu conglomerate, and recently retired METI bureaucrat. In 1967 I-san graduated with a Law degree from Tokyo University and joined MITI in the same year. As is the custom with elite-track bureaucrats,

Table 4.1 FEA[a] and TEA[b] rates, by country rank, 2002–2003

Ranking	Country	FEA rate (average 2002–3)	TEA rate (average 2002–3)	(FEA + TEA)
1	Uganda**[d]	2.78	29.30	32.08
2	Venezuela**[d]	2.72	27.30	30.02
3	Chile	6.06	16.30	22.36
4	Thailand*[c]	1.17	18.90	20.07
5	India*[c]	1.78	17.90	19.68
6	Korea*[c]	4.02	14.50	18.52
7	Argentina	1.39	17.00	18.39
8	New Zealand	2.79	13.80	16.59
9	Mexico*[c]	2.80	12.40	15.20
10	Brazil	1.87	13.20	15.07
11	China	2.56	12.00	14.56
12	USA	2.37	11.30	13.67
13	Iceland	2.19	11.30	13.49
14	Australia	1.84	9.90	11.74
15	Canada	2.33	8.50	10.83
16	Ireland	1.85	8.60	10.45
17	Norway	1.24	8.10	9.34
18	Switzerland	1.29	7.30	8.59
19	Denmark	2.27	6.20	8.47
20	Israel	1.37	7.10	8.47
21	Hungary	1.71	6.60	8.31
22	Spain	1.89	6.30	8.19
23	UK	2.09	6.00	8.09
24	Greece	1.27	6.80	8.07
25	Singapore	2.35	5.40	7.75
26	Finland	1.93	5.70	7.63
27	Slovenia	2.70	4.30	7.00
28	South Africa	1.12	5.70	6.82
29	Germany	1.46	5.20	6.66
30	Italy	2.05	4.60	6.65
31	Sweden	1.87	4.10	5.97
32	Hong Kong	2.56	3.30	5.86
33	Belgium	2.22	3.40	5.62
34	The Netherlands	1.44	4.10	5.54
35	Taiwan	1.08	4.30	5.38
36	Poland	0.41	4.40	4.81

Table 4.1 (cont.)

Ranking	*Country*	*FEA rate (average 2002–3)*	*TEA rate (average 2002–3)*	*(FEA + TEA)*
37	Croatia	1.12	3.10	4.22
38	France	1.54	2.40	3.94
39	Japan	1.36	2.30	3.66
40	Russia	1.02	2.50	3.52

Notes:

[a] FEA rate (Firm Entrepreneural Activity Rate) = [(# of entrepreneural firms/# of all firms)/(# entrepreneural jobs/# of all jobs)]/ 2*[c]. *"Entrepreneural firms" are defined as firms (as reported by the owner-managers) having a major impact on the market (e.g. firms that are providing goods or services new to the market).*[c]* *0 point = 2 to avoid negative numbers.*

[b] TEA rate (Total Entrepreneural Activity Rate) = # of adults out of every 100 adults that were involved in operating or starting a business less than 3.5 years old.

* TEA 2002 data.

** TEA 2003 data.

All other data averaged for 2002–3.

he was soon dispatched for his two-year rotation (to obtain a masters degree from a prestigious American or British university). I-san received an MPA from the Kennedy School of Government at Harvard University.

He quickly moved up the ranks at MITI and was seconded to projects in energy, SMEs, national security, R&D, and intellectual property rights (IPR). He served as commissioner of the Japanese Patent Office and the director general of several bureaux, including the International Trade Policy bureau and the Trade Administration bureau during the Hashimoto (1996–8) and Obuchi administrations (1998–2000).

Nearing the end of his tenure at MITI, I-san represented Japan at APEC and WIPO meetings in the mid-1990s and later was a chief architect of the Asian Economic Recovery Plan during the Asian Economic Crisis. Retiring from MITI in 1999, I-san spent a year at Stanford University as a Visiting Scholar in the Asia Pacific Research Center. He assumed his post at his current firm in September 2001. I contacted him in 2003.

One sunny July day in 2003 I was whisked up a private elevator of I-san's corporate office in Tokyo's Ginza. Stepping off the elevator into

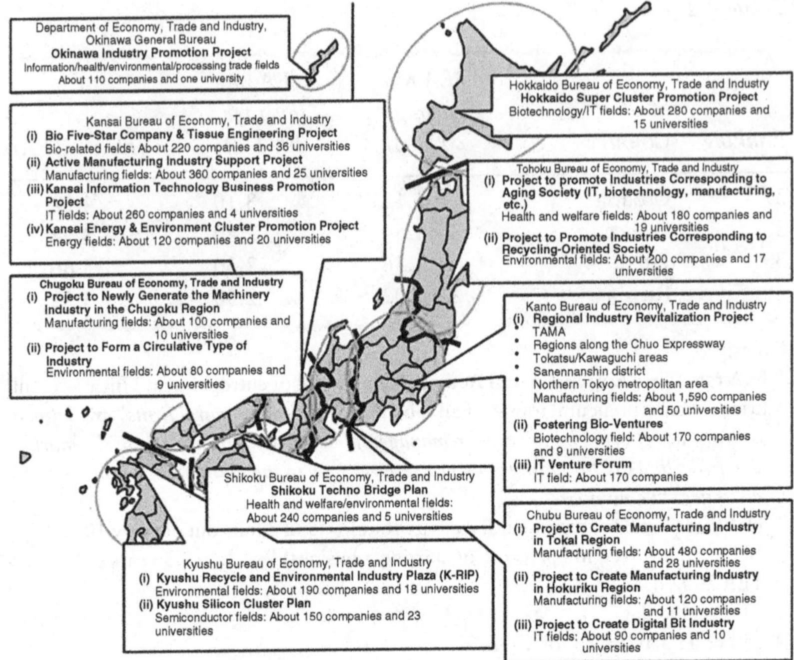

Figure 4.2. Map METI Cluster Plan, 2003

a wide hardwood-paneled hallway, cool and quiet, I was escorted into I-san's private conference room. As I sat waiting, natural sunlight poured in through the many windows, and a smartly dressed OL brought me some tea.

I-san came in at the appointed hour and after a few pleasantries, I began my questions, which centered on his perspective on METI's ambitions with the new "Cluster Plan." While I-san does not doubt the sincerity of the intentions of his former colleagues, he is doubtful that this "new" plan will be a success. I-san's critique of the national approach to the Cluster Plan is threefold: its insensitivity to regional history, its inconsistency, and its hubris. First, national bureaucrats tend to be insensitive (and often ignorant) of the utility of tailoring policy to the historical context of each region. I-san noted that Japan's regions have a 2,000-year history from which particular kinds of region-specific industries have emerged. Within Japanese regions themselves, the indigenous capacity to produce products varies widely. For example, he compared Ota Ward (in Tokyo) with regions outside of Tokyo. Ota was developed by national policy fiat, in a previously undeveloped physical space (during Japan's post-war heavy industry-based high-growth period). Because of this dependence on the national government Ota has always lacked self-reliance (*jiritsu sei*). Though this lack of self-initiative may be characteristic of the once-numerous firms located in the environs around METI offices, this is not the nature of industry in most places outside of Tokyo.

This notion brought I-san to his second critique of current METI policy – its inconsistency. In the past, the shortest implementation timeline for a given policy was five years, usually it lasted more than ten. Now, METI changes policies every few years. What was once serious and patient is verging on the dilettantish.

I-san's most virulent critique is leveled against what he describes as "national hubris." "Public officials have hubris when tackling policy issues, they think that whatever they decide at the national level can be done at the regional level." He agrees, though, that the national government should play a supporting role in regional development, particularly through financial and infrastructural measures. Unfortunately, according to I-san, national-level bureaucrats have a control problem. "They often interfere with regions when regional problems should have regional level solutions." I-san concludes that "to have central government control of the Cluster Plan will certainly fail." Having interviewed a number of METI officials already, I noted that they seem to be working so hard, and with such sincerity, that there must be some possibility of success. I was dispatched by I-san to METI's "Cluster Plan Promotion Office" to find out for for myself.[3]

I left I-san's pristine corporate headquarters and made my way on a hot July day in Tokyo over to METI's *Bekkan* (annex). The Japanese describe the retirement of elite ministry bureaucrats into corporations at the end of their long service as bureaucrats as *amakudari*, or the "descent from heaven." I couldn't help but think that I was not going to the "heaven" of one of the most elite ministries in Japan, rather I was descending into the bowels of some Kafkaesque hell. This was the working environment of a mid-level bureaucrat in Japan's elite national ministries.

The *Bekkan*, a dreary, grayish 1950s-style building is where scores of METI offices staffed with cadres of the best and brightest minds of Japan toil away doing the grunt work of METI policy design and implementation. On this day in the *Bekkan* at METI's "Cluster Promotion Office" the air conditioning was out, though the windows remained sealed shut. Dim fluorescent lighting illuminated the steel gray rows of desks, at each of which was huddled a METI functionary, dripping with sweat. Perhaps Japanese decorum kept these men from even loosening their ties or rolling up their long (no longer crisp) white shirt sleeves.

I gratefully accepted from a uniformed OL, a *mugicha* (summer tea), in a small glass with a large chunk of ice. I was there to meet M-san, who immediately launched into the standard "chronology and contents of this project" speech. I dutifully took notes and waited for my opportunity to ask questions (hopefully before my allotted time ran out). I was particularly interested in how this ambitious new policy was designed, which models and scholars were the most relevant, who participated in the process, and so forth. I was also interested in learning how the project would be evaluated as it progressed.

The surprising answer to the first question was: "Michael Porter's clusters was our inspiration." M-san knew of no other scholar's perspectives. Precisely as I-san said, M-san described a vast nation-wide METI-led framework, albeit with regional variations on the national model. Maybe it was the heat, perhaps the topic, but by the end of the interview our heads were hovering inches above the coffee table, M-san was leaning close and speaking in a whisper: "If we don't start supporting the smallest of the SMEs – and not just the established medium-sized (*chuuken*) which are reaping the most benefits from this project, the Japanese economy will fail." I asked if he thought then that the "Cluster Plan" would fail. He smiled sardonically and said nothing (M Interview 2003).[4]

One example of the "regional variation" of the Plan is the way in which the national METI has gone about implementation at the regional level. According to T-san of the regional METI Kinki office, their so-called national cluster project is actually a home-grown "Strategy Project." T-san was adamant in stating that, first of all, his organization started the project in the mid-1990s, long before this new national plan emerged. The local METI Kinki project itself originated out of an earlier study group looking into the micro-foundations of entrepreneurial success in local cities. From this, the regional bureau created a package of policies geared at supporting *existing firm-level initiatives*, including the Kyoto Shisaku Net (discussed in chapter 5). T-san was also adamant that their approach was nothing like the current "mega"-level cluster plan of the national METI. In fact, T-san reported that a few years ago, national-level representatives suddenly "informed us that *our* project was now a 'national' project and would henceforth to be called 'Cluster Project'".[5] Perhaps the fever pitch at which the national METI is going about imposing the Cluster Plan throughout the regions is a function of how desperate the situation really is. A look back at the policy environment from which the "Cluster Plan" emerged is informative.[6]

4.3 1990s: bad policy, poorly implemented

In the late 1990s, as the Japanese recession neared a decade in length, the government tried to implement a series of policies to jump-start innovation and foster new business creation. Unfortunately, their efforts resulted in bad policies which were poorly implemented. For example, in October 1998 MITI (then still the Ministry of International Trade and Industry) announced a new policy ostensively to support struggling small business, 40 trillion yen in government backed loans was earmarked for SMEs, intended for investment in new equipment and technology.

Before the ink was dry on the legislation, however, firms were finding themselves approached by bank representatives, urging them to apply for the funds. Firms noted that these were the same representatives who six–eight months earlier had abruptly cut off funds and called in existing loans. Bank representatives were reported to have told firms that if they applied for this new program (with the bank's assistance), they would be certain to get the funds. In return, firms were expected to use these funds to pay back old loans. Since the program was backed by the Ministry of Finance (and administered by MITI), there has been speculation that the so-called "program for SMEs" was actually a veiled bailout of sorts for the banks.

The sheer speed with which banks at the local level all over Japan were able to obtain detailed information and applications for the program (within days of the announcement of the MITI policy) is highly suggestive in this regard. At the same time, there are reports of "strong-arm" practices being used by banks to collect funds of called-in loans. One bank employee, interviewed anonymously, told of a

"Collections Manual" that showed how medium-to-smaller-sized firms were specifically targeted. Mistakes in reporting and the like were identified (*ochido*), and used as excuses for sudden call-in of loans. "Negotiations" would then begin with firms for the return of funds. In actuality, these "negotiations" were unilateral demands by the bank for unrealistic monthly payments. Many firms reported harassment and even threats of violence by bank operatives.

In November 1998, MITI introduced measures aimed at promoting new business formation. Loan guarantees would be offered to regional credit associations, to be used to assist new start-ups (though funds would be limited to those that already had part of the funds needed to start-up their businesses). In November 1999 the Japanese government announced an 18 trillion yen stimulus package, the largest ever. The "new" measures included expanding the amount currently allocated to credit guarantees for small business, loans to encourage more start-ups, and the like. 2000 brought yet another similar ineffective and ill-fated stimulus package.

Another policy involved the *Industrial Revitalization Law* (IRL, effective from October 1999) (*sangyo katsuryoku saisei tokubetsu sochiho*). The Law had a number of good components. First, it seemed to be a genuine attempt at patent reform. For example, firms approved under IR would spend less time in the patent queue. Also, the fees for obtaining patents were reduced (in particular, those potential innovations demonstrating an industry–private industry link). Second, it supported technology licensing organizations (TLOs), also for promoting university–private sector new product R&D. Lower fees would be collected from patent applications generated from these collaborations in the hopes of promoting technology transfer from universities to industry. Thirdly, there would be life after business failure through the *Civil Reorganization Law* (CRL, *minji saisei ho*, enacted in April 2000). The CRL was modeled on the old Chapter 11 Code in the USA in that a business owner was not, upon declaring business bankruptcy, forced to also declare personal bankruptcy. These efforts were to be coordinated under the related Industrial Revitalization Corporation (IRC).

Unfortunately, as is often the case in Japan, the ideals of the legislation often broke down in implementation in the private sector. For example, the first "approved" firms were the usual suspects – the big industrial monoliths and the least likely place for quick and nimble new business creation: Sumitomo Metal, Fuji Heavy Industry, Tokyo

Motor, and Mitsubishi. Of the ten new business models touted by METI's international public relations arm, the Japan External Trade Organization (JETRO), seven were Tokyo firms, and the remaining three firms were located in Osaka, Saitama, and Akita. It seems the intended far-reaching national impact of the IRL did not reach so far from Tokyo after all.

The recipients immediately made mass layoffs in guise of returning to "core competences" (under the auspices of the IRL and IRC). "Restructuring" (*resutura*) was now spun as core competence. In return, these firms got tax credits and holidays, such as the "Angel Tax" of a quarter of capital gains. The Angel Tax was intended to jump-start high-risk/high-return investment through venture capital funds (its name is a misnomer, as "angel investors" are individuals rather than firms). Second, the IRC also helped to soften the burden for large firms of their earlier bad investments (it also camouflaged MOF's failure in this regard). These trends in consolidation in the biggest Japanese firms also occurred in the context of the 1997 repeal of the law preventing pure holding companies (zaibatsu).

After suffering through these policy failures in the 1990s, the new and revamped METI also moved away from its "network creation" in the 1990s (as it had from earlier "technopolis formation" in the 1980s). By the early 2000s, METI's new catchphrase was "regional clustering."[7] How did METI come up with the most ambitious policy package since the 1960s? It outsourced.

4.4 2000s: when all else fails, go to Harvard

In 2002, Harvard Business School alum and Hitotsubashi professor Yoko Ishikura was selected to head the "Cluster Plan Research Group." In autumn 2002, she was dispatched to Cambridge to attend courses and workshops under the tutelage of Michael Porter (who had trained originally in mechanical engineering at Princeton University). Porter's name had become synonymous with "clusters" through the popularity of his "diamond model" of innovation (Porter 1990, 1998).[8]

The "diamond model" shows the main foundations of successful innovative clusters of firms, akin to the basic ingredients (or conditions) outlined in this book's Introduction.[9] "Clusters" are spatial agglomerations of interconnected firms and institutions in a particular field, linked by commonalities and complementarities (Porter 1998).[10]

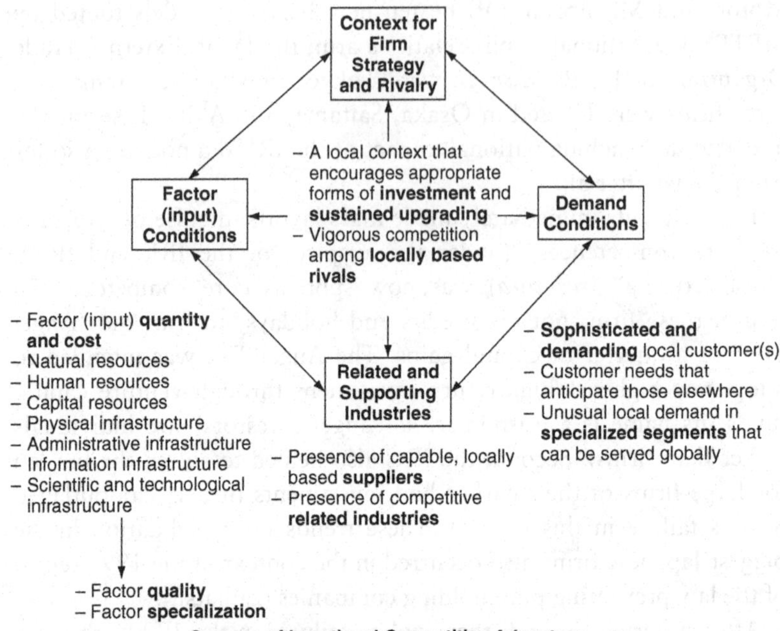

Figure 4.3. Porter's diamond Model
Source: Porter (1999, p. 211).

The availability of various factor input conditions (tangible and intangible resources), supporting industries (suppliers), and demand conditions (customers) all interact to create an environment conducive to innovation and cooperation within local firms (see figure 4.3). I address the local context at the heart of successful (diamond) clusters below.

Three influences of successful clusters on competition are, for Porter, increasing productivity, increasing capacity for innovation, and stimulating new business formation. These happen to be the three goals of METI's new Plan. In 2000 Porter, with Hirotaka Takeuchi and Mariko Sakakibara, had published the results of an eight-year research project on Japan's economy. (Porter *et al.* 2000)[11] Around the same time, Porter's ideas gained salience in the policymaking groups that orbited around METI.

In March 2003 a group of some 500 Japanese bureaucrats and academics, mainly from the top ministries and universities in Tokyo, attended the first "Industrial Cluster Conference," whose keynote speaker was Porter himself. By this time, METI had a new plan, one that seemed quite like the ones that came before it – although no self-respecting bureaucrat in Tokyo could be found uttering names such as "Technopolis" and "Brains Location".[12] This one, however, had the Harvard moniker, which carries much weight among Japan's economic and political elites. In fact, in all of the volumes of METI "Cluster Plan" documents there is a noticeable absence of any reference to any other perspective than Porter's. A fact check confirms the eerie similarity of structure and content of Japan's most ambitious national policy initiative in thirty years to a single chapter ("Clusters and Competition") in Michael Porter's *On Competition* (1998).

In emulating Porter's approach to clusters, however, METI has lost in translation several critical factors that energize cluster development and sustained innovation. Porter observes that even in spatial agglomerations of firms that appear to have all the requisite basics (factor, support, demand), innovation and new business creation do not necessarily follow:

> While the existence of a cluster makes such [personal] relationships more likely to develop and effective once in place, the process is far from automatic. Formal and informal organizing mechanisms and cultural norms often play a role in the development and functioning of clusters.[13]

The core of the diamond is the "local context," comprising the social relationships described above. This core is said to encourage appropriate forms of investment and sustained upgrading. This context is not purely cooperative. In fact, according to Porter, the most innovative communities are charged with vigorous competition among locally based rivals. Further, the emergence of clusters is often inextricable from particular local histories (e.g. the presence of certain natural resources) and chance (e.g. the happenstance of a particular firm having located its operations and then spurred later unanticipated spin-offs in a certain sector).

These social and cultural factors are described by Porter (1998) as the "socio-economy of clusters". I would add that entrepreneurs within a given "local context" are embedded in a complex environment of socio-political relationships. These relationships – and the social capital (investments in trusting, reciprocal arrangements) that abounds within the most successful clusters – are the stuff of sustained community-wide innovation. Civic entrepreneurs (enterprise mavericks engaged in activities that benefit the community as a whole in the long term and often benefit their firms only indirectly) have stores of social capital and often serve as brokers of tangible and intangible resources between community stakeholders. How these complex socio-political relationships (between particular types of people) translate into innovation and competitiveness through the activities of civic entrepreneurs is the subject of chapters 6 and 7 of this book.

Analysis of these complex – and region-specific–socio-political relations is lacking in cluster research to date in Japan. While the Japanese government seems to ignore the socio-political context of successful clusters, it also fails to heed Porter's specific admonitions about the kind of role government should play in cluster development.

According to Porter (and based on case studies in twenty-nine countries) successful national-level policies geared at developing clusters: (1) have been attuned to local-level perceptions (aiming at shared understandings of the need for clusters); (2) include traditional, and even declining sectors; (3) are inclusive not exclusive (even of difficult individuals); (4) are private sector-led and ideally will take place through an entity *independent* of government; and have (5) neutral facilitators of interpersonal communications that lead to trusting personal relationships. As METI is only mid-way through its implementation, the full impact of the Cluster Plan cannot be judged. However, we can get a sense of how METI has gone about emulating "Porter-style" cluster development. At this point (2004), we can evaluate the Plan in two major areas: its divergence in practice from the prescriptions of Porter and its distinctions (if any) from METI's earlier policy initiatives.

Japan's METI diverges in several ways from the Porter-style approach. First, the Cluster Plan is not only a government project but a national government project to boot. Worse, this national control is being attempted in a situation where national–regional–local government relations in Japan are sometimes contentious and cannot be described as entirely trusting. Further, the Plan is wholly focused on high-tech industry, and traditional/declining sectors are negligibly incorporated, if at all. Finally, the "coordinators" of inter-firm, interpersonal networking in Japan's Plan are largely METI bureaucrats, hardly neutral parties. Japan's national bureaucracy also seems to miss the region/enterprise (and often wholly organic) nature of the world's most successful clusters.

For example, of the three American regions that METI models – Silicon Valley, Austin, and Philadelphia – only the Philadelphia area has direct links to federal government programs.[14] Even the Cluster Research Group's leader Ishikura admits that the Japanese national government is attempting – by policy fiat – to create clusters following innovative communities in the USA that emerged without one iota of federal government initiative. For example, Silicon Valley emerged from an organic process (university-initiated, local firm linked, with virtually no government involvement in the early stages). Austin, though supported by the local government, was also enterprise-initiated (by Teledyne). The state took a hands-off approach.[15]

Consequently, I would argue that Japan's national METI clusters fall short on the most critical factors (i.e. the socio-political, region-initiated, and "local"-led context) that make clusters competitive in the most successful situations world-wide. In essence, METI's Plan diverges in critical aspects from the bases of successful efforts elsewhere. At the same time, METI has been unable to break out of its historical (top-down, centralized) management style and create truly new and improved policy.

4.5 What's "new" about the Cluster Plan?

In a government-backed book on the Cluster Plan 3 (Ishikura *et al.* 2003) the authors outline five "differences" between the new Plan and its predecessors:

- First, the method of targeting firms and institutions for clustering is said to be different: METI has supposedly shifted to a region-initiated policy. Until now, according to Ishikura *et al.*, Japanese national government policy has been characterized as "*mura okoshi, baramaki*" (the central state trying to force major change on sometimes intransigent regions, while trying to please all parties by spending money recklessly).[16]
- Second, the goals and expectations are said to be higher. In other words, process improvements to existing technology will no longer suffice. METI acknowledges that to emerge as a competitive and innovative country, Japan's national government must provide incentives for new product innovation.

- Third, the boundaries (limits) of the industrial targets are broader than ever before. In doing so, METI is expanding the "value chain" of clusters by emphasizing not only the need for technological development, but also for marketing, management, and finance.
- Fourth, METI promises that they are committed to the Cluster Plan for the long haul: twenty–thirty years.
- Fifth, METI is being more selective in its targeting. This selectivity has two implications. On the one hand, METI will no longer start from nothing through green field or brown field investments. Instead, it has focused on identifying existing agglomerations of firm-level potential. On the other hand, METI's biggest bet is being put on high-tech industry, particularly IT and bio-pharmaceuticals. In 2004, the Plan was through the second of its four stages: preparation, formation, clustering, and establishment. The budget for these activities in the first two years was 44.8 billion yen (2002) and 41.3 billion yen (2003).

Stage I (preparation) began officially in 2001, though a special budget allocation was not received until 2002. In preparation for cluster formation, METI officials searched for (new) spatial agglomerations of cooperative, complementary related firms in bio-pharmaceuticals, IT, and high-tech manufacturing. The three largest of the nine regional clusters are Tokyo, Hokkaido, and Kansai (Kinki), outlined below (Inoue 2003).

Tokyo's Tama

Tokyo's clusters are located in the northwest environs of Tokyo's metropolitan area (West of Shinjuku station on the Chuo line to Hachioji city): colloquially referred to as "Tama." By the Second World War, the Tama area had become home to numerous small manufacturers, many of whom had relocated from the Keihin (Southeastern Tokyo) coastal area. These manufacturers produced electrical and precision machinery as well as transportation equipment. In the mid-1990s Tama was targeted by METI's SME Agency for high-tech-based network formation. By the late 1990s, network policies targeting Tama firms incorporated universities, government organizations, and others. By 2003, the Tama Regional Cluster, spread between cities such as Hachioji, Sayama, and Sagamihara, included 260 firms, seventeen local governments, twenty-eight universities, and other support institutions (public research institutions, incubators, financial firms).

Between 2001 and 2002, 1.73 billion yen of public monies were invested in fifty-six companies and seventeen universities to promote the management consulting and technical assistance of appointed "coordinators."[17] Inter-firm networking was promoted through "order-exchange" and "technical assistance" meetings as well as through promotional websites. Paradoxically, according to Koji Wada, an academic expert on SME policy, the result of increased funding has been to scuttle what was once a promising local initiative. Instead, "people who like money" but lack creative and innovative ideas but happen to be well-versed in government application procedures have joined the mix. "What the region needs is to develop existing inter-personal relationships – not more money".[18] Tama's cluster origins couldn't be less like those of Hokkaido's.

Hokkaido's IT/Bio

Hokkaido's IT/Bio-tech Clusters ("Hokkaido Super Cluster Promotion Project") includes 230 firms (fifty of which are bio-tech), fifteen local governments, and a number of support institutions. The IT cluster is situated around Sapporo Station and has high concentrations of bio-tech enterprises (e.g. sugar-chain engineering in glycobiology). Following the national cluster model, activities include database development (for promotion of local firms), exchange meetings (like that in Tama) and "diversified business support networks." In fiscal year 2001–2 2.18 billion yen was invested in projects involving seventy-three firms and twenty-six universities.

Hokkaido's IT cluster emerged, however, in the 1970s through the efforts of university researchers at Hokkaido and other universities in conjunction with entrepreneurial firms such as Hudson, Softbank, Tomcat, BUG and later (in the 1990s) Cyber Trust and Soft Front. Informal networks and initiatives by the local university faculty (e.g. the microcomputer workshop at Hokkaido University). Unlike the hodge-podge of Tokyo Tama cluster firms, numerous spin-offs from these entrepreneurial start-ups stimulated further cluster development after the 1980s. In sum, Hokkaido's clusters have evolved out of an organic process. The origins of Kinki's clusters are more like Hokkaido's and less like Tama's.

Kinki's bio

Kinki's bio clusters include 200 firms, nine local governments, thirty-six universities, fourteen public research institutions, twenty incubators, and twenty-four financial firms. Its two technological cores are pharmaceuticals (four firms) and tissue engineering, in firms located in and around Kobe, Kyoto, Nara, and Osaka. Cluster activities include exchange meetings, technical assistance workshops, and web/email clustering mechanisms supported by METI's national Plan. In fiscal year 2001–2, 3.18 billion yen of public funds were invested in eighty-one firms and ninety-three universities. Kinki's clusters are examined in greater detail in chapter 6.

These three regions (Tokyo's Tama, Hokkaido's Sapporo and Kinki) exhibit several regional variations on the national cluster model. For example, Hokkaido's clusters appear to have emerged from an organic process (universities and firms in the 1970s), while Tama's seems like a hodge-podge of various-sized manufacturers dispersed across a number of industries and cities. As a result, Tama's clusters seem to lack a cohesive "cluster core" around which complementary, cooperative clustered firms are said to revolve (in the national model). In Kinki's clusters there appears to be more cohesion in the technology core (bio-pharmaceuticals), and also much greater diffusion of this technology across firms. Reports from firms and Kinki regional government officials (such as T-san's above) indicate that a number of these "new" agglomerations were well known to local officials, and had proven track records in the very areas that the new Cluster Plan is said to promote.

On the one hand, this selection process (attaching the "national" label to existing agglomerations and local-level initiatives) guarantees the ability of national METI (and Ministry of Education, Science, Culture, Sports, and Technology – MEXT) bureaucrats to report success in their Tokyo "Cluster Seminars." On the other hand, it has further undermined trust (and morale) in the sincerity of national-level efforts to actually shift to a so-called "region-initiated policy." Having "prepared" the regions in Stage I, METI moved into Stage II.

Stage II (formation) involved regional METIs conducting extensive surveys of industry, semi-government, and private research institutes related to the targeted sectors in each region. For example, Kansai's METI (METI Kinki) conducted a survey of 701 firms and 170 organizations, of which 153 and 53 responded (response rates of

21.8% and 31.2%, respectively).[19] The nature of the survey questions indicate that at least the MITI Kinki office is assessing the firm-level needs and then responding with appropriate policy mechanisms (though they were doing this before the new Cluster Plan anyway). If the regional METIs are actually able to draw significant amounts of national-level resources into enterprise-based policy (say, for development of a web-based communications backbone for inter-firm exchange, collaborative manufacturing, and the like) then this might actually distinguish this Plan from its predecessors. By 2003, METI, having completed reports that outlined the spatial conditions (and expressed needs) of firms in the targeted sectors (Stage II), was ready to begin clustering.

Stage III (clustering) focuses on the clustering of firms and institutions through facilitating (human) networking. This involves two main activities: sending emails to target firms with various industry and topical information; and encouraging firm managers and technologists to get together for symposia and workshops. These networking workshops are often moderated by academics and occasionally a successful local entrepreneur will give a talk.

Reports from the entrepreneurs of this study indicate that the most innovative firms ignore the emails. Further, they report that they do not see any value-added in attending cluster workshops. The productivity of their already established personal networks is just fine. If asked to attend as a keynote speaker, however, they become interested. Talking to a workshop about their own firm has PR value, and a new client might come out of the hours spent on the activity. This interaction between established entrepreneurs and brand new start-ups might result in the establishment of truly new (and value-added) networks – for the new entrepreneurs at least (but we already know that the main beneficiaries of the Cluster Plan so far have been established, medium-sized firms). As of this writing, METI was struggling to get the right mix of attendees (and in the right numbers) at the regional workshops.

Stage IV (establishment) involves activating industrial clusters through building density, encouraging international inter-cluster exchanges, and expanding their scope (Inoue 2003; Ishikura *et al.* 2003). In the Plan, density is built in two ways:

- First, firms are expected to use support personnel, such as "coordinators" more frequently. Perhaps this is intended as a government-manufactured proxy for "Angel investors," consultants, and civic entrepreneurs who are abundant in successful clusters elsewhere (and who act as internal and external brokers of community resources). I would argue that it is around these "brokering" activities that innovative communities emerge and coalesce.[20] It also helps if these interactions are charged with a shared vision and rest on trust. Consequently, if the national METI can manage to get their coordinators placed in the right way (selecting home-grown civic entrepreneurs with proven track records would help) in local clusters, it might work.

- Second, confidentiality agreements are expected to increase inter-firm cooperation. Domestic density will ideally (for METI) be complemented by international openness.

International inter-cluster exchanges are expected to accelerate technology transfer and inward foreign direct investment (FDI). The scope of Japan's clusters, if all goes according to the Plan, should be expanded in three ways: creation of trial product manufacturing inter-firm networks; creation of (financial, personnel, management consulting) service networks; increased involvement of trading companies and other demand-side entities crucial to Porter's "feedback" mechanism ensuring ongoing competition and quality improvements. My observations on the ground on the state of METI's Plan in 2004 echo the sentiments of METI's own commissioned research.

4.6 Mid-2000s: checking on the patient

METI commissioned several private sector studies currently being under taken by Mitsubishi Research Institute (MRI) and UFJ (one of Japan's major banking groups) to assess the project mid-stream. By 2004, the nineteen regions had entered Stage III, where human networks were being facilitated by getting interested business people together with government and university people (Ishikura *et al.* 2003; METI Kinki Region 2003). Unfortunately, METI doesn't seem to be heeding the findings of its research commissioned earlier.

One such study done by MRI (a private sector research organization, with perhaps the closest ties to METI) found that despite the sincere efforts by central-state bureaucrats to both design and implement "network-creating" policies throughout the 1990s, the state largely failed. This comprehensive study conducted in the mid-1990s found that networks sponsored by *any level* of government fared poorly. Network creation from the perspective of (METI's supposed target) entrepreneurial firms is examined in depth in the next chapter.

4.7 Conclusion: too much *Gesellschaft* and not enough *Gemeinschaft*

Attempts by Japan's national government to create Silicon Valley-like clusters focused on the basic ingredients for innovation (e.g. infrastructure and formal institutions), outlined in this book's Introduction. Unfortunately, METI was not very effective at developing sufficient conditions such as fostering a shared (national–local) vision among community stakeholders (and facilitating civic entrepreneurship). The flipside of this problem is that the national METI lacks social capital in the regions to even plug into existing coalitions of community stakeholders. In short Japan's Cluster Plan is heavy on fabricating the *Gesellschaft* (formal institutions) undergirding clusters and light on nurturing the *Gemeinschaft* (informal social relations) that energize clusters.

Successful innovative networks (or "clusters") are infused with intangible know how (and vision) possessed by community members, and socio-political savvy on the part of civic entrepreneurs in brokering resources. These informal relations provide both the glue and the electricity – the conduit – between institutions and people. Manufacturing *Gemeinschaft* is proving to be a daunting task for Japan's METI Cluster Plan. I return in chapter 5 to these issues through a look at case study firms in the context of innovative networks in Kyoto, Osaka, and Tokyo.

Notes

1. This underscores the point that innovative capacity does not necessarily translate in an automaton fashion into entrepreneurial strength. For example, according to The *Global Competitiveness Report 2002–2003* (2003), Japan ranks fifth (behind the USA, the UK, Finland, and Germany) out of fifty-eight countries in terms of national innovative capacity. This capacity is a composite of measures of scientific and engineering manpower, innovation policy, cluster innovation environment, innovation linkage, and company innovation orientation. See Porter and Stern (2002, table 1, p. 229).

2. Chalmers Johnson's seminal *MITI and the Japanese Miracle* (1986, 1st edn., 1982) explores MITI's role in the industrial targeting behind Japan's high-growth period.
3. I Interview, Interview 2004.
4. M Interview, Interview 2003.
5. T Interview, Interview 2003.
6. The 1990s have been described as "Japan's lost decade" (Fumio Hayashi 2003).
7. METI (2002a, 2002b, 2002c).
8. Apparently, the *Global Competitiveness Report* issued by Porter's Council on Competitiveness also had a significant impact on the Cluster Research Group. The Report outlines various (particularly macro-) structural factors supporting competitiveness across seventy-four countries. Measures included patent figures, IPOs, opinion surveys to business executives on perceptions of competitiveness and the like. *The Global Competitiveness Report 2002–2003* (2003).
9. One method of measuring the potential for and/or existence of innovative and competitive regions (spatial clusters) is to identify the composition of its *value chain* (vertical alliance of enterprises optimizing internal and external supply chain functions) in traded clusters (trading products and services outside the region, in contrast to local clusters, whose producers serve exclusively local markets). For example, if the bulk of a region's firms produce goods (collaboratively and competitively) that compete with goods produced elsewhere for national and international markets, then that region can be said to have a successful "cluster" in a particular good or goods (Bergman and Feser 1999; available from http://www.rri.wvu.edu/WebBook/Bergman-Feser/contents.htm). A further step in analyzing a region's relative success is in comparing local firm output and sales, by industry, compared to the national average. See the *Battelle Report* for an example of this analysis applied to the industrial cluster in and around St.Louis, Missouri (Battelle Technology Partnership Practice 2003).
10. Porter cites Alfred Marshall's nineteenth-century writings on the externalities of specialized industrial locations as laying the intellectual foundations of clusters (Porter 1998, p. 256).
11. Porter and his research team found that in aggregate Japan's post-war national targeting produced more uncompetitive industries than successes. On the other hand, industries that *were not* targeted (motorcycles, 1960s; audio equipment, 1970s; autos, 1980s; game software, 1980s) emerged as Japan's most competitive industries.
12. The laws underlying these policies were enacted in 1983 and 1985, respectively.

13. Porter (1998, pp. 213–214).
14. A few European cases are also referenced (Finland, France, Germany). In May 2004, the *New York Times* reported that the USA was slipping from its position as world innovative leader. (See Broad 2004).
15. It should be noted that Texas is one of America's most fiercely independent states, where the mere mention of (particularly federal) government intervention elicits derision.
16. Not surprisingly with a bureaucratic project of this magnitude in Japan, there also seems to be some inter-ministry rivalry. Within months of METI's launching of the "Cluster Plan," MEXT launched its own "Knowledge Clusters" project. Some interviewees noted that METI, in its cluster initiative with its emphasis on greater university–industry collaboration, was intruding on territory traditionally under the purview of the former Ministry of Education. Nakagawa (2003).
17. Coordinators appear to be culled from the ranks of METI bureaucrats, firm managers, and university professors (Ishikura *et al.* 2003, p. 32).
18. Koji Wada, Interview 2 August 2004.
19. METI Kinki Region (2003).
20. Informal investment (assets of family and friends) is said to comprise the vast majority of start-up capital for entrepreneurs, far outweighing the role of "Angel investors" and Venture Capital (VC). See *Gem 2003 Executive Report* (2003, p. 64).

5 Networks and firms

5.1 Introduction

BUSINESS networks in Japan exist as hierarchies. These have operated in place of horizontal, loosely connected, inter-firm relations and have served the usual functions of networks (Powell 1990).[1] The machinations of bureaucrats and big business representatives have created these hierarchies over time, with the support of politicians. Nevertheless, a number of prominent studies have upheld Japan as a "network society" and as an exemplar of how networks can succeed as an alternative to markets and hierarchies in production and innovation (Dore 1986; Kumon 1992; Morales 1994; Sako 1994). Most have argued that a core element of these networks is long-term trust-based relations (in contrast to spot-market, contractual agreements) between large finished product producers and smaller suppliers. Recent research in Japan belies existing claims about the positive nature of the structure of Japanese business networks (Ayuzawa 1995; Wang 1998).[2]

In this chapter I show that, in contrast to standard portrayals, firms that have been *less* beholden to parent–child (*oya–ko*) subcontractor links in the past have been *better able* to form and sustain productive inter-firm networks – with other SMEs as well as with large firms at home and abroad. In sum, the less linked to parent–child-type subcontractor relations, the more innovative firms are in general, and network-enabled in particular. There also seems to be regional variations in the degree of "civic entrepreneurship" on the part of SME leaders. Firm-level leaders often say that they create and lead networks, apart from strategic reasons, to meet what they perceive as their civic responsibilities to support regional industrial success. Civic entrepreneurs have a keen sense of "giving back" firm- and individual-level wealth and experience to the larger community, for mutual long-term gain. In contributing to their communities, these entrepreneurs draw on banks of social capital (shared norms such as reciprocity that encourage cooperation between actors). Their status as successful entrepreneurs allows them to act as brokers between government resources and new start-ups, for example, – the former are perceived to know how to pick the next regional winners.

Leaders in Kyoto, for example, are less likely than their counterparts in Tokyo or Osaka to say that they have felt obligated to enter into long-term relational contracting agreements with large firms. At the same time, these leaders express strong community or civic consciousness. Osaka is a middle or somewhat independent case, while Tokyo area firms fall at opposite ends of the spectrum of independence. The character of Kyoto firm leaders appears to be infused with both entrepreneurial independent (and maverick) mindedness and civic notions of contributing to their local communities. I discuss the implications of this civic entrepreneurship later.[3]

First, my findings show that a small number of networks have flourished, despite the overwhelming control of the central state and big business over network forms. These networks typically have their origins in local spatially clustered firms (Whittaker 1997). The persistence of these horizontal networks despite the biases in the system toward hierarchical forms points to the limits of hierarchies in Japan. At the same time, research in the 1990s on the dearth of successful business networks in Japan, particularly among small firms, illustrates the overwhelming (structural and institutional) odds against the successful formation of horizontal networks (MRI 1996).

Second, I show that certain emerging network forms indicate small openings in Japan's extant network hierarchies. I examine networks – from the perspective of member firms – in each of three regions (Tokyo, Osaka, and Kyoto) that are representative of the dominant network form in its area. These network cases were selected after identifying and reviewing at least twenty-five randomly selected networks in each region, interviewing industry leaders (both within and outside of the three selected networks), and consulting with local government officials and government statistics. Aggregate cross-regional surveys showing the negative relationship between hierarchical linkage and innovation support the findings here (MRI 1996). Networks often provide critical supports for firms in producing innovative outcomes.[4]

Each network has a distinct relationship with the central state and local government. Each case also illustrates the challenges involved in state-level strategic planning, and local governments' ability to provide a supportive climate for firm networks. "O net" in Tokyo has the closest links to the central state (and big business), and its structure and level of activity reflects this strong link. Higashi Osaka's "TOPS" is a middle case, having some links with METI-sponsored network creation programs and informal links with the Osaka regional government through its sponsorship by the Osaka Chamber of Commerce. "Kiseiren" in Kyoto has the least formal links with either the central state or local government. Each will be discussed in terms of their structure (what they look like from the outside) and what they do (what they look like from the inside and whether or not it works).

While firms in Kyoto tend to be less linked to large–small firm hierarchical structures (e.g. subcontracting ties), a firm's locale (region) itself *is not* significant in determining whether or not it will be able to access (and/or form) innovative networks. Instead, the degree of *vertical linkage* (characteristic of the dominant network form in Ota, for example) is the largest structural–institutional barrier to innovation at the firm level. In sum, there remains hope, even for those firms located in more vertically structured regions, once they manage to de-link from these structures and foster productive ties with other firms.

Despite the sincere efforts in recent years by central state bureaucrats to both design and implement "network-creating" policies, the state has largely failed. As discussed in chapter 4, the new and revamped METI has moved away from its "network-creation" initiatives as it did from earlier "technopolis formation" policies to focus now in the early 2000s on regional clustering (METI 2002d; METI Kinki Region 2003). I find that the networks with the fewest historical links with the central state have been the most successful in promoting innovation and growth. Here, it is useful to define what precisely is meant by the term "network."

Networks: what are they and what are they for?

I use the term "network" here to indicate inter-firm interaction for an explicitly agreed-upon purpose by members, usually to engage in joint R&D and new product creation. Benefits of network membership are measured by the subsequent increase in sales (of jointly developed new products) resulting from such cooperative activities.

In Japan, the "network" label has often been pasted on groups of firms (whether actually "networked" or not) to suit the needs of government bureaucrats and big business – as the example of O-net shows. In contrast, the examples from Kyoto show that network founders have found it much easier (than founders in Ota) to rally member firms around civic notions of community. The presidents of Kyoto firms often describe their role in network participation as part of their civic responsibilities to ensure the future industrial success of the Kyoto city/region. Later I discuss the implications of this civic entrepreneurship in the context of case studies in Tokyo, Osaka, and Kyoto. Before doing so, it is useful to begin by noting the role that *hierarchy*, *trust*, and *local and national governments* often play in the success and failure of inter-firm networks. At the same time, there has been a neglect of the critical role that *power* also plays in the context of hierarchy, trust, and government–business relations. First, hierarchy – and its inherent power asymmetries – undermines the free flow of information within and between inter-firm networks; trust, by contrast, is said to facilitate this flow. Second, "trusting" relations in Japan have always been layered on top of a more pernicious presence of power and control (Sakai 1990; Ayuzawa 1995).[5] Third, the undermining effects of hierarchy and "trusting" relations that mask power asymmetries are exacerbated by the often befuddled meddling – albeit well intentioned – of local and national governments.

Whither Japan?

In the 1990s, research on Japanese business networks began to analyze the failures in existing networks, while attempting to identify the replicable characteristics of the handful of successful networks. For example, a 1996 study by MRI went about the task of identifying the factors behind the success or failure of various business networks throughout Japan.[6] MRI researchers reviewed thousands of networks in Japan based on success in R&D output, management, production, human resources (HR), and information exchange. Thirty networks were selected for detailed case study, based on their successes in these areas. MRI grouped case studies into three categories: independently created by firms (nine), networks emerging out of producer associations and existing inter-industry groups (ten), and networks established by local governments and/or public institutions (eleven) (MRI 1996).[7]

The report found that based upon measurable results such as new product development, the most successful networks were those that were formed independently by firms. The least successful, on the other hand, were networks sponsored by government. One reason for failure was that governments, in attempting to please everyone with broad and extensive policies (*sobana teki na tori kumi*), ended up doing poorly in each specific area. This weakness was exacerbated by the decrease in available resources resulting from the prolonged recession in the 1990s.

In each of the three types of networks in the MRI study (independent, association, and government), a factor behind success was the "wide-area" nature of horizontal ties (*koiki teki na nettwaaku kochiku*). First, firms are using networks as an opportunity to establish JVs with firms outside their locales. These JVs have been the basis for further trust-based relations (*shinrai kankei*) between firms. Network members have reported that long-term collaborative relations have been fostered and that they feel comfortable in openly exchanging opinions with other network members. The author of the study argues that, in this context, local and regional governments can be useful in administering the collaborative activities of firms (*unei*) through providing infrastructure such as meeting places, and the like. Unfortunately, these basic services appear to be the extent of local government capacity in this regard.

The MRI study finds horizontal network formation to be a critical step toward realizing success potential for SMEs. In order for these networks to exploit opportunities, however, the goals and characteristics of participating firms must be distinct from one another, and clarified at the onset. Several problems remain, mainly in the areas of establishing trust and the barrier to network solidification that distance creates. Table 5.1 lists the main problems firms have reported having in trying to establish networks that include members from outside their locale.

Also in the 1990s, in addition to the domestic comparisons such as the MRI study cited above, a number of Japanese works on networks have compared network formation in Japan with that in Silicon Valley in the USA, with the goal of drawing lessons from successes in Silicon Valley networks. The question driving these works, however, is: how can the Japanese central state create local-level inter-firm networks by policy fiat? That is, they have been aimed at suggesting government policy rather than at understanding how successful networks are developed. A 1998 study by Imai (1998b), for example, focused on the need to

Table 5.1 Problems in achieving goals of (wide-area) network formation

Network goal	*Problem*
Establishment of trust	Cannot divulge proprietary information Feel resigned to one's own passive mindset (*ukemi no shisei ni amanjiru*)
Clarifying network objectives	Unclear objectives, exchanges take place with firms and people that we do not know
Evaluating merits of exchange	If we begin to have our own troubles, we will not be able to evaluate others effectively Overestimate the merits of doing business with network partners
Research and preparation (needed for dealing with network partners)	Do not engage in any preparations before dealing with exchange partners (*ba atari*) Too busy to prepare in advance
Long-term engagement (with network partners)	Only short-term expectations Only thinking of how to take advantage of other members, not thinking of how partners can succeed together (and have win–win outcome)
Existence of point person (i.e. key person, coordinator of network activities)	No-one available in the area Lack awareness that point person is necessary
Making formal (*teiketsu*) agreements with network partners	No interest in making formal agreements Poor mutual understanding of objectives and contents of agreements

Source: MRI (1996).

nurture a venture community as well as the need for the development of a pool of venture capitalists in Japan.[8] Two major barriers to the creation of a supportive environment around firms in Japan, however, are the lack of horizontal, inter-industry personal networks and the lack of institutions that support innovation:

Not only does Japan lack the personal networks that act as a supporting mechanism in capital sourcing (like that in Silicon Valley) it lacks networks of professionals (lawyers, accountants, consultants). Supporters (*shiensha*), advisors, and institutions to support entrepreneurs are few in Japan (Murakami 1998)

The Imai study also finds few people in management who believe that technologists contribute to the profit of firms. This is one reason that existing institutions in Japan fail to provide an environment supportive of venture business:

Part of the American culture is that people respect in others what they lack in themselves. For network formation to be possible in Japan, management must develop respect for technology departments. That is, [in Japan] it is easy to support something you understand, and much more difficult to support something you don't (Okazawa 1998)

Another reason for Japan's general failure to encourage horizontal network formation is the high social sanction on business failure. Within business networks in the USA, young entrepreneurs can learn from the successes and failures of their seniors. In Japan, however, failure carries with it not the possibility for learning from mistakes but an enormous amount of shame; this limits open discussion in obvious ways. Studies have concluded that new network formation is more likely within the less hierarchical structure in Kansai than in or around Tokyo (Oguri 1998). Over time in Kansai, for example, there has been less deference to keiretsu production hierarchies coupled with greater risk-taking behavior on the part of entrepreneurial mavericks. The downside of this has been the perception outside of Kansai that in the event of business failure the tendency of business owners is to shirk ultimate responsibility (*yo nige*) while their counterparts in Kanto take that shame to their deathbeds.[9]

Failures in network formation and productivity have not gone unnoticed by policymakers in Japan. The central state has made numerous attempts to create networks among SMEs in its efforts to jump-start innovation and job creation among local businesses, as seen in chapter 4.[10] In seeking METI funds, regional and local governments have responded to calls from the central state for network creation by doing just that, at least on paper. Unfortunately, measurable output from these "new" networks in the form of new business creation and product formation has been limited. Despite the barriers to innovative

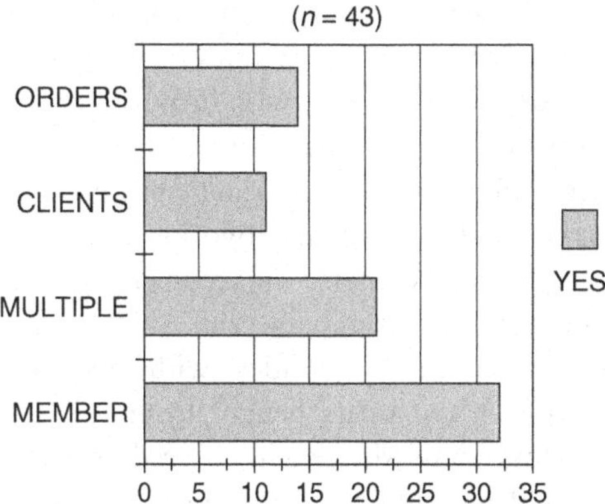

Figure 5.1. Network membership and use

inter-firm interaction imposed by hierarchy, pernicious power asymmetries masked in the veneer of trust, and government failure, there remains hope for the emergence of innovative inter-firm networks. Let us now consider the narratives of struggle in innovative network formation in Tokyo, Osaka, and Kyoto, taking into consideration the national and regional industrial milieu in which these networks are situated (Aggregate trends in Japanese industry (investment, production) were discussed in the Introduction and chapter 2.)

5.2 Overview of firm experiences

Of the forty-three case study firms, thirty-two, or 74.5%, were active in at least one network (see figure 5.1). Of this number, 65.5% were active in multiple networks; 34% of those active in networks found them helpful in accessing new clients, while 44% shared orders (e.g. outsourced) with firms within their networks. Measurable network benefits were concentrated in Higashi Osaka and Kyoto.

On the other hand, firms reported that networks helped them come up with product improvements and new product ideas to a lesser extent. Only 20% of Ota firms considered themselves active in multiple networks, despite listing numerous networks in which they were labeled (e.g. by local government) as "members." At the same time, over 77% of firms in Higashi Osaka and Kyoto regarded themselves as active in multiple networks.

The key finding about network usage is that active networks enable newcomer firms to de-link from production hierarchies – by helping firms in accessing clients and aiding collaboration with firms of similar size for production. Members have cited information exchange on the business practices of large assemblers as a major benefit of network membership. The benefits in the most productive networks often pass from senior to junior members, or "newcomers." Newcomers benefit from the expertise of senior network members who successfully struggled to become independent in earlier decades, with fewer or no network supports at the time. Newcomers benefit from the lessons learned from the struggles for independence of their predecessors. De-linked firms have contributed to building institutions, including certain forms of business networks that enable firms to enhance technical skills and innovative potential. It follows that an analysis of successful innovative communities and the institutions that support them – from the perspective of firms themselves – will yield better strategies for firms and their local communities.

In other words, it is not network membership *per se* (a superficial measure often used in aggregate reports) that assists firms, but the structure and quality of interactions with other network member firms that matters – factors best measured by a firm-centered analysis. Such analysis shows that inter-industry networks are helpful while intra-industry subcontracting networks (the kind encouraged by parent firms) are not. Networks in Higashi Osaka and Kyoto were more diverse than their counterparts in Ota, in both membership and origin. For example, there were many more active, firm-initiated networks than government- or parent firm-led networks in these regions than in Ota. This diversity is perhaps one explanation why firms in Kyoto, in particular, found de-linking from (production) hierarchies – or avoiding hierarchies altogether – easier than in other regions.[11] What follows is a comparison of networks representative of the dominant network form in each of three industrial regions: Tokyo, Osaka, and Kyoto. After briefly situating each network in its immediate socio-economic environment, each is evaluated based on what it has accomplished for its member firms.

5.3 Networks in Ota Ward: O-Net

Ota Ward in southeast Tokyo has some of the oldest small manufacturers in Japan, boasting the highest concentrations of small manufacturing firms in the nation. Approximately 80% of Ota firms produce machinery and metal products. High-tech SMEs in Ota were firmly assimilated into keiretsu "pyramid" production structures in the post-war period. Manufacturers in Ota and Tokyo city-wide have been in steady decline over the 1990s. In Tokyo (city), total exports, the value-added of exports, firm numbers, and number of employees declined between 40 and 50% between 1991 and 2001. The decline of the 1990s continued into the 2000s. Between 2000 and 2001, the total number of firms dropped 10.1% (30,096–27,066). Employment dropped 4.7% (550,633–524,570). Exports decreased 7.8% (¥17.9 trillion–¥16.5 trillion). Total value-added of product also declined 4.0% (¥7.5 trillion–¥7.2 trillion) (Tokyo Manufacturing Summer Report 2001).

Under the close eye of the central bureaucracy, Ota firms have been the first and most affected by the centralization and rationalization policies of the central government ever since the days of wartime control associations (*toseikai*). The presence of large, powerful "parent" firms has proved a force in undermining horizontal network formation in Ota Ward. A majority of SMEs in Ota in the post-war period became exclusive subcontractors for keiretsu groups – that is, most of the sales of a given firm go to one buyer. Large firms have used their (*de facto* monopsony) leverage against subcontractors who have tried to organize independently of peak associations and keiretsu-sponsored subcontractor networks. According to Tomohiro Koseki, an outspoken critic of keiretsu practices in Ota Ward, small firms have in the past been intimidated from forming horizontal networks (e.g. subcontractor unions). Koseki cites interviews with many local businessmen who said that firms around them, "after trying to organize – or merely vocalize the unfair treatment by large keiretsu firms – were forced under" (i.e. driven into bankruptcy) (Koseki 2002).[12]

Historically, across regions, firms have found it difficult to access technological information beyond the confines of their subordinate links to main buyers and parent firms. A 1994 survey of 426 machinery manufacturers (with an average number of 92.5 employees) in Kanto and Kansai, among other regions, found that the primary source of SME network formation and technological information in general came from their parent firm/main buyer (35.7%). In contrast, direct network links with nearby firms were scant (1.2%). The Internet remained an insignificant source of network formation/information (0.9%). (*Chushokigyosogokenkyukiko* 1995)

In recent years, however, small firms in Ota have begun to break away from exclusive subcontractor relations. These firms survived the "hollowing out" that hit the Ota region hard as their biggest clients moved operations overseas – in the 2000s, mainly to China. Based on what these firms refer to as their "independent technological strength," these enterprises have begun to "resist existing domination of keiretsu."[13] Independent technological strength can mean the ability of a firm to protect its proprietary technology from expropriation by large firms. It can also mean establishing a unique product niche based on its patented technology. Besides an active Association of Small and Medium-Sized Enterprise Entrepreneurs (SME Doyukai), local neighborhood networks are beginning to develop. Activities of local business networks have included forming "buyers clubs," which help to control the cost of insurance and other overhead costs among firms.

A major initiative by the local government has been the establishment of an online network for local firms. With backing from the Chamber of Commerce, KDD, NTT, and Fujitsu, among others, "O-net" was incorporated in 1990. O-Net is housed in the "PiO" (Ota City Industrial Plaza) and administered by a board of directors having executives from KDD, NTT, Fujitsu, and a few local medium-sized firms. The network boasts 7,000 members – most enterprises in Ota. The sheer size of this "network" of course raises doubts as to how much it can function like a network, despite the fact that the network founders were very successful in obtaining seed money from the Tokyo government. The two major objectives of the O-net are to provide public relations for local firms and to act as go-between for international trade for local high-tech SMEs. Activities have included the publishing of a detailed trade directory and creation of a website promoting the O-net and local SMEs.[14]

Several interviewees have said, however, that little new business has come as a result of O-net activities. One source said that O-Net was yet another example of the "form over substance problem" in the execution of METI policy initiatives. One small manufacturer complained that it was a waste of time for him to get involved.[15] At the same time, interviewees report that informal networks among manufacturers have fared somewhat better. For example, firms that established early ties with other SMEs both within and outside Ota have been less vulnerable to the fallout after the collapse of the "bubble".[16] The high public profile of the O-net has tended to obscure (in the standard literature) the presence of these less formal networks among the small businesses themselves.

5.4 Networks in Higashi Osaka: TOPS

Like Tokyo's Ota Ward, Higashi Osaka consists of spatially concentrated clusters of small manufacturers. Higashi Osaka prides itself on being the center of "supporting products" for Japanese industry. Around half of all firms there produce machinery or metal products. Around 10% of firms produce plastics, and Higashi Osaka firms have somewhat lower technology levels than their compatriots in Ota and Kyoto.

Networks in Higashi Osaka tend to be less formal and hierarchical than in Ota, though the presence of major keiretsu groups is still felt. As of 2000, local firms were yet to make widespread use of Internet technologies. On the other hand, SME owners, known for their sales acumen, spend most of their day "pounding the pavement" in search of new customers. Since they are always meeting new people, their personal networking skills are high (Nonami 1998).When asked if networks helped firms to obtain new customers, most interviewees said that formal networks (which are linked to the local government and Chamber of Commerce) do not help in new customer acquisition. Instead, interviewees credit informal personal networks for new customer access:[17]

> Networks in Ota are more formal and linked to government services. It is in this respect that Ota firms can get more from the government, like the industrial plaza (PiO). Higashi Osaka networks are much more fluid (*sugoku yawarakai*) and thus must struggle much more for government services (*junansei ga aru*).[18]

Akihiro Kitabatake founded and served as president of Sanyo Vacuum until 2003, when he retired and turned the firm over to his son. Kitabatake senior shared his experiences with Higashi Osaka networks. Founded in 1963, Sanyo employs 220 people and produces sputtering machines used in thin-film application technologies (e.g. for liquid crystal displays) and etching technology. Kitabatake noted that although there are many networks in Higashi Osaka, in comparison, the quality of personal networks in Kyoto is higher: "This is because in Kyoto networks are generally established and run by the owners/managers of small firms. In Higashi Osaka, many are created by bureaucrats, who have the best intentions but do not understand market needs." Although Sanyo has had many interactions with METI, Kitabatake finds that bureaucrats in METI also lack an understanding of the market and the needs of SMEs. He gets the impression that METI bureaucrats come around not to help in network formation, but instead primarily to look for post-retirement *amakudari* posts ("*amakudari*" is the "descent from heaven" of bureaucrats into the private sector).[19]

With the support of the local Chamber of Commerce, Higashi Osaka firms have established a national network of SMEs. Since 1997, SMEs from ten major industrial regions have come together for the annual Small and Medium Size Enterprise City Summit (Japan Association of Small and Medium-Sized Enterprises 1998). The local Chamber of Commerce has also sponsored the establishment of fifteen inter-industry exchange network groups. Most of these networks were founded in the late 1980s and during the 1990s. The Chamber of Commerce coordinates these networks under the auspices of the Higashi Osaka Inter-Industry Liaison Council (*Renraku Kyogikai*). On its formation in 1996, the Council set out to achieve four main goals: (1) to publish informational materials on Chamber of Commerce-sponsored inter-industry network groups, (2) to facilitate exchange among local inter-industry networks, (3) to provide infrastructural support for the annual general meeting of sponsored inter-industry networks, and (4) to provide for network management and other tasks.

According to outside sources, the most active of the fifteen Chamber of Commerce-sponsored networks is the "TOPS Higashi Osaka" network. TOPS was formed in 1997 and is an amalgamation of the top fifty producers, as measured by sales, in the area. Most members are either metal goods producers or machinery makers. Yoshihiro Ishizaki, the president of Takako, the lead firm in TOPS, said that this network had been created on the initiative of the Chamber of Commerce, based on the sales success of member firms. With respect to public relations for Higashi Osaka firms in general, Ishizaki says that the network has been successful, but he had little to say about the likelihood of new products coming out of joint activities of network members.[20] Other interviewees confirm that few new products have come out of the joint efforts of these Chamber of Commerce- sponsored networks.

Two exceptional, though much smaller, Chamber of Commerce-sponsored networks, by contrast, are the "Gyatech" and "Mekatro 21" groups. Gyatech's seventeen members are divided relatively equally among metal goods producers, machinery makers and plastics manufacturers. Within sixteen months of its formation in 1996, Gyatech had jointly developed a product called "*Tafupaakingu*," based on technology for recycling industrial materials. This and other product innovations prompted member firms to form a marketing JV firm. Mekatro 21 was formed in 1991 by twenty-three firms, mostly electrical machinery producers and metal products makers. Under the guidance of a professor at Kinki University, the group has worked with university students on new product research development, and the group has jointly developed a robotic hand. This is one of few local networks in Higashi Osaka to have a formal link with a local university.

5.5 Networks in Kyoto: Kiseiren and its spin-offs

Kyoto's high-tech SMEs are scattered over an area in the southeast portion of the region, in small townships such as Kuse and Uji. Kyoto firms have largely avoided hierarchical links with major keiretsu groups.[21] Kyoto manufacturers are not likely to have been integrated into a "parent–child"[22] subcontractor relationship in the past, owing to the historical weaker presence of big (keiretsu) firms in the Kyoto area.[23] Throughout the region of Kyoto, firms produce high-value-added electrical machinery, semiconductor and silicone products. Kyoto firms tend to maintain a good balance among sales ratios (the ratio of sales between the largest client and other clients). Several interviewees noted that small firms in Kyoto have avoided becoming subordinate to parent firms through their unique technological expertise.[24] A 2002 study by METI lauded Kyoto for being a model "venture area," citing its highly productive networks (METI 2002a).

Several interviewees (outside of Kyoto) commented on the fact that Kyoto business networks are much less numerous than in other locales. One executive from the Osaka government admitted that although networks in Ota and Osaka are quite numerous, many are inactive. Kyoto networks, on the other hand, tend to remain active once formed. Other interviewees alluded to a "form over substance problem" in network formation by most local and regional governments.[25] That is, in response to METI calls for network formation, local governments have rushed to throw networks together without thinking through organizational goals.[26]

One example of innovative networks in Kyoto is the Kyoto Liaison Council for Small and Medium-Sized Producers of Machinery and Metals (*Kyoto kikai kinzoku chusho kigyo Seinen Renrakukai*, "Kiseiren"or KSR).[27] Kiseiren was formed through the initiatives of local firms, with infrastructural support from the Kyoto regional government (Kyoto prefecture).

In 1982, Yoshinori Nagashima, the founder of Nagashima Seiko (a producer of lathe machinery) got together with like-minded entrepreneurs to form Kiseiren. In the 1970s, Nagashima Seiko was recognized internationally for producing ultra-precision lathe machinery. As managing director for the first two years of Kiseiren's formation, Nagashima provided a model for members of success based on independence and hard work. Further, Nagashima can be considered a civic entrepreneur because of his maverick leadership and his wish to give back to the community in which his firm prospered.[28]

Kiseiren was named for its membership base of young managers of small and medium-sized Kyoto area machinery makers and metallic processors. Keenly aware that while they knew how to make things, and make them well, few knew how to really sell their product and services on the open market, Kiseiren was thus envisioned both as a marketing platform for members and also as an opportunity for small firms, including the Akita Works (introduced in chapter 2) to break out of vertical production relationships and forge horizontal inter-firm networks. Kiseiren's founders were so adverse to hierarchy, in fact, that they instituted a policy of the mandatory "graduation" of members upon turning forty-five years of age. In the early 2000s KSR had some 100 members.

The founders of Kiseiren infused the organization with a spirit of "let's grow up, let's nurture [our businesses], let's succeed together" (*sodato, sodateyo, sodachi ao*).[29] Yasuhiro Ikuta, coordinator of Kiseiren's activities in the late 1990s, commented that this spirit had been maintained throughout Kiseiren's history. In fact, members had consistently striven to become independent of big business and peak associations. These firms had fought to maintain their independence on many levels. Early leaders of Kiseiren built the network based on the principle of open exchange with competitors, as friends (*harawatta*). In the context of Kiseiren's formation in the 1980s, young managers, lacking the experience of doing business during the high-growth period of their predecessors, began to take the helm of existing SMEs and also form new ventures. These new leaders wanted to share their experiences of struggling (*ikizama*) for success in the changing marketplace.[30]

From the beginning, the founders of Kiseiren sought to form an organization unlike the majority of existing business networks. Earlier networks had been formed based on predetermined (and often central-state dictated) notions of how firms should interact (i.e. as subordinate members of peak associations controlled by big business, *unmeikyodotai*). Instead, Kiseiren formed a network based on the mutual benefit of members (*kyoseigata*, literally "a symbiotic model"). *Mutual benefit* was the ideal goal, and the organization did its best to put it into practice. That individual members "graduated" and left the network upon reaching the age of forty-five distinguished KSR from other networks. The rationale was that camaraderie would be enhanced and hierarchies avoided if there were no significant difference in age among members. "Graduated" members may maintain informal links to the network and volunteer as advisors to current network members.

Kiseiren has provided an environment where firms can learn from each other's successes as mistakes. Meetings, held on a monthly basis since the network was formed, have focused on practical issues. These issues have included: forming a buyer's group (for sourcing raw materials and other inputs), strategies of overcoming recessionary environments, legislation to end slow payment of debt by big firms, new product development, the training of technicians, how to start venture businesses, international exchanges (e.g. with Taiwanese firms), the role of SMEs in the global economy, capital mergers, employee management issues, tax problems, improving the quality of information exchange, and developing firms' public relations. Several members said that they had obtained new customers through the Kiseiren web page.[31] One member said that firm sales had increased threefold since joining the network.[32] Another recounted that:

> Kiseiren has really helped. During the three years [our firm has] been a member, we have obtained a lot of industry and government information that we would not otherwise have received. Information comes into Kiseiren.[33]

One of the main organizational goals of Kiseiren in the late 1990s was to support the technological upgrading of member firms. In order to support the development of a healthy and prosperous business climate, recent network objectives have included organizing new product R&D on a larger scale than before, establishing a regional network of employment, further developing networks among employees of member firms and supporting continued trust-based network formation. Though Kiseiren has no formal link to government, several members noted that the regional government-level Kyoto General SME Center is good at passing on information to local firms.[34] Representatives of the General SME Center have also acted as advocates for local SMEs at the central-state level, as well as promoted local firms and networks nationally and internationally. Kiseiren remains an open network, for example, through encouraging spin-off networks; Koji Akita's experiences in Kiseiren provide an example.

Akita spent some time in the first year after joining his parents' business and the Kiseiren network commiserating with other young presidents – who, like himself, were either struggling to start their own firms or to keep small family businesses alive after taking them over from their parents. Akita came to the conclusion that Akita Works would have to move on from sheet metal processing into more lucrative areas, higher up the production ladder. How could Akita make the jump from sheet metal processing?

Soon after Akita "graduated" from the Kiseiren network (upon reaching the age of forty-five in 1999), he joined with nine other Kiseiren firms to establish a spin-off network. They based "Kyoto Shisaku Net" on the Internet platform of Kiseiren's Peter Drucker Study Group, but it took an entire year to work out the details and complete the web design for the new network. Shisaku was launched officially on July 1, 2001 with firms from various machinery manufacturing, processing and design fields. Its website constitutes the network's main marketing interface. The distinguishing feature of Shisaku is that potential customers can place orders on-line (for final goods produced collaboratively by network member firms). Users merely upload their product specs and are guaranteed to receive a quote within two hours. To enable such a rapid turnaround time, each member carries his or her cellular phone at all times. In fact, Akita says that the key to the success of collaborative network-based R&D and production in Shisaku Net is this constant real-time communication between network members.[35]

The next year (2002), 250 customer leads from the web site had been established and of these leads, fifty had placed orders. By 2003, a number of new products and patents had come out of the network, which by that time had established ties with the engineering departments of several local universities such as Ritsumeikan. Shisaku Net's latest collaboration (begun in 2003) includes the engineering department at Ritsumeikan and Matsushita to develop nanotechnology. Shisaku Net has drawn the attention of engineering faculty at Kyoto University, who have expressed interest in collaborating with Akita and Shisaku in the future. The network eventually got the attention of Drucker himself, and Akita has since met the author.

Throughout the 1990s and early 2000s, Akita continued to invest in software development, and now focuses on designing custom-made control function software for robotics and testing equipment in key manufacturing industries. In the early 2000s, both Akita Works' and Act's sales had moved heavily into mechatronics. Akita remained active informally in Kiseiren after his "graduation," often serving as a mentor for newcomers and helping them to establish their own networks. Other firms have similar success with enterprise-initiated networks like Kiseiren and its spin-offs, while the Kyoto local and regional governments act as a kind of advocate.

One such example is Ikuta Manufacturing. Ikuta produces manufacturing machinery and is currently involved in a research and development JV with a German firm. Ikuta uses over thirty Kansai area subcontractors, and its largest client takes up 20% of sales. The founder and president, Yasuhiro Ikuta, finds that both Kyoto city and the Kyoto regional government have been helpful in obtaining R&D capital for local businesses. Ikuta has found it much easier to obtain information on government funding programs since joining KSR in 1995. Ikuta finds that the Kyoto regional government is very effective at acting as a "window" to various government-sponsored assistance programs. Ikuta has found, however, that government representatives lack the ability to assess the viability of firms' technology. Consequently, the government still gives money to failing firms – for example, in the construction industry – based on those firms' connections to the central government.[36]

As the experiences of Akita and Ikuta firms have illustrated, Kiseiren and similar networks continued to operate on the tenet of "open exchange of information." Ikuta, Kiseiren's coordinator in the 1990s, observed that as traditional hierarchies in Japan's economy break down, firms are again asking, "what [kind of enterprise] am I?" (*onore wa nani mono ka*). That is, small business leaders are reassessing, and reasserting in public spheres, their structural role in the Japanese political economy. These firms are working hard to develop marketing skills and access new clients, independent of big business-linked distribution hierarchies. For Ikuta, these struggles herald a return to a more independent basis for firms, particularly small enterprises, competing in the Japanese political economy.

Like the original founders of Kiseiren, current members are proud of having established their independence (*ko no jiritsuka*) from both big business and the state. In the recession-plagued environment since the 1990s, firms fostering practical know how (*sonzai igi*) and showing that it is possible to realize entrepreneurial dreams independently from existing hierarchies in Japan, have been significant in providing direction for newcomers. Ikuta was impressed by the many young managers enthusiastically participating in a Kiseiren "Vision Symposium" on management strategies. In addition, member firms have successfully developed products and secured new clients together with greater frequency in recent years:

> I am fifty-two years old, and now I see younger people coming in and voicing their opinions. This is a wonderful thing. We have made steady progress over time in nurturing the younger generation of entrepreneurs [*juncho sodateita*].[37]

Kiseiren has been so successful in achieving its organizational goals that it has attracted national attention. In an article on the critical role of success stories (*monogotari sei*) in encouraging entrepreneurialism and innovation in the Japanese economy, Imai highlighted the efforts of Kiseiren: "Kiseiren has created, independently of other organizations, an environment for its firms that has this kind of linkage [based on mutual success stories]."[38] Table 5.2 shows how the networks representative of each region compare.

5.6 Conclusion: seeds of change

Participation in local business networks, often supported by local government, has helped small SMEs to survive – that is, remain in

Table 5.2 Networks in Ota Ward, Higashi Osaka, and Kyoto

Network	O-Net	TOPS	Kiseiren
Year established	1990	1997	1982[a]
Formation initiated by	Local government, Chamber of Commerce, large firms	Chamber of Commerce	Local firms, supported informally by regional government
Funding	Chamber of Commerce, large firms	Chamber of Commerce	Self-funded
Main characteristics of member firms	Location in Ota Ward	Top fifty producers in Higashi Osaka	Location in Kyoto
Activities	Inactive, some trade fairs	Public relations for members	Marketing, new product development, management training

[a] Though the oldest network among the three, the Kiseiren policy of "graduating" members (mandatory exit) upon turning forty-five years of age continually renews the youth of the network as well as reducing internal hierarchies.

business. These networks have provided a critically important context for the exchange of information about management techniques and the market. Local networks also provide a conduit for information on practices of which to be aware, and wary of, by large (keiretsu) makers.

While maintaining neighborhood ties, business networks have become increasingly fluid in recent years, expanding across industries, domestic regions, and internationally. Kansai networks have historically been more fluid than their Kanto counterparts. Ota and Higashi Osaka firms are likely to participate in one or more local networks. These networks, however, tend to have few higher-value-added manufacturers as members, and thus lack "technology mentors" and therefore have few members who can serve as civic entrepreneurs. Kyoto networks, by comparison, seem to enjoy far greater access to traditional sources of information. Networks in Kyoto, for example, appear to be more savvy at obtaining information about and access to government-sponsored programs. Industry and government sources estimated that less than a third of firms in Ota are involved in a local business network, though the local government has labeled many firms as "members" of certain networks. More firms in Higashi Osaka were active in one or another network, while Kyoto firms tended to list a small number of networks in which they considered themselves active. It may appear upon superficial comparison that Kyoto firms do not find networks useful. A closer look reveals that, though numerous, networks in Ota and to a lesser extent Higashi Osaka, are often inactive. Successful models such as the Kyoto Kiseiren network deserve further attention in the future.

In sum, most business networks in Japan, particularly those closely linked to central government and big business groups, are inactive and lack focus. In a few places, however, business networks in Japan have improved in number and substance in recent years. Independently formed (firm-initiated) networks have been the best at delineating and attaining clear and manageable goals for their members, including improving marketing skills and enhancing technical human resources. These highly successful networks have served as institutions enabling member firms to become more innovative and competitive, often with the informal support of local or regional governments. It is in these firm-initiated business networks – led by civic entrepreneurs – in which the seeds of change lie in the small enterprise sector within the Japanese political economy. The Kyoto region seems to excel at this innovative network formation – and chapter 6 explores why – at the firm and regional levels.

Notes

1. A comparison of the characteristics of markets, hierarchies, and networks shows how on each point, so-called "network forms" in Japan are in reality hierarchical. Powell 1990, table 1, p. 300.
2. See Ayuzawa (1995) for a discussion of the existence of social stratum-based (pyramid) organizational forms v. true network organizations in Japan; Ayuzawa finds that there are few of the latter. See also Wang (1998).
3. I thank Seiritsu Ogura and Hugh Whittaker for pushing me to refine this notion.
4. As previously mentioned, innovation is of two kinds: "product" (e.g. that never before produced, new products in new sectors) or "process"

(improvements to the steps of production of an existing product). "Innovation" refers here to that resulting in new products. Innovation is measured in this study by patent and new product R&D output.

5. Ayuzawa (1995), for example, conducted a survey with 253 firms in March 1995 and found that over 45% had taken precautions against increasing their dependence on exclusive buyers (*tokutei hanbaisaki*) through the use of horizontal networks. In terms of future business strategy, 48% of firms were planning to focus on getting out of exclusive buyer relationships.
6. See also Edgington (1999).
7. The author notes that these networks should not be viewed as representative of networks in each area. They are instead exceptional cases (MRI 1996, n. 2–2).
8. Imai (1998b).
9. Suicide soon after business failure is not unheard of. Dramatically increasing suicide rates in Japan in the 1990s and 2000s, particularly among young people and (failed) businessmen, has become a major concern for citizens' groups and government alike, as well as the subject of television "dramas" See Lies (2003); Health and Welfare Ministry (2002).
10. Policies to support network formation among SMEs were a central focus in 1998 for MITI's SME Agency. See for example, *Dai Issho Souron Monodzukuri Nettowaaku Shien*, Japan Small and Medium Size Enterprise Agency (1998).
11. That Kyocera, one of the few independent firms to grow to be a high-tech leader rivaling large keiretsu firms emerged from Kyoto is worthy of note.
12. Tomohiro Koseki, fax November 23, 2002.
13. Koji Akita, Interviews 1998, 2002.
14. Whittaker notes the early stages of O-Net's establishment as a "technology-based information network" (see Whittaker 1997, p. 124).
15. Interview 1998. Another interviewee commented: "There are countless networks in Japan that have no purpose whatsoever" (Hirotada Takenaka, interviews 1998, 2002).
16. An Osaka study found that the greater the firm was horizontally networked the less affected it was by economic fluctuations in other firms (such as a parent or main buyer). The study found that Higashi Osaka firms were more effective at networking horizontally, and consequently were less affected by industry downturns in the 1990s. Osaka Small and Medium-Sized Enterprise Information Center (OSBIC) (1997).
17. Higashi Osaka firms have also established more personal international networks than Ota firms, especially with firms in Asia. In a 1997 study, more than 9% of Higashi Osaka firms surveyed had international network partners compared to 6% in Ota. See OSBIC (1997).

18. Yasuhisa Nakano, Interview July 27, 2004.
19. Akihiro Kitabatake, Interview 1998.
20. Yoshihiro Ishizaki, Interviews 1998, 2003.
21. Some have argued that Kyoto's current independent business environment has its origins in its historical artisan-based business community. Toshihiko Asai of the Kyoto Regional General Small and Medium Size Enterprise Center (*Kyoto fu chuushoukigyou sougo sentaa*) noted that between the Heian (794–1185) and Edo periods (the Tokugawa period, 1603–1868) Kyoto was the center of Japanese culture and industry. (Toshihiko Asai, Interview 1998). The emperor and court of Japan were located in Kyoto for over a thousand years; in 1868, it was officially moved to Edo, now Tokyo.
22. Many interviewees took offense at the mention of the term "parent–child" subcontracting relations (*oya-ko gaisha*). Several said that this term has always been a misnomer, as large assemblers have rarely acted in a manner towards their subcontractors remotely resembling the benevolence of a "parent" figure.
23. In terms of their own use of subcontractors, of the forty-three firms, 84% (36) used subcontractors on a regular basis, while an additional 10% (4) used subcontractors on an occasional basis. Only two firms had never used subcontractors. About a third of firms used fewer than ten subcontractors on a regular basis while another third used up to fifty subcontractors; 14% of firms used over 100 subcontractors on a regular basis; 44% of firms used subcontractors in the same city, district, or region, while a growing number of firms were branching out to other regions and also internationally (37% and 7%, respectively).
24. B said that the technological expertise and independence of Kyoto firms has not gone unnoticed: "We have many large firms coming to see why it is that we have survived and continued to prosper, despite the recession."
25. For example, B said that "there may be more networks in Tokyo, but you must look inside, at what (the networks) really can do. That is why you see fewer networks in Kyoto. The number means nothing."
26. X Interview, Interviews 1998, 2003.
27. Other examples include the "Kyoto shisaku net" (*Kyoto-shisaku.com*), and "Kyoto 21" networks discussed later.
28. Koji Akita of the Akita Works, founder of the Shisaku net, is a more recent example of active civic entrepreneurship in Kyoto.
29. Yasuhiro Ikuta, Interview July 29, 2004.
30. Yasuhiro Ikuta, Interviews 1998, July 29, 2004.
31. 00 Interview, Interviews 1998, 2002.
32. X Interview, Interviews 1998, 2003.
33. Seiritsu Ogura, Interviews 1998.

34. Yasuhiro Ikuta, Interviews 1998, 2004; Takafumi Kinugawa, Interviews 1998.
35. One of the stated aims of Shisaku net is to establish more so-called "Kyoto Brands" that can compete with increasing competition from cheap Chinese manufactures.
36. One of the most bothersome things for G is that not only are the procedures for applying for government programs time-consuming, many planned programs never come to fruition, making applying for them a waste of time. While G is hopeful about planned bureaucratic reform, he has yet to see a change in central government–SME relations. Instead, he sees paralysis (*kankakumahi*) in these relations.
37. Sa, Interview 2002.
38. Kenichi Imai, Interview 1998. See also Imai (1998b) for a detailed discussion of the significance of success stories or "*monogotari sei*" for venture businesses.

6 The Kyoto Model

6.1 What is the Kyoto Model?

A number of regions in Japan have been heralded as a home-grown "Silicon Valley" by local promoters and observers alike. Examples include Hokkaido's Sapporo bio-tech cluster (introduced in chapter 4) and Tokyo's Akihabara electronics retail district that spawned later developments in software. Even far-flung Kyushu has laid claim to the title.[1] Kyoto prefecture is itself situated within Japan's "Keihan Valley" and the economic performance of its vibrant entrepreneurial (particularly high-tech) community of firms has given rise to the notion of the "Kyoto Model." For example, throughout the 1990s and 2000s the performance of these Kyoto firms in return on investment (ROI), sales, and profit have continued to outpace Japanese giants headquartered in Tokyo such as Hitachi, NEC, and Sony.[2]

One might ask whether this new so-called "model" is so distinct from the much-belabored Silicon Valley or Third Italy archetypes. For example, all three regions (Palo Alto, Tuscany, and Kyoto) share similar structural–institutional characteristics common to innovative communities world-wide. These characteristics include being situated far from the national political order and being abundant in indigenous resources that fueled initial economic development (e.g. mountain streams to power textile mills).

A number of features about Kyoto make it uniquely able to produce comparatively large numbers of world-class companies owned and managed by entrepreneurial mavericks. This regional success has spawned a number of works in Japanese that have sought to define the Kyoto Model and present its exemplar firms (Ishikawa and Tanaka 1999; Horiuchi 2001; Imai 2004; Inoue and Tsuji 2001). These works have tended to focus on the largest Kyoto firms such as Kyocera and Omron, which have become familiar names even outside of Japan. The case study-style stories about a handful of Kyoto firms have painted an intriguing picture of the Kyoto region. These stories, however, have not analyzed in depth how firm-level success might be somehow linked to the nature of the regional political economy.

This chapter addresses three things: what makes the Kyoto region a model of entrepreneurship and innovation, which Kyoto firms fit the model and why, and if the Kyoto Model can indeed be emulated in other places, even in Japan. I will begin by reviewing the unique political–cultural history of Kyoto that has been serendipitous to its current status as an innovative region. Second, I outline the three levels at which the model is manifested: region, firm, and entrepreneur – using examples from my own cases and others. Third, I review measures of regional economic success, highlighting the performance of top Kyoto firms. Fourth, I complement the existing literature's focus on the largest Kyoto firms by introducing small entrepreneurial firms including the Samco and Akita cases from earlier chapters. I also consider why it is that there seems to be more active civic entrepreneurship in Kyoto than in other places in Japan. I conclude with some thoughts on Kyoto as a model for other places.

6.2 Serendipity in history

Kyoto was the political, economic, and cultural hub of Japan for over a millennium, until the Meiji restoration in 1868 that shifted economic, political, and military power to Tokyo.[3] Kyoto's history as a cultural and technological center has never been usurped, however, and Kyoto University has produced numerous Nobel laureates. The city remains a center of fine arts including ceramics, tea, sake, and silk. This artisanal culture and abundance of technological skill, such as attention to precision-level detail, have combined to make Kyoto a breeding ground for high technology entrepreneurs.

Kyoto prefecture is spread out over about 46,000 m^2, of which 610 km^2 comprises Kyoto city. In 1999, Kyoto prefecture firms employed nearly 300,000 people and generated export revenues of over ¥8.8 trillion. Home to about 2.6 million people (1.4 million of whom reside in Kyoto city proper), the region generated a trade surplus of ¥24 billion in 2000. Total personal income in the region topped

¥79 billion in 1998. In 2000, its manufacturing enterprises (7,641) employed over 177,000 people and generated gross export revenue of ¥5.4 trillion (*Japan Industry Revenue Bulletin* 1999; *Japan Industrial Statistics Bulletin* 2000; *Japan National Census Bulletin* 2000; *Worldwide Agriculture and Forestry Bulletin* 2000).

In contrast, Tokyo became Japan's financial hub in the period of rapid industrialization following the shift in political power after 1868. By the turn of the twentieth century, zaibatsu (large financial combines) rose around the new political capital and fueled growth in heavy industry. Kyoto was no longer a financial center and zaibatsu main banks therefore never had a major presence in the Kansai region. Consequently, Kyoto entrepreneurs had to rely on what can be called "pocket-money finance," from friends and relations.

After Japan's defeat in 1945 the American military dissolved the zaibatsu. As a result, "keiretsu" – or loosely organized groups of firms revolving around one main bank and cross-shareholding–emerged in and around Tokyo to take the place of zaibatsu in fueling post-war Japanese growth. Like zaibatsu, keiretsu tended to have insular, vertically integrated trading and production hierarchies. In Kyoto, however, keiretsu, like zaibatsu before them, never took root. One result is that the region's firms lack the business benefits of relational (in-group) contracting ties and concomitant main bank finance. Lacking these supports, Kyoto firms have struggled in a fiercely competitive environment. This adversity-turned-opportunity is another reason why Kyoto has come to be known as a center of independent, maverick-type firms.

Losing its political (and military) eminence in the late 1800s in fact became a blessing in disguise for Kyoto. While Tokyo was decimated by firebombing in 1945, Kyoto's industrial structures and cultural institutions emerged unscathed. Tokyo's post-war industrial communities, such as Ota Ward, relied heavily on the central state for their very existence; it is no surprise, then, that Ota has been a major recipient of government subsidies and the bureaucratic red tape and hassles that follow. The weakness of inter-firm networks in Ota, discussed in chapter 5, attest to the difficulties many Japanese firms have faced in trying to stay independent from government dictate. Like innovative regions in other countries, Kyoto has been relatively free from the distractions of bureaucratic oversight and national political intrigue.

6.3 Model firms

This historical–institutional confluence (or serendipity) of cultural eminence, precision technology, pocket-money finance, and political (and social) freedom created a particular *socio-cultural milieu*. This milieu has produced (and attracted) world-class firms and the entrepreneurs at their helm: Horiba's Masao Horiba, Kyocera's Kazuo Inamori, Murata's Akira Murata, Omron's Kazuma Tateisi, and Rohm's Ken Sato. With all of these regional historical–structural–institutional characteristics supporting local firms, one might guess that they have had an easy time of it. One theme that emerges from the stories of these entrepreneurial firms, however, is how they turned adversity into opportunity. Masao Horiba offers one example.

Adversity into opportunity: Horiba

Masao Horiba was released from compulsory military service after the official surrender of Japan on September 2, 1945. He then tried returning to Kyoto University's particle accelerator lab to complete his doctoral thesis research. The American Occupation Authority, however, soon destroyed all research and testing equipment that might have use in the development of nuclear technology. The particle accelerator central to Masao's experiments was gone, and along with it his ability to complete his thesis in the university lab.

Horiba was not deterred. Within a month, he had started his own "lab" – an 80 m^2 space in an old wooden building, yards away from Kyoto's Karasuma *gojo* (Imperial Villa). Horiba quickly completed his thesis, now focused on low-tension electricity technology, better known by its common name "radio." He soon saw the commercial applications of his work. Horiba's first product was a small back-up battery to power a light bulb in the event of a power failure.

Horiba soon faced a conundrum, reminiscent of the challenges faced by Murao of Namitei, introduced in chapter 2.[4] Horiba was contracted to make a medical pulse transmitter, but found that the capacitors (two or more conducting plates separated by insulating material to store an electric charge) he was using for his transmitter were of poor quality. One problem was ensuring the pH consistency in the process of making oxide film. At the time, US-made pH meters dominated the world market; these American meters however, were very expensive while at the same time not being designed to withstand the humidity common in Japan.

Collaborating with professors from Kyoto University and Kyoto Medical University, Horiba and his research team soon developed a vastly improved pH meter. This led to later developments in devices for medical diagnostics, semiconductor production and design, and electrical engineering. In 2004, Horiba's net income reached a record high of ¥2 billion. Like Masao Horiba, Akira Murata's story shows how, given the right kind of drive and perseverance, Kyoto entrepreneurs have refused to settle for average-level success.

Refusing to settle for the average: Murata

Akira Murata was sickly as a child and never quite made it to the college track of Japan's education system. In fact, by junior high Akira had dropped out of school to work as a salesman in his father's small ceramic shop near Kiyomizu *dera* (temple) in Kyoto. The Kiyomizu district is symbolic of Kyoto's spiritual history and historical home to Kyoto's many ceramic artisans and sellers.

Akira's father made money making and selling fine table ceramics, with a side business in small ceramic insulators. Akira, though, was not about to settle for a life growing old as the proprietor of a small mom-and-pop ceramic shop. In 1944, he founded Murata Manufacturing, whose first product was a ceramic condenser. Murata, lacking in specialized training in ceramic technology, instead obtained ad hoc training at the National Ceramic Research Institute and at the Kyoto Industrial Research Institute (Taneda 2003). He also collaborated extensively with Tetsuro Tanaka, a faculty member in the electrical engineering department at Kyoto University.

By 1950 Murata's firm was incorporated with paid-in capital of ¥1 million. Murata Manufacturing has since become a world leader in ceramic condensers and other components used to regulate the flow of electricity in products such as laptop computers and cell phones. Murata's net income in 2003 was over ¥39 billion on ¥394 billion of sales – an increase in profit of nearly 13% from 2002. In 2003, 65% of Murata sales were overseas. Akira's first son Yasutaka now runs the company. Other events leading to serendipitous outcomes played a role in the evolution of the high-tech community in Kyoto. For example, early in

Omron's development, the firm was forced to re-locate from Osaka to Kyoto.

Serendipity of adversity: Omron

Kazuma Tateisi was born in 1900 in Kumamoto in Western Japan, first son to a family of traditional sake cup makers. In 1908, Tateisi's father died suddenly and the family business declined. His mother was forced to open a boarding house to support the family and Tateisi delivered newspapers to help bring in extra money. From an early age Tateisi learned the value of hard work and independence.

In an attempt to lessen the burden on his family, in junior high school he studied hard and tried for a spot at the prestigious Kumamoto Naval Academy. He failed to pass the physical test but earned top marks on the entrance exam. Though Tateisi was denied entry to the Naval Academy he immediately found another way to pursue his dreams of financial independence. He was soon accepted into the electrical engineering program at Kumamoto Technical College (now Kumamoto University), where he quickly learned to read both English and German. After graduating in 1921 he worked briefly for the Hyogo prefectural government and in 1922 started with Inoue Electric as a project engineer. He worked primarily on a project reverse engineering American prototypes of electrical relays, but was out of a job soon after the Stock Market Crash of 1929.

Tateisi had meanwhile invented a trouser press and soon was selling this and later a knife grinder. He peddled his wares by bicycle and in open market stalls in Kyoto's Todaiji temple, located just south of Kyoto Station. Tateisi was still looking for his chance to make it big. A friend gave him an idea for a timer for X-ray machines and he was soon at work on a prototype. Tateisi found that the skills developing relays that he had learned at Inoue were of great use, and he soon had a prototype X-ray timer.

Omron was founded as "Tateisi Electric" in Osaka in 1933. Tateisi was soon producing original equipment manufacturing (OEM) devices for clients in Osaka and Tokyo. As the firebombing during 1945 worsened, Tateisi decided to build another factory in Kyoto. By the end of the war, the Osaka plant and Tokyo office had been completely destroyed but the newly built Kyoto factory was untouched. Tateisi decided to relocate manufacturing and the head office to Kyoto.

The move to Kyoto became the most important turn of events in the firm's history. Marketing their products from Kyoto became more of a logistical challenge – Osaka remains the trading and distribution center of the region. On the other hand, the firm was now free from the big city constraints of Osaka. His son Yoshio reflected on the significance of the move to Kyoto after the war in a 2001 interview for the *Japan Economist*: "Had Omron not moved to Kyoto, it would have surely become an exclusive subcontractor for the post-war fast-growing keiretsu in Osaka: Matsushita, Sharp or Sanyo" (Inoue and Tsuji 2001). Now, Omron's multinational business focuses on sensing and control components and operates in thirty-five countries with over 23,000 employees. Omron's net sales topped ¥500 billion per year over 1999–2003.

Omron's R&D philosophy prioritizes the anticipation of social needs. This way of thinking has resulted in its developing and marketing of the world's first automatic traffic signals, automated cancer cell diagnostic equipment, and an on-line cash dispenser. Tateisi established Omron's corporate motto: "a civic minded company" (*kigyo no kokensei*) and left an indelible mark on the company in this regard. His son Yoshio says that he feels so strongly about his team working to serve society, that "this civic mindedness has become part of the DNA of the firm" (Inoue and Tsuji 2001). Asked if he would ever consider moving from Kyoto, Tateisi replied that Kyoto's deep history as well as forefront technology is what made Omron what it is today. Further, according to Yoshio Tateisi, Kyoto's brand image in the world is one of the highest quality and frontier technology. For of these reasons, Tateisi says, "we will never leave Kyoto." This feeling is echoed in the sentiments of two other Kyoto high-tech mavericks: Nakanuma Art Screenings' Hisashi Nakanuma and Tose's (of Nintendo software development fame) Shigeru Saito.

A little help from other entrepreneurs: Nakanuma

In 1954, Hisashi Nakanuma was a twenty-one-year-old student in electric engineering at Kyoto's Ritsumeikan University when he decided to have a go at starting his own business. At the time, Nakanuma was more interested in his two passions: photography and silk-screening. He grew up in the North of Kyoto, center of the famous Nishijin style of textile dying. For the first decade after starting his company, Nakanuma made silk screens for applying designs to clothing such as T-shirts.

In 1979, Nakanuma got involved with a local chapter of an entrepreneurs' association – the SME Doyukai (*chushokigyokadoyukai*, SME DYK). The DYK is a national association of entrepreneurs, formed in 1957 in direct opposition to rising domination of state-sanctioned and "guided" peak associations, the latter run by former wartime keiretsu (zaibatsu) wartime giants (Ibata-Arens 2000). Kyoto's DYK has, like chapters of the association throughout Japan, been entirely independent and autonomous from the central state. Nakanuma attributes the inter-industry exchange facilitated by DYK to introducing his firm to technologies in plastics and metals that helped him develop products with broader, higher-value-added applications, particularly in the rising electronics market in Japan. In 1979, Nakanuma had forty employees and profit of ¥3 million. By 2004 he had 168 employees and a profit of ¥50 million, a fourfold and fifteenfold increase, respectively. In 2004, Nakanuma was named managing director of the Kyoto DYK. A number of junior firms in the organization cite Nakanuma's natural curiosity and estheticism (*tanbishugi*) in providing just the right combination of drive and creativity for becoming the outside spokesperson for DYK initiatives. Nakanuma recalls that during the post-war period in Kyoto there was a family-type of atmosphere surrounding new business start-ups. People were competitive, to be sure, but it seemed like they were all in it together.

Nakanuma sought to develop an ever-increasing level of detail in his screening designs, eventually moving into the screening of small-scale keypads for computer games and later pocket-sized cellular telephones. It was only a matter of time before his firm developed macron-level detail in its screening technology. He laughs, "we were doing nanotech before such a thing had a name." He notes, however, that universities were slow to come around to the idea of developing precision level detail at the nanotech level.[5]

Nakanuma points out that the newest METI Cluster initiative merely adds a new label to the SME DYK's long-standing inter-industry exchange activities (*igyoshukoryu*). Only the name has changed, not the people involved or the activities themselves (*nakami*). What is different is that universities and big firms have become interested in these kinds of on-the-ground activities.

He confirms that Nakanuma Art Screening is indeed in the new "Cluster," at METI's behest. METI has come around to visit Nakanuma quite a lot in the last year or so, but Nakanuma complains: "they move around so fast, flit around to other offices of other companies, then a few months later someone else comes in, asking the same questions, and we have to start again with them from scratch." This has left Nakanuma a little jaded about METI: "though they say that we are in the cluster, we continue to do the same things that we were doing before – the new relation with METI makes no difference to us" (Nakanuma 2004). Tose's Shigeru Saito, of Kyoto's younger generation of mavericks and fellow Ritsumeikan alum, also chose the path not taken.

The pull of Kyoto: Tose

Upon graduating from Ritsumeikan University with a degree in electrical engineering, then just shy of twenty-three years old, Shigeru Saito joined his father's firm Toe Seiko. Toe Seiko had worked closely with Matsushita for a number of decades and the business was solid, but not terribly exciting. Shigeru volunteered to take over the firm's side business in arcade games. At the time, arcades were perceived as "dark, dirty places." Saito, said, "Well, if I am to make my own mark on the company, I will go to the dirty side." In 1979, "Tose" split off from its parent.[6]

He and a few technologists had soon developed the "Sasuke and Commander" arcade game machine whose high sales established Tose in the business of gaming software. Soon thereafter, Saito managed an introduction through his bank to Nintendo and together the firms pursued ideas for creating hand-held electronic games that could be played anywhere. What started as an attempt to develop products not associated with "dark, dirty gaming centers" transformed the market for gaming software in Japan and the world. By 1983, Tose had switched completely to the software gaming field. Revenue was used to purchase the company's current corporate headquarters in the heart of downtown Kyoto. Saito's family was from the northwest of Kyoto, an area known for its country charm. Ritsumeikan University, itself on the outskirts of the city northwest, was a big first step for a country boy to the big city. Purchasing a building in the center of town was a major milestone for Saito; needless to say, he is not pleased about the expected shift of the engineering faculty of Kyoto University to that institution's new campus in far-flung Katsura in the city's southwestern environs.

As the gaming business declined in Japan in the late 1990s, the firm started making inroads into the emerging cellular telephone-based gaming software industry. By 2001, Tose was upgraded to the first listing on the Tokyo Stock Exchange. Meanwhile, in 1993, Tose had closed its US office (because of poor sales) and opened one in Shanghai in the same year. The company has since made major investments in China and plans to do all software development for the Chinese market in China by Chinese technologists. In 2001, Tose added a second R&D center in China's city of Hangzhou, just outside Shanghai.

A member of the Kyoto Venture Forum and the DYK, Saito is proud to be a Kyoto native. As such, he subscribes to the view that Tokyo – and, by relation, METI policy – is irrelevant to the past and future of Kyoto's culture, politics, and economy. Saito cites the fact that Kyoto has never been under the sway of the Liberal Democratic Party (LDP), which dominated Japanese politics for the entire post-war period, until the mid-1990s. LDP had some support, as had the new Democratic Party and the Communist Party in earlier years. People say "*Kyoto biki*" (the pull of Kyoto) to indicate the lure of Kyoto's enduring artisanal culture and history for visitors, foreign and Japanese alike (*Kichiri to yatteiru: bunka mamorinagara*). Often companies will go out of their way to have a little business in Kyoto so that they and their families can take advantage of what the area has to offer culturally.

Kyoto is not without its detractors, however. Negative images of Kyoto include the perception that its residents tend to be unpleasant and disagreeable in general (*iyarashisa*). "Kyoto jin" or "Kyoto-ites" are also perceived by other Japanese as "too independent" and "conservative" (in the social sense and also of the "pull yourself up by your own bootstraps" variety). Japanese mass opinion surveys have found that people who do not define themselves as "fiercely independent" hate living in Kyoto (Suematsu 2002). It could be said that the feeling is mutual. Kyoto businessmen seem to have a particular disdain for lawyers, the type of professionals that dominate the political and economic institutions in Tokyo. Interestingly, of the regions promoted by the national METI, Kyoto is noticeably absent from the national Cluster Plan introduced in chapter 4.

The historical institutional features and socio-cultural characteristics that have supported the performance of the leading firms introduced here form the basis for what has come to be called the "Kyoto Model" of entrepreneurship. The model can be described at three different levels: region, firms, and entrepreneurs.

6.4 Levels of the Model: region, firm, entrepreneur

Region

The Kyoto region, partly for the reasons outlined above, is characterized by horizontal production, pocket-money finance, inter-firm networks, collaborative manufacturing, and innovative coalitions:

- First, due partly to the absence of keiretsu groups, production (and trading) relations between firms tend to be horizontal and fluid.
- Second, the lack of main banks as a source of business capital encourages "pocket-money finance." Entrepreneurs depend on small amounts of money from friends and relations for start-up capital and also to buttress them against dips in cash flow. This informal system of finance spreads the burden and the risk across a wide community of investors.[7] It also keeps entrepreneurs from becoming beholden to banks and thus subject to underhanded bank tactics, as the stories in earlier chapters of post-"bubble" bank loan and collection practices attest.
- Third, as discussed in chapter 5, Kyoto has active inter-firm (and inter-industry) networks that facilitate in particular the flow of information (thereby compensating in part for the lack of benefits from hierarchy).
- Fourth, active networks have provided a forum for the forging of collaborative manufacturing relations between Kyoto firms and also between Kyoto firms and firms outside the region and Japan. These collaborative manufacturing ties have proven competitive in world markets against their perceived-to-be more effectively organized keiretsu competitors.
- Fifth, firm managers, local government officials, academics, and community leaders work together in broad innovative coalitions. These coalitions have been effective, for example, at drawing resources from the national government while avoiding the worst effects of bureaucratic oversight. Shisaku Net, led by Koji Akita (the online collaborative manufacturing network introduced in chapter 5) is one example

of such efforts. These regional trends stem from patterns in firm-level business strategies.[8]

Firm

The success of world-class Kyoto firms – or "Kyoto Model" firms – outlined above have been driven by six management strategies: core technological competence, niche specialization, overseas market targeting, openness, financial independence and autonomy, and R&D focus.[9] First, successful Kyoto firms have emphasized maintaining complementary and expert-level skills (i.e. core competence) enabling the creation of competitive products and processes that set world standards. For example, Samco's Tsuji could have made more money on his firm's JV with Kirin Beer by attempting to coat Kirin's bottles with his carbon film in a new or expanded in-house plant. He decided against it because he did not want to get away from the company's core competence in developing thin-film technologies.

Partly as a consequence of their strengths in maintaining core competence, Kyoto firms create specialized products for niche markets. Niche markets by their very nature are often too small to attract large mass-scale producers. High technology niche specialization by Kyoto makers provides crucial components in a variety of capital goods (small lot sizes are compensated for by profits from high-value-added). Essentially, Kyoto firms have parlayed their core competence into niche market dominance. Kyocera's fine ceramics, Samco's thin film, and Rohm's custom integrated circuit (IC) technologies are only a few examples.

Third, by default and by choice, Kyoto producers have tended to avoid exclusive sales arrangements with Japan's keiretsu giants (the story of Osamu Tsuji of Samco with which this book began shows how its initial failure to sell to Japanese companies turned into long-term advantage for this Kyoto firm). Attention to quality and precision-level detail by Kyoto producers have made them champions in overseas markets. Less dependence on Japanese buyers also means more cash at hand from overseas customers. As shown in the Introduction and chapter 2, unlike Japanese buyers, foreign customers usually pay their bills on time, often paying 50% up front.

Fourth, in contrast to the insular, hierarchical structure of their keiretsu competitors, Kyoto Model firms have striven to remain open – both domestically and internationally. Kyoto makers have not been constrained by pressures from keiretsu management to "keep the business in the group." They have also been more transparent with their accounting practices and finances – critical for attracting foreign investment. This transparency has paid off. Rohm boasts that 40% of its shareholders are from outside Japan, one of the highest ratios among Japanese firms. Kazuo Inamori of Kyocera had an experience similar to his friend and colleague Osamu Tsuji of Samco. In 1959, after founding Kyocera, Inamori had a hard time getting Japanese firms to even consider Kyocera's first product, parts for TV tubes. Like Tsuji, Inamori was driven abroad by the buying recalcitrance of the Japanese electronics giants.

By 1966, Kyocera had managed to make the company's first major sale of IC parts, amounting to a quarter of the operating profits for that year. The buyer? IBM. Suddenly, Kyocera's credibility in the domestic market – questioned at first – was no longer an issue for Japanese buyers. Kyocera now sells to major German and Japanese electronics producers. In the 1970s, the oil shocks forced Kyocera to diversify into ceramic cutting instruments and medical supplies. In 2003, 49.5% of sales were from the company's equipment business. Fine ceramics and electronic devices made up 22% and 21%, respectively. Total sales in 2003 were nearly ¥483 billion, with net income of ¥27.9 billion. Kyocera, Samco, and others have also stayed independent from the banks.

Fifth, Kyoto's entrepreneurial mavericks have insisted on financial independence and autonomy. In doing so, they have emphasized keeping a healthy cash flow and profit margin. Kyoto firms avoid being at the mercy of the slow-payment behavior of Japan's keiretsu buyers (discussed in the Introduction) by simply not selling in unbalanced sales proportions to them. This allows Kyoto firms to have more cash up front to pour into R&D, further enhancing core competences and therefore long-term profit margins. Plugging into Kyoto's system of pocket-money finance has allowed its entrepreneurs autonomy from the banks.

Finally, Kyoto firms have the will to maintain and enhance core competence and the wherewithal of cash at hand facilitate continuous upgrading of products (and the development of new niche products) through substantial R&D spending. Samco has established research institutes in Cambridge (ceramics) and the USA (nanotech) that draw

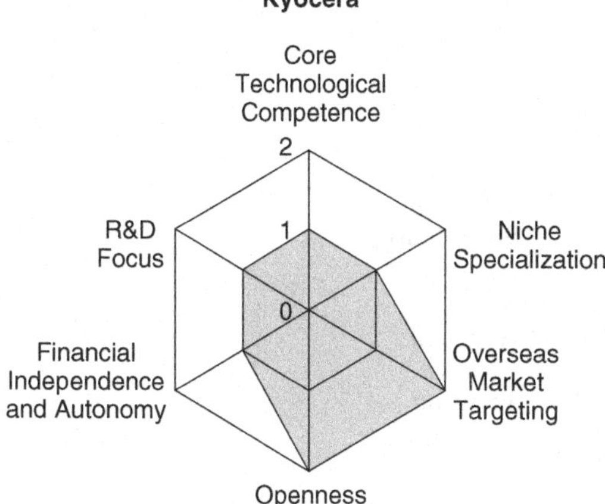

Figure 6.1. Management strategies of Kyoto Model firms: Kyocera

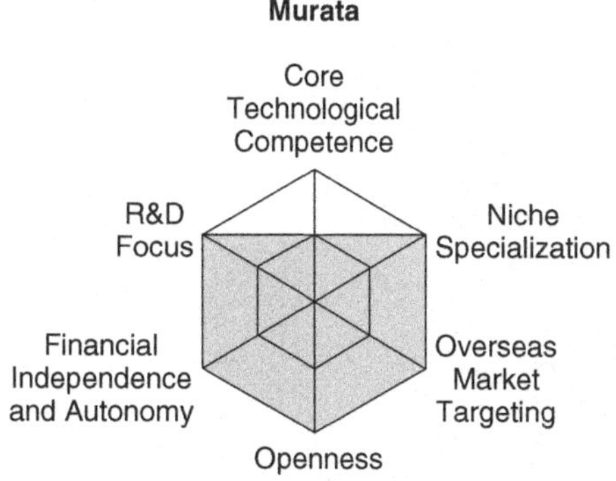

Figure 6.2. Management strategies of Kyoto Model firms: Murata

from the unique capabilities of the research communities in these countries. Figures 6.1–6.5 illustrate how top Kyoto firms fit the Kyoto Model in terms of the six major management strategies: core technological competence, niche specialization, overseas market targeting, openness, financial independence and autonomy, and R&D focus.[10] The five firms of Horiba, Kyocera, Murata, Omron, and Rohm are considered to be most representative of Kyoto Model firms. Firms demonstrating the highest degree of emphasis on each of the six strategies include Murata, Rohm, and Samco.

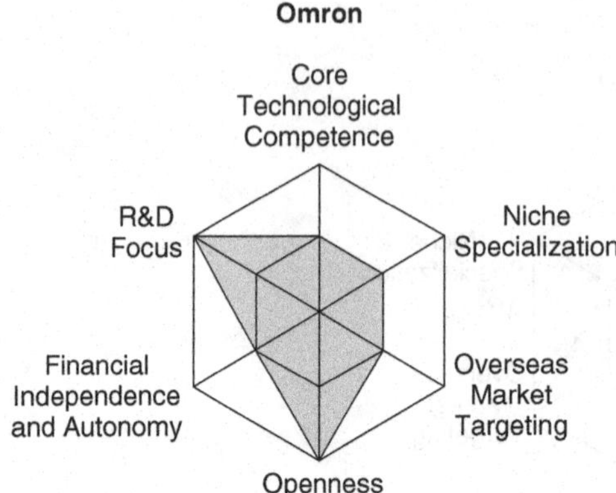

Figure 6.3. Management strategies of Kyoto Model firms: Omron

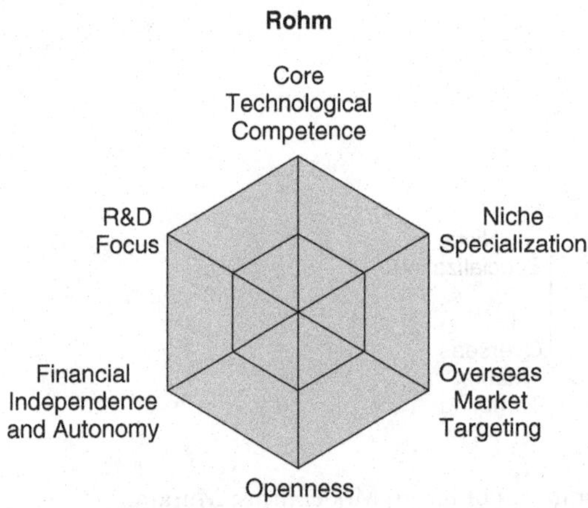

Figure 6.4. Management strategies of Kyoto Model firms: Rohm

Based on the management strategies outlined above, other researchers have grouped firms into two groups: Kyoto Model and Semi-Kyoto Model (Higuchi and Whittaker 2003). These "semi"-Kyoto Model firms include Shimadzu, Nichicon, Japan Battery Storage, and Nintendo. Appendix 3, Figures A3.1–A3.5, illustrate which management strategies make these other firms somewhat representative of Kyoto-style management. Still others group these firms together along with this study's Samco and Tose and Nichicon (Kunii 1999;

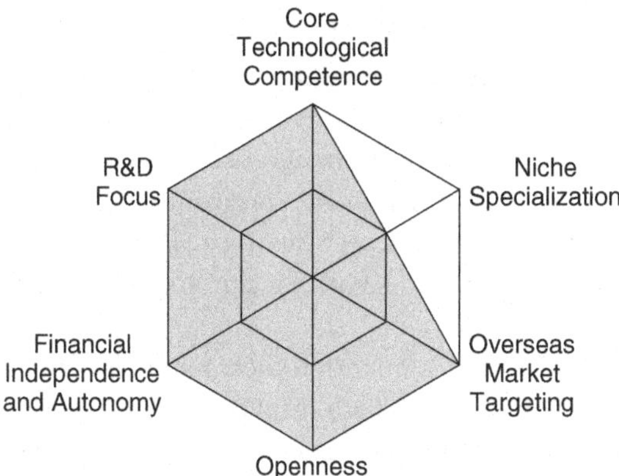

Figure 6.5. Management strategies of Kyoto Model firms: Samco International

Suematsu 2002; Okamura 2003; Tanaka 2003; Taneda 2003). At the very least, we would all agree that these leading Kyoto firms have been founded by a certain kind of entrepreneur.

Entrepreneurs

What kind of person creates a world-class firm from scratch – with pocket money? Kyoto entrepreneurs have three distinctive characteristics: fierce independence, stellar technological skills, and civic mindedness. First, as previously mentioned, Kyoto businessmen are viewed outside the region as being fiercely independent and even difficult to work with. Unlike their counterparts in Tokyo who are bound by considerations of maintaining good in-group relations, Kyoto businesspeople tend to enter into arrangements based purely on a given deal's merit. This makes for dealings that are on the upside extremely efficient, but on the downside often viewed as ruthless. (Suematsu 2002; Inoue and Tsuji July 24, 2001).

Second, Kyoto is home to more than thirty-six universities and produces a large share of the nation's top-notch scientists and technologists. One example is Ken Sato, founder of Rohm, who developed the smallest, lightest resister while still a Ritsumeikan University student in 1958. Sato worked part-time for a radio shop after school and noticed that most of the broken radios being brought in for service had faulty resistors. He was confident he had a fix for these bad resistors. Sato started his company Rohm ("R" is for resistor and the "ohm" signifies the unit of electrical resistance) in a friend's house in the Nishijin district of Kyoto. Unlike his keiretsu competitors, Sato has made a point of staying away from mass-produced dynamic random-access memories (DRAMs) and went into custom integrated circuits. Rohm leads the market in these circuits and was at the forefront of commercializing the new ferroelectric random-access memory (FRAM) chip. Kyocera's founder is another example of Kyoto's technologists-turned-entrepreneurs.

In the late 1950s, Kazuo Inamori, founder of Kyocera, left his former employer after his boss at Shofu Co., a Kyoto insulator manufacturer, rejected his idea for a cathode-ray tube for the emerging TV industry. By 1959, along with seven friends, he had founded Kyocera and since built the firm into the world's top maker of ceramic chip systems (Kunii 1999). Kyocera's net profit in 2003 was ¥41.2 billion, up 35% from the previous year (Taneda 2003).

Yet another example of Kyoto's technologists-turned-entrepreneurs is Osamu Tsuji of Samco, whose skills in chemistry and thin-film technology gained at Kyoto University and NASA served him well in leading the development of products in ICs and semiconductors. Also unique to Kyoto, according to Kenichi Imai, an expert in Japanese industrial relations, is the social progressiveness of the region. For example, Imai noted in an article about the sources of entrepreneurialism in Kyoto that there are increasing numbers of women in the "spirited graduate student" cadres abundant in Kyoto (Imai 2004). In essence, Kyoto remains at the forefront of technological *and* social change in Japan.

*Philanthropy (*shakaikoken*)*

Thirdly, Kyoto entrepreneurs are not content to rest on their laurels once they attain success. Instead they have given back to the community that nurtured their talent (*onkaesu*). Successful entrepreneurs have spent time volunteering to critique business plans for new start-ups and acting as informal business consultants to their junior colleagues. One such effort, in the late 1980s, was initiated by Samco's Tsuji in collaboration with his colleague Masao Horiba, both troubled that Kyoto's scale of new business creation was low. About sixty firms joined the

Kyoto Venture Business Club whose membership was limited to small, truly new start-ups (0–10 years) in a number of industries, including manufacturing, services, and consulting. The goal of the club was to have members meet monthly to jointly figure out the venture business game through hashing over the successes *and* mistakes made by member firms.

The Club has since evolved into a formal arrangement between the Kyoto city government and investment groups. Successful initiatives have resulted in the establishment of the Kyoto Research Park, other incubators, and VC supports for new start-ups (Ishikawa and Tanaka 1999). In 2004, the "Kyoto Venture Forum" had over 100 members. Tsuji volunteers along with colleagues like Horiba, Inamori (Kyocera), and Murata in providing personal feedback on the business plans of new start-ups. Fledgling entrepreneurs can submit business plans and then present them to the Forum's monthly sessions. Tsuji says the process can be quite brutal for the new entrepreneur, who is often very nervous: "We can tell in about 20 minutes if they have what it takes in terms of technological know-how and gumption to make it as a new business." Tsuji has also lent himself to a few Management of Technology (MOT) projects with local universities. He agrees that though most Japanese entrepreneurs are skilled technologists, few can manage technology, which is the deficiency that MOT projects have attempted to deal with. This civic mindedness is echoed in the community-level initiatives of Kyoto's Murata, Omron, and Horiba.

Concerned that Japan was behind the world in basic science research, in 1985 Murata established the Murata Science Foundation (*Murata kagaku shinko zaidan*). The foundation supports research in natural science and humanities. Between its founding and 2004 Murata had granted over ¥1 billion to support individuals, research labs, and overseas study in basic science and humanities research.

Omron's efforts are more grassroots. Its "company citizen activities" (*kigyoshiminkatsudo*) are focused on local community development and revitalization. Activities range from planting trees to establishing a "welfare plant" (*fukushikoba*) that employs the "severely handicapped" (*judoshintaishugaisha*); 90% of the plant's employees are handicapped, but it does not operate as a charity. In fact, the plant has operated in the black since its first year and a number of its workers have become executives at Omron. The success of these efforts have led to the establishment of similar "welfare plants" at Honda and Sony.

Founder-owner-managers of smaller Kyoto firms have also demonstrated civic entrepreneurship. Yasuhiro Ikuta and Norihito Azuma offer two examples.

Yasuhiro Ikuta, president of Ikuta Manufacturing, served as the managing director of KSR (Kiseiren), the network introduced in chapter 5, for eight years (1996–2004). Ikuta joined KSR early in his career at his father's firm. Soon after joining, however, his father died and Yasuhiro was forced to take the reins of the firm. At the time, the average age of his employees was fifty-five and firm "veterans" were suddenly in the position of taking orders from someone twenty years their junior. It was a struggle at first, as these people had built the firm with his father over many years. It seemed that he would lose many of his key people[11], so Ikuta sat down with them and had a heart-to-heart. He recalls saying to them that he knew that he had much to learn, but with their help the company could pull through and continue to grow. In the end, only one of them left. Ikuta told them that he would work hard to draw on his personal and social resources outside the firm – for example, through his KSR network contacts.

While a member of KSR, Ikuta also participated in technology exchange via the national NC Net (www.nc-net.or.jp). Ikuta is also a member of the Shisaku net and argues that Shisaku-like collaborative manufacturing networks will become the new model for inter-firm networking in Japan. Slowly but surely, Ikuta has expanded his customer base through Shisaku's web page.

At the same time, Ikuta has nurtured links with China. His experience as an undergraduate exchange student in the USA taught him the value of being open to other countries. Ikuta was grateful to have had the US experience and thought that he should return the favor in some way (*on o kaesu*). In the early 1990s, Ikuta hosted his first exchange student through a local YWCA program; the student happened to be from China. He kept in touch with the student over the years and met many people in China as a result. Around the same time, Ikuta started to go to China to try to sell his products, but realized that lacking a local contact communication with potential customers would prove difficult.[12]

In 1998, he decided to take the plunge and hire a Chinese technologist. After a few years, Ikuta and the technologist decided to spin off part of the company's production to mainland China and start a joint partnership. While Ikuta says that it is a challenge in terms of training the Chinese workers, that they work very hard to catch-up to the technology protocols of his firm and sales in China continue to grow. Ikuta's approach to maintaining fluid, overlapping, and international networks is typical of Kyoto entrepreneurs. His approach to giving back to the local community is mirrored in the activities of his junior colleague at KSR, Norihito Azuma.

For Norihito Azuma of Seiwa Manufacturing, camaraderie is important at both the firm and network level. Azuma had worked for his senior colleague (*senpai*) at Ikuta's firm after graduation until he turned twenty-nine. Returning to his father's firm, he realized how far behind the times the firm had become. In the early 1990s, the skill levels of Seiwa employees were dismal and his father had just about given up on the business altogether.[13]

Azuma was discouraged. He discussed what would have to be done to turn the company around – long hours, only coming home to eat and sleep, and the like – with his wife. Fortunately, his wife, a monk by training, told her husband not to give up (*omo kiri kokai shinai yo ni*). Azuma soon thereafter joined KSR (1992) and found that he was not alone in his firm-level struggles. He was also relieved that there were older network members and graduates around who could give practical advice about worker re-training tips and the like. After a few brutal months, Azuma managed with KSR's help to develop a new product (he recalls at the time regretting never going to class in college). Soon, thanks to KSR introductions, Seiwa was expanding sales enough to hire two new people within the same year. Azuma became associate director (*fuku daihyo*) of KSR in 1998; in 2000, he became director.

In the 1990s Seiwa grew from ten to twenty-two employees. Sales are threefold what they were in the early 1990s and net profit is up fivefold. His only dilemma is whether he should keep growing at the same pace or to be more conservative and stay small and nimble. Either path has its risks. The more people on the payroll and the more investment in sunk assets, the greater the risk of going under. If Seiwa remains small, however, in twenty years the firm will be in the same position it had been in 1990, with an aging, out-of-touch skill base. Ideally, Azuma would like to maintain an employee base of about twenty. With twenty employees Azuma says they can stay nimble and take an entirely different direction if the opportunity presents itself (*sei no ... pun*). With thirty, this might be difficult. Plus, the firm's motto is "the fastest in Japan." Every year, the employees get older. Azuma says, "I could '*restra*' [institute layoffs] and get rid of some old blood for new, but that would destroy the '*wa*' [harmony] of the firm."[14]

This notion of "*wa*" is also important to Azuma in Seiwa's inter-firm relations. A while back another KSR member had a problem with a shipment of defective goods that was due at the customer the next day. Seiwa took the shipment in and fixed the problem. It took all night, but the shipment was delivered at the customer's doorstep in time and Seiwa did not accept a single yen in return.

Informal, local-level efforts such as those of KSR are usually overlooked in national-level reports, says Samco's Osamu Tsuji.[15] He notes that many foreigners perceive that METI controls everything. In reality, the best programs for helping SMEs are created at the regional level.[16] Fortunately, the Kyoto region in particular has been effective at drawing from METI project funds, while saving local firms the hassles of direct METI regulation. Tsuji compares the Kyoto regional government's activism with similar successes in Malaysia:

> Mahathir knows the Japanese system in terms of its regional strengths. This is the aspect of the Japanese system that he re-created in his country. (Tsuji, quoted in Ibata-Arens 2001, p. 132)

In fact, Tsuji says that the Kyoto region as a whole is an ample source of human resources and institutional supports for venture firms, as successful venture firms help newer start-ups. Tsuji was helped in this fashion, and he is supporting newcomers in the same way his firm was supported in the past. This keen sense of giving back to the community that supported their fledgling businesses makes Osamu Tsuji and other Kyoto business leaders of civic entrepreneurs in the best sense.[17]

Entrepreneurs-turned-philanthropists

Kyocera's Inamori is perhaps Kyoto's ultimate example of an entrepreneur-turned-philanthropist. In 1984, Inamori prepared to step down from the head of Kyocera. In the same year, he founded the Inamori Foundation of which he currently serves as president. Inamori personally contributed ¥10 million of seed money and has since provided large cash infusions from his own funds to support the foundations mission (e.g. ¥200 million in 1984, ¥210 million in 1977) (Ishikawa and Tanaka, p. 158). The foundation's "Kyoto Prizes" have come to have cultural status in Japan of the caliber of the Nobel Prizes. Kyoto Prizes are awarded in several disciplines: advanced technology, basic sciences, and arts and philosophy. Kyoto Prizes have been bestowed upon scientists and artists from all over the world since 1985. Laurates receive a medal and an unrestricted cash reward of ¥50 million.[18] Past recipients include Noam Chomsky (Basic Sciences, 1988) and Jane Goodall (Basic Sciences, 1990). After building a multi-million dollar firm and philanthropic foundation, Inamori has recently become a Buddhist monk. Only in Kyoto are stories such as Inamori's "entrepreneur-turned-philanthropist-turned-monk" commonplace.[19]

6.5 A model for other places?

The experiences of Kyoto firms such as Kyocera, Samco, and others tell a story of entrepreneurship and innovation unparalleled in any other place in Japan. Is this a new model for other regions to emulate?

The intense efforts in the 2000s by the national METI to build institutions and networks in Japan's regions seem to indicate that at least the people in the Japanese national government believe that innovation and entrepreneurship can be manufactured by policy fiat. As documented in chapter 4, rather than emulate its home-grown success regions, these national policymakers have instead chosen to follow a (I would argue cookie-cutter) US/Harvard style approach. At the same time, what these policymakers have not so easily dealt with are those fuzzy – and thus not easily quantified – characteristics such as serendipitous (and also barrier-laden) historical contingencies (e.g. Kyoto's fine arts escaping unscathed from the Second World War) as well as the role of personal characteristics (fierce independence while at the same time civic mindedness).

Which aspects, if any, of the Kyoto Model can provide a template for other places? A look at factors underlying recent successes in fostering innovative community development in other countries may yield insights. It is these efforts in the American Midwest, particularly St. Louis, that are the subject of chapter 7. Lessons from less than successful efforts in Cleveland and elsewhere are also informative. I also situate Kyoto/Kinki and these Midwestern American locales briefly within broader comparative context, set against regions in China and Germany.

Notes

1. Kyushu has a vibrant semiconductor industry.
2. Suematsu compares the performance over time of ten Kyoto firms (Kyocera, Rohm, Nihon Densan, Murata, Horiba, Omron, Tose, Nichicon, Nihon Denchi, and Samco) with Japan's brand-name makers: Hitachi, Toshiba, Mitsubishi, NEC, Fujitsu, Matsushita Denki, and Sony. Suematsu 2002).
3. In 1868, the Shogun was deposed and the Emperor Meiji was "restored" to the throne, ushering in the political and economic dominance of the bureaucratic–industrial complex that still exists today (see chapter 3).
4. Namitei, another Kansai entrepreneurial firm, designed a device to clean its inter-continental lengths of telecommunications cable in a compact, self-contained manner. Namitei's president, Masatsugu Murao, soon saw the inter-industry applications of the new product. In 2004 the "Namijet"comprised some 30% of total firm sales (see chapter 2, p. 38).
5. Hisashi Nakanuma, Interview July 30, 2004.
6. Shigeru Saito, Interview July 26, 2004.
7. Samco's Tsuji says that Kyoto businessmen liken this system to "winning at the track." That is, if you succeed at your business and make a few extra bucks, you share your good fortune, however small, with others.
8. See also Sakaguchi *et al.* (2003) (PDF file) (cited May 9, 2004); available from http://www.mtc.pref.kyoto.jp/shien-kenkyu/2003/.
9. By contrast, "old-growth" Japanese companies such as NEC have relied on mass production of a continuously expanding scope of products, in-group suppliers, and distribution networks, and have depended heavily on main bank financing.
10. Kyoto Model firms can also divided into three periods: post-war start-ups (Kyocera, Rohm), 1970s boom start-ups (Samco), and 1990s Internet/E-business start ups (ACT).
11. Yasuhiro Ikuta, Interview 1998.
12. Yasuhiro Ikuta, Interview July 29, 2004.
13. Norihito Azuma, Interview July 27, 2004.
14. Norihito Azuma, Interview 2004.
15. Osamu Tsuji, Interview 2002.
16. Tsuji notes that the local METI representatives are often constrained by the national bureaucracy. For example, if a METI representative has an idea to go somewhere in Japan or abroad to learn about a new business or technology trend, they must complete a pile of paperwork requesting permission and so forth, and then wait about three months for it to make its way up the chain for approval. "If I want to go somewhere, I can leave the next day" (Osamu Tsuji, Interview 2003a).

17. Funabashi attributes the philosophy behind this civic mindedness to the teachings of Sontoku Ninomiya. Ninomiya coined the concept of "*suijo*" which meant "be thrifty at home and philanthropic toward society." The teachings of Ninomiya were later named "*hotoku.*" (Funabashi 2002).
18. Inamori (2002) noted that many recipients have donated their cash prizes to charity.
19. Funabashi likens the "spirit of diligence" that emerged from the teachings of the Edo Period (1603–1868) spiritual leaders and philosophers such as Rennyo, Shosan Suzuki, and Baigan Ishida, as similar to the "Protestant work ethic" that emerged later in Max Weber's observations on Western industrialization.

7 Regions in comparison

7.1 Introduction: building innovative communities

PROPONENTS of national-level approaches to studying innovation policy may ask: What is the point in understanding a regional innovation system (RIS) in its entirety, a task requiring detailed, in-depth case study analysis over time, if few useful comparative lessons can be drawn? I respond to such criticisms by showing how places as far-flung as Kyoto in the heartland of Japan and St. Louis in the American Midwest – though vastly different in terms of national culture – have similar features that have led each region to the forefront of innovative communities world-wide. Granted, they each possess the basic building blocks underpinning innovative communities: research universities, strong regional (if not local) governments, established service industries, and so forth.

Many regions have such basic building blocks, yet have faltered at the game of sustainable innovative community development. For example, in Cleveland, Ohio, despite world-class academic institutions and the presence of major manufacturing firms, civic factionalism undermines the region's development potential (Chu 1999; Gilman 2001). Similarly, the prevalence of bureaucratic initiatives over informal enterprise-led cooperation has led to some costly and failed attempts at economic revitalization in Flint, Michigan and Omuta, Japan. Firm-initiated projects have fared better in both regions (Gilman 2001).

What sets Kyoto and St. Louis apart from the pack are features that are to a great extent socially (and politically) driven. As such, these regions may provide valuable insights for regions elsewhere that are trying to stimulate innovative activity. Politically savvy entrepreneurs and civic leaders energize the basic building blocks and foster creative approaches to sustainable community development through two main strategies:

- First, these communities – with local entrepreneurs and civic leaders at their helm – are effective at building broad-based coalitions between community stakeholders. Further, these coalitions are focused on a few specific tasks such as drawing venture capital (VC) to the region.
- Second, these communities are adept at parlaying (perceived) local strengths to draw national and international resources to the region. Civic entrepreneurs and other community stakeholders draw on local civic consciousness and social capital while being politically savvy in pursuing innovative goals. Civic consciousness is an individual's awareness that they are embedded within a larger community (and polity) within which they possess certain rights and responsibilities toward reaching common goals (clean air, universal education). Social capital indicates shared norms such as reciprocity that encourage cooperation between actors.

Community (firm, civic) leaders demonstrate political savvy in various ways. This may in some cases mean simply staying under the radar of national scrutiny or using brokers in local and regional government to draw on national resources. In these regions, successful entrepreneurs, local government officials, and university faculty have a kind of civic, yet strategic vision that inspires others and attracts fresh talent to the region. New talent invigorates local networks and helps avoid resting on laurels and subsequent institutional stagnation (stasis) in the long term (Florida 2002). One consequence is that these relations are relatively free of the problematics of insular (keiretsu, familial) networks that in the long term undermine innovation. To what extent are these patterns unique to their cultural and national environments?

Cross-national comparison is useful in identifying certain patterns of social and political embeddedness (how enterprise is situated within complex socio-political institutions) that at the same time may transcend national/cultural environments (Granovetter 1985; Kumon 1992; Grabher 1993; Uzzi 1996, 1997; Oguri 1998). In other words, understanding enterprise embeddedness in comparative perspective can help explain how complex political, social, and cultural contingencies affect economic outcomes, while yielding practical policy prescriptions that have relevance across national borders.

Examining these processes in St. Louis and Kyoto make for a valuable comparison. First, St. Louis and Kyoto are located in traditional (American and Japanese) industrial heartlands. These regions are home to final goods producers in heavy and light manufacturers, including metallics, machinery, electronics, and their suppliers. Second, each region has been similarly impacted by the move overseas (to Mexico and China, respectively) of manufacturing production and concomitant high-wage jobs. Thirdly, the metropolitan areas of St. Louis and Kyoto are being forced to re-tool themselves and adapt to international market pressures, or risk falling behind their larger competition (Chicago, Tokyo). This chapter has three main themes: identifying the core institutions and types of people behind successful innovative community building, posing a set of hypotheses about how these institutions and people relate in generating positive socio-economic outcomes, and cross-national comparison of these patterns.

First, I review core constructs underpinning innovative community building in these seemingly disparate regions (St. Louis and Kyoto): entrepreneurial mavericks, civic entrepreneurship, political savvy, social capital, and innovative coalitions. I then pose hypotheses about possible causal relations between these people and activities and innovative outcomes. Second, I examine the role that people and local institutions play in building sustainable innovative communities through discussing the emerging innovative community in and around St. Louis, Missouri, in the American Midwest. I then return to Kyoto, noting the similarities between these Japanese and American regions and comparing and contrasting briefly with other communities in Germany and China. I conclude the chapter with a discussion of if, and how, this locally informed political economy approach can be a template for other regions, noting best practices and the pitfalls to avoid.

7.2 Core constructs

Core constructs in innovative community building can be divided into two main levels – individual (entrepreneur, stakeholder) and region (institution, coalition). Before outlining these terms it is useful to clarify what is meant here by "innovative community." An *innnovative community* is more than merely a spatial cluster (agglomeration) of competitive enterprises. Rather, these communities are geographic concentrations (city, region) of like-minded (e.g. enterprise mavericks) stakeholders (entrepreneurs, workers, residents, government officials) in the economic outcomes of local enterprises. Community members identify with shared goals of creating new products in growth sectors.

Sustainable innovative communities are innovative communities that adapt over time to externalities (e.g. international market competition). These communities manage to exit maturing sectors and enter new ones.

Individual level

Enterprise mavericks are individuals who stake out new business territory on their own (usually through a new product that they have invented, designed and created themselves). These entrepreneurs identify and capitalize on "structural holes" (Burt 1992) or process needs (Drucker 1993). They are driven and have a particular vision. They also tend to possess personality traits that clash with bureaucratic managerial types in large corporations and academic institutions. Once they succeed in business, however, it is their success stories (*monogotarisei*) that lead to emulators within their regions and also attract newcomers (skilled technicians and next-generation entrepreneurs) to the region (Imai 1998a, 1998b). One example is Inamori, the founder of Kyocera, who left his employer to form Kyocera after his idea for a cathode-ray tube was rejected by his boss (chapter 6). These individuals tend to avoid hierarchy imposed on them or imposed by themselves on their employees. *Civic entrepreneurs* are savvy enterprise mavericks with a keen sense of "giving back" firm-level resources to the wider community for mutual long-term gain. These enterprise mavericks acting as civic entrepreneurs demonstrate political savvy in their activities.

Political savvy is the common-sense ability to identify and "read" or comprehend the powers-that-be (e.g. government resources and permissions gatekeepers). This involves knowing which to avoid, and which to pay at least lip service to. In Japan, this means that firms that are approached by METI for a survey generally comply, but most are averse to taking METI funds (without a go-between), as they are aware of the bureaucratic hassles that inevitably follow. In the USA, this may necessitate hiring lobbyists.

Regional level

In *innovative coalitions* civic entrepreneurs and local civic leaders coordinate their efforts within loose innovative coalitions of stakeholders – that is, across local groups of people with a vested interest in positive socio-economic outcomes. These relations are less formalistic and long-term than an alliance or JV, and include broad-based membership of community stakeholders (e.g. Kyoto's Venture Forum, St. Louis' Coalition for the Plant and Life Sciences). Members are not just owner-managers or government officials. Another way of describing these coalitions is as a network of people and their institutions that forms, usually on the initiative of a local entrepreneur (or university faculty), around a specific task, such as establishing a venture capital community (Samco's Osamu Tsuji and Horiba's Masao Horiba, Washington University's William Danforth). Outside of coalition activities, member firms may compete head-to-head. In successful communities, innovative communities appear to be infused with a certain civic consciousness. Meanwhile, the fact that these communities are populated by entrepreneurial mavericks enhances competition between community members, further stimulating innovation.

Taking these constructs as a basis, we can begin to situate the process of innovation at the firm level into broader community-level trends. We can also start to identify potential causal mechanisms through posing hypotheses about how these socio-political processes relate to innovative outcomes.

7.3 Hypotheses: people, institutions, and innovation

The reality of sustainable innovative community development – adapting to changing externalities in order to have innovative and competitive outcomes over time – is neither a purely organic process (firm- and market-driven) nor can it be accomplished by political fiat. Instead, the most successful communities, sometimes through trial and error, have managed to balance entrepreneurial/firm-level demands with the constraints and opportunities afforded by their national contexts.

The critical question then is: is there a certain (replicable) pattern or balance between enterprise-initiated and government policy-driven measures that result in innovative outcomes community-wide (i.e. across broad groups of stakeholders) and over time? Identifying/specifying (network, coalition) patterns that might transcend national (particularistic, cultural) contexts is facilitated by posing three main hypotheses:

Hypothesis 1

Civic entrepreneurship enhances innovative outcomes at the community level.

Civic entrepreneurship is the tendency of civic entrepreneurs to actively engage in efforts supporting community-wide economic development. Civic entrepreneurs are defined as politically savvy enterprise mavericks having a keen sense of "giving back" firm and individual wealth and expertise to the larger community, for mutual long-term gain. These individuals have amassed ample stores of (positive) social capital, enabling them to galvanize other firm owner-managers behind collective efforts. Social capital indicates, as mentioned previously, the existence of informal norms that promote cooperation between two or more individuals. Community stakeholders include entrepreneurs, business executives, workers, community activists, residents, and local government officials – that is, those with a vested interest in positive socio-economic outcomes. Innovative outcomes at the community level are measured by sales generated by new (tradable) products and new business creation. Tradable products are those sold outside the region, with the bulk of product revenue returning to the region.

Hypothesis 2

Broad-based coalitions of community stakeholders unified behind community-wide efforts for new product and new business creation (developmental coalitions) facilitate innovative outcomes.

"Broad-based" is measured by the frequency of interaction for the purpose of generating useful policy between three or more groups of community stakeholders.

Hypothesis 3

Developmental ideas (or visions) shared by (resonate with the interests of) cross-cutting groups of community stakeholders keep stakeholders "on task" in facilitating innovative activity.

Certain civic leaders and entrepreneurs provide a kind of vision that plugs into latent civic pride to advance the interests of broad groups of community stakeholders: firms, workers, and residents.

Comprehensive testing of these hypotheses would require a complex historical–institutional study of key players, networks, socio-political, and spatial relations using a combination of quantitative and qualitative measures and is beyond the scope of this chapter. We can, however, obtain a snapshot of important linkages and cross-national trends through case study analysis of key players in successful local communities of firms. We can also identify promising areas of future research. With this in mind, what follows is a discussion of case studies in civic entrepreneurship and developmental vision-driven local stakeholder coalition building from three perspectives – entrepreneurs, firms, and regions. This is accomplished through examining these processes in the emerging bio-technology and life sciences cluster in St. Louis, Missouri and comparing these patterns to the processes behind the proven track record of Japan's most innovative local community, Kyoto.

7.4 St. Louis: the bio-belt of the American Midwest

Building blocks for innovation

Since the mid-1990s, St. Louis has tried to compress several generations of innovative community development into a decade. The region's leaders eschewed the "Porter-style approach" – lately a favorite of national level bureaucrats in many countries including Japan, in attempting to foster innovation (Porter *et al.* 2000; METI 2002e).[1] Instead, St. Louis has embarked on a gamble on life science and bio-pharmaceuticals, though its dense local industrial, political, and other networks were heavily tied to the American auto industry. The result is that St. Louis in the early 2000s is emerging as a cluster of bio-pharmaceutical and life science start-ups, backed by a concerted effort and coalition of community stakeholders from local firms up to state government. One measure of this success is the fact that by 2003 St. Louis had 161 life science manufacturing firms employing 12,921 people (Battelle Technology Partnership Practice 2003). In 2004, including plant sciences, the region had 390 enterprises with 22,000 employees (*Biobelt Website* 2004).

St. Louis is located just south of the confluence of the Missouri and Mississippi rivers. A fertile river valley, the area was home to a succession of peoples, including a large Indian civilization of "mound builders," then settled in the mid-1700s by French fur traders. Named after Louis IX, the area was at the time still part of Spanish territory, and was later sold by Napoleon to Thomas Jefferson (1803). The area remained a major transportation hub for the fur trade as well as a stopping-off point for westward-bound settlers. By the mid-nineteenth century, the city was home to settlers from France, Spain, Germany, and Ireland. The city continued to grow with the advent of steam boat and rail and later established several universities, including Washington University. In 1904, St. Louis hosted the Summer Olympic Games. Eventually, the city lost ground to Chicago as the Midwest's major transportation, trade, and financial center, but among locals the historical memory of St. Louis as "world-class city" remains.

In the 2000s, St. Louis, like Kyoto, had the basic building blocks for innovation: research universities such as Washington University, St. Louis University (SLU) and University of Missouri, St. Louis. Washington University's Medical School is routinely ranked among the top four medical schools in the USA and draws National Institute of Health (NIH) funding levels often surpassing those of Johns Hopkins University. St. Louis University has an active virology research program. The region can also boast a top-notch private school system, not a draw for 20-something technologists but a major plus for 30-something chief executive officers (CEOs) and technology managers looking to set down roots in a place where they can raise their children.

In 2002, St. Louis county, within which St. Louis city is located, had more than 178,236 firms (STLRCGA, St. Louis Regional Chamber and Growth Association 2004). Only eighty-seven of these firms employed more than 1,000 people. The bulk of St. Louis county industry is in services and retail trade, with manufacturing representing a mere 5% of the economy. In 2002, the region's 3,137 manufacturing firms employed 146,573 people. In 2003, fifty-one aerospace and defense firms employed over 20,000 people, 311 chemical and plastic producers employed 13,000; 936 machinery and metalworking employed 37,504 people (mainly serving the auto industry); while 161 life science manufacturing firms employed nearly 13,000 (US *Economic Census*).

Starting with the narratives of entrepreneurial struggle of three start-up high technology firms gives us an idea of the opportunities and barriers in one of America's emerging cluster regions.

Entrepreneurial firms: laying the foundations for civic entrepreneurship

Political savvy at national level: Chlorogen

David Duncan is current CEO of Chlorogen, a bio-pharmaceutical start-up established in 2001. Duncan worked for Monsanto for twenty-two years, starting right out of graduate school in product development, then moving into research administration and government relations. In the mid-1990s Duncan spearheaded Monsanto's four-way JV (with three major global paper companies) aimed at improving productivity in forestry product production. After this, he decided that he wanted to run his own company "instead of fixing someone else's." The idea for Colliant (a now-inactive firm) soon followed. The idea was to take unused Monsanto gene technology (gene traits) and license them to industries farther afield from Monsanto's core focus in corn, soy, and cotton products. It took an entire year to negotiate the licensing agreement with Monsanto's legal team, but finally Colliant was ready for its first series of VC funding. By this time, unfortunately, the VC had dried up for these kind of deals, in part due to the negative image emerging about plant bio technology – in Europe in particular.

By 2002, the Colliant–Monsanto deal was dead in the water, but Duncan had no intention of returning to the corporate rat race. Instead, he re-fashioned Colliant into a consulting firm and began taking on projects in business planning and syndicate VC finance. Through this work, he was introduced to the principals at Chlorogen who were looking for someone to run the business side of the organization while they focused on the research side. Choosing a market niche for Chlorogen's products was an initial challenge.

Chlorogen's chloroplast technology is suited for a variety of market applications, including bio-agriculture, bio-polymers, and bio-defense. The first thing Duncan did when joining Chlorogen was to decide on a core competence for the firm. They decided to target bio-pharmaceuticals and out-license the other areas. The idea was to get rid of the distraction of the non-core ideas, but to make money on them nonetheless. The lessons learned by Duncan while at Monsanto in the negotiations for Colliant's use of Monsanto technology helped immensely in this regard.

Chlorogen's products under development use proprietary technology to produce human albumin serum (HAS) which itself has two main applications. First, it enhances cell growth (e.g. growing skin). It also has applications in blood replenishment; because it is grown on tobacco leaves rather than using animal or human tissue (Duncan's graduate work in plant physiology is helpful here) they do not have to go through the most extensive type of Food and Drugs Administration (FDA) approval process. This means that the product can come to market in two years – as opposed to five to seven in other areas that require clinical testing. The technology has potential to be used in so-called "blockbuster drugs". Preliminary tests at Washington University's Medical School proved promising in this regard.

Duncan uses the lab facilities of NIDUS (the non-profit plant and life sciences incubator at the Monsanto campus in St. Louis, MO), the local incubator in which his firm is currently housed as well as relying on the Danforth Life Science Center's greenhouse space (discussed later) in coordination with Washington University faculty.

Duncan is not new to the government lobbying game, either. For six years he represented Monsanto's interests at local-, state-, and national-level government. In July 2004, Duncan had just returned from Washington, DC where he had talked to a number of politicians about Chlorogen. Duncan says that he was helping them to understand that they "need to help me" through tax credits and the like. One consequence of his and Chlorogen's on-staff lobbyist's efforts was that he was able in 2004 to obtain close to $5 million in bio-defense funding from the Defense Department.[2]

Duncan observes that the biggest obstacle to taking his company to the next level in St. Louis is the reluctance he sees on the part of the state (Missouri) to take the plunge into developing properties suitable for wet-lab space and production of plant science-based products. Missouri's competitors such as South Carolina, Florida, and Kentucky have lobbied his firm hard to make the move. According to Duncan, these other states have made it clear that they are in the business of supporting their tobacco farmers and they see the value in providing facilities to house Chlorogen, a potential large-scale employer. In the fortunate position of being courted by several state governments, Duncan is confident that he will obtain optimal terms from whichever state in which he chooses to operate. The ability of the St. Louis region to retain Chlorogen and other entrepreneurial high-tech firms such as SpectrAlliance could be a challenge.

Growing organically in a fledgling market: SpectrAlliance

Susan Bragg received her PhD in astrophysics in 1981 from Washington University and turned down a tenure-track position in the Physics Department at University of California, Berkeley in favor of a position in the research group of McDonnell Douglas (MD). In the 1980s, McDonnell Douglas' research group was run like an academic research institute with distinct project teams: satellite lasers, optical physics, and chemistry – even a "Star Wars" group. Bragg's specialty was in spectroscopy – the science that makes sure that a laser is not absorbed by the earth's atmosphere.

Things went well for the first eight years after joining MD, but in 1990 as "Star Wars" and other defense funding fell off, MD's vice president gathered all the researchers together and said that "there is not one of you who shouldn't be sending out résumés." In the end, Bragg was offered a position elsewhere in MD's divisional operating company, but by this time she had been approached by a small firm called Metaphase to oversee instrumentation design as their director of research. A lot of Metaphase's work was as a subcontractor to Alcon (a US manufacturer of prescription therapeutics, equipment, and consumer vision products). Bragg's designs started to create a buzz in the industry. In 1994 she was approached by another colleague about working together on a subcontracting project designing OEM fiber optic sensors for a measurement system.

Soon Bragg had a small workshop set up in the attic of her three-story house and was producing a number of these sensors, while working closely with the end-user. In 1998 the colleague agreed to start SpectrAlliance as partners "in order to improve my revenue result," she says. The idea was to develop a brand-name spectrometer that could handle all wavelengths at the same time. Bragg was to be the scientific brains of the operation, while the partner was to handle the day-to-day business and sales. Meanwhile, Bragg's development and production operation was rapidly outgrowing her attic and beginning to take over the basement and hallway of her house.

It was time to make a move, and the partner chose a strip-mall location. Bragg disagreed; their clients were large firms like Pfizer, Merc, and Glaxo Smith Kline and Bragg was sure that the appeal of a strip-mall outfit was not suited for this level of client. Relations with the partner turned sour after this and they decided to part company. What followed was an expensive buyout and the move of

SpectrAlliance to incubator space in the Center for Emerging Technologies (CET), near downtown St. Louis.

Asked about the market space for SpectrAlliance products, Bragg explained that the market for analytical instrumentation is huge and is currently dominated by major world players such as Agelent and Shimadzu. Their products can be classified as lab-based analytical instruments. SpectrAlliance occupies a niche in this market, as the spectrometers they produce go directly to the factory floor. The SpectrAlliance spectrometer provides real-time measurements to improve the process of manufacturing.

Recently, serendipity has played a role in the success of SpectrAlliance of getting over the first few hurdles and continuing to grow organically (i.e. without the crutch of VC funds). The FDA has dictated to pharmaceutical companies that they can no longer assay (analyze the composition of) a few pills out of millions for QC (quality control) testing. Instead, products must be monitored for integrity along the entire production process. SpectrAlliance's signature product is an analytical measurement system for production processes using a combination of patented hardware and trade secret software. The system stores gigabytes of information measuring all aspects of a unit of product, from temperature and density to the concentration by micron of inputs. SpectrAlliance is the only firm in the USA to have this technology.

Like Duncan at Chlorogen, Bragg's SpectrAlliance is poised to outgrow its incubator environs. For Bragg, however, the fact that St. Louis has yet to establish a critical mass of high technology firms poses a potential longer-term problem. If SpectrAlliance interviews a potential spectrocopist, they might have what is called a "techno-trailing" spouse – that is, a technologist also needing employment. The St. Louis region as a whole doesn't have enough firms to create an environment whereby job applicants see local career opportunities for their partners – or for themselves should things not work out at a given firm.

On the upside, Bragg notes that St. Louis is a very affordable place to live. Relocating the firm to Boston or San Diego would become a very expensive proposition. Further, Bragg senses a level of energy in the civic community in and around St. Louis that was not present during her graduate school days in the 1970s at Washington University. The local and regional government now seems to be strongly focused towards building a bio-technology corridor. For Bragg, this is not generic biotech, but it seems to be very focused on agricultural bio-technology, drawing from the strengths of the Danforth Plant Science Center and Monsanto. At the same time, Bragg notes that the area must combat its "slow to commercialize technology" image. Bragg has a number of colleagues out of places like MIT and Stanford who have been involved in technology spin-offs.[3] In contrast, the spin-offs out of Washington University could still be counted on one hand in the early 2000s.

Washington University should be active in this regard, but to date it has not fostered significant commercialization of faculty-developed technology. On the one hand, St. Louis lacks the physical infrastructure to retain growing firms like Chlorogen and a critical mass of firms – enough to attract the nation's best and brightest minds to high-tech firms like SpectrAlliance. On the other hand, the region's dense, hierarchical social networks are a turn-off to newcomers, as the experiences of Kereos shows.

The paradox of dense social networks: Kereos

Robert Beardsley holds a PhD in biochemical engineering from the University of Iowa and an MBA in finance from the University of Chicago. He was recruited by one of the major VC funds behind Kereos to manage the start-up as its CEO. Kereos is a St. Louis developer of therapeutics and imaging agents that detect and attack cancer and cardiovascular disease. As late as 2004, Beardsley was one of a small but growing number of professional CEOs recruited from outside St. Louis to lead start-ups. Like other emerging markets, Beardsley sees the lack of enough skilled "national-caliber" CEOs as a weakness. Though the region has its share of technologists, it does not yet have technology managers, or those who can do things like creating a national image for the St. Louis business community as a place that is interesting and vibrant.

Beardsely, who has experience studying and working in Japan, likens the climate around Washington University to the rules of the Japanese network paradigm. If you have personal connections inside the institution and know "who, where, and when" to approach the institution about your projects, you can curry favor. At the same time, Washington University is one of the last great bastions of faculty control. Unlike places such as MIT or UCSD that form entrepreneurial firms to commercialize faculty research, "Wash U" people seem to feel that commercialization sullies their academic image.

Beardsley views St. Louis' immediate challenges as threefold. First and foremost, national VCs have a fear of flying. VC managers are worried about the "midnight phone call" from their firms – calls that they have to deal with right then and there. If the fund and the firm are located around Boston, New York, or San Francisco then this is not a problem. St. Louis, as will be discussed below, is for a number of reasons one of those "can't get there from here" places. "This is why you see a lot of syndicate (rather than direct) financing going on in St. Louis right now. VCs get together and have the local partner deal with emergencies".[4]

Second, like SpectrAlliance, a major challenge for Kereos is being able to hire the right people. St. Louis must improve its image nationally in order for local firms to be able to recruit top national talent. One drawback is that social hierarchies are hindering regional development. The first thing a local inevitably asks of a new acquaintance, for example, is "where did you go to high school?" The response allows the local to situate the other person into the complex local social ranking of schools and districts. Most locals are at a loss if a person cannot provide a codeable answer. This can be viewed as a double whammy. On the one hand, local social networks are insular and provincial, making it difficult for newcomers to become assimilated. On the other hand, outside talent, on being exposed to this provincialism, are inevitably turned off the region. Unfortunately, these social hierarchies are extremely entrenched.

St. Louis is said to have the most trust funds *per capita* than any other place in the USA. This is one way of saying that a lot of political decisions are made by people who have been in St. Louis for many years. On the upside, these established social networks help to perpetuate a strong sense of civic pride. That the civic community in St. Louis is unified behind the push to establish a bio-technology corridor is therefore significant. In St. Louis, civic leaders have the will *and the wherewithal* to put their ideas into practice. The trick for new talent to the region is to somehow get plugged into these old networks. This is no easy task.

Another downside to these dense social networks permeating the region is that, according to Beardsley, classic maverick entrepreneurs couldn't hack it. Luckily, he says, life sciences and bio-tech are industries best suited for what can be called anti-maverick entrepreneurs. The kind of scientific mind behind product development in these industries is suited for the "check off the boxes" process of FDA approval. There is no secret about what the FDA wants to see in a new commercialized bio-pharmaceutical technology; unfortunately, technology management (e.g. strategic decisions about new R&D

expenditure) and marketing requires a different skill set. In addition to these socio-political barriers St. Louis has logistical issues.

The 2001 buy-out of TWA by American Airlines and subsequent downgrading of St. Louis from hub to secondary hub has translated into a major logistical impediment. This means that in 2005 a person cannot get on a plane from San Francisco after 12 noon and expect to arrive in St. Louis before midnight. St. Louis suffers badly from the "can't get there from here" syndrome, and the current state of the US airline industry doesn't look promising.

7.5 Entrepreneur and firm-level challenges: a summary

The challenges faced by these three entrepreneurial start-ups – Chlorogen, SpectrAlliance, and Kereos – are indicative of the overall socio-political institutional environment within which entrepreneurial firms must operate. The dense networks rich in social capital and civic pride have been an important support in creating an atmosphere that seems to be behind the idea of creating a critical mass of high technology firms – by putting local money behind development projects. Public relation campaigns bankrolled by local groups have put St. Louis on the radar screens of national VC and professional CEO/technology managerial talent. Newcomers, while being impressed by the strong civic pride behind these efforts, are also turned off by the inherent provincialism of these same social networks. St. Louis is at a crossroads and local civic leaders and their organizations are working intensely to surmount these barriers and bring St. Louis to the next level of entrepreneurship and innovation. The activities of a number of institutions in this regard complement the picture of St. Louis presented by the stories of individual entrepreneurs as well as fleshing out the regional context of firm-level innovation.

The regional context: support institutions

In their efforts to build a critical (and self-sustaining) mass of firms, the region's social and physical capital has been focused in recent years on the first two stages of support for fledgling businesses. First, two incubators were established, Nidus and CET, with major bankrolling by Monsanto and the support of state government, respectively. Second, as start-ups outgrow incubator space, local leaders have tried to persuade developers (still gun shy from the burst of the "tech bubble" in the 1990s) to build larger spaces that are wet-lab ready.

NIDUS

Bob Calcaterra (DSc in chemical engineering, Washington University) directed the NIDUS Center in 1998. NIDUS is a private sector complement to St. Louis' other incubator, CET, established in 1998, which is more closely tied to local and state government. NIDUS is a start-up incubator in St. Louis, backed by Monsanto. The Center began accepting tenants in 1999; Calcaterra was recruited to run NIDUS from the Arizona Technology Incubator (ATI), which he ran for seven years. Prior to ATI, he founded and ran the Boulder Technology Incubator (BTI) for three years. Calcaterra offered his take on the differences in civic culture behind entrepreneurialism in Boulder and Phoenix, and how his experiences in these very different places have informed his approach in St. Louis.

Boulder

Calcaterra found Boulder to be very entrepreneurial. Inter-industry exchange was strong, especially in electronic devices and software. Further, there were a lot of VC people in the area. IBM had major operations, and this helped to foster the growth of the local data storage and hardware market. Interestingly, the vibrant entrepreneurial community bred an anti-incubator attitude. People would ask Calcaterra as he was trying to set up BTI "why do we need an incubator?" He sensed the underlying opinion that only firms that could not succeed on their own would go to an incubator. As a result, it was an uphill battle in the early years. However, once a number of successful entrepreneurs joined the board, it worked better, as newcomers and local naysayers followed their lead. In the end, BTI was successful. For example, out of sixteen companies housed in the incubator while Calcaterra was there, four have gone public. Arizona was a different story.

Arizona

According to Calcaterra, Arizona in general has a very difficult culture in terms of support for entrepreneurs. In Phoenix, for example, there is very little VC. There are few start-ups, and only a handful of interactive activities to get entrepreneurs together. Instead, during Calcaterra's tenure, the whole state economy seemed to be driven by tourism and real estate. ATI was adjacent to Motorola's electronic device center, in an old unused Motorola building. Arizona State University gave ATI verbal support in the beginning, but no real commitment followed. There were neither networks to support entrepreneurs, nor a civic climate that seemed to care. Coming to St. Louis was a welcome change in this regard.

St. Louis

Calcaterra sees St. Louis entirely differently. He notes that, unlike big firms in other places, Monsanto has put an incredible amount of support behind the idea of establishing an enterprise community and has been very committed to it. For Calcaterra, this means that the people in Monsanto's executive offices understand the value of creating a critical mass of entrepreneurial companies:

> They [Monsanto executives] follow through on their commitment by pulling together a number of community stakeholders onto evaluations committees and so forth. Therefore, the committee members deciding on where to put community money in support of new business creation have a vested interest in what is going on. The community commitment is much stronger than I expected to find, especially after my experience in Arizona. In St. Louis, you have a number of old-line people who have stayed in the community and supported it in the long-term. Here in St. Louis, if these folks commit, then the community falls in line.[5]

One primary example of the role of civic leaders in this regard is Bill Danforth, whose family made a fortune from the vast foodstuff conglomerate Ralston Purina. Danforth's soft-spoken and modest demeanor commands so much respect in the community that Calcaterra says: "if he calls you up and asks you to get on board with something, you simply cannot say no." In the mid-1990s it seems that Bob Shapiro of Monsanto, Peter Raven of the Missouri Botanical Garden, and Bill Danforth, then Chancellor of Washington University, got together and decided that there was simply no reason why St. Louis could not become a bio-tech center. Grand ideas are fine, but putting them into practice is another matter – no matter how rich in positive social capital and civic pride and leadership a region might be.

Turning these grand visions into action is often credited to Dick Fleming of the Regional Commerce and Growth Association (RCGA).

Fleming is said to have been blunt with the other folks: "it is fine for us to have an idea – but we need a plan." The Battelle Report, the most comprehensive study of St. Louis' industrial structure and cluster potential, was commissioned by Fleming. This was long before the Battelle Institute had made a name in the business of regional studies. In fact, St. Louis was among the first three regional studies that Battelle did. By 2004 Battelle had completed over forty such regional studies in the USA. The Battelle Report was jointly funded by the Kauffman Foundation (Kansas City) and the Danforth Foundation (St. Louis) in cooperation with the RCGA and Civic Progress. It took about two years to complete the research and produce the report, published in 2003 (Battelle Technology Partnership Practice 2003). As the Battelle research was underway, people asked why St. Louis didn't go to a big name like Michael Porter's Institute for Strategy and Competitiveness, an organization with more experience in "cluster" studies. Fleming at the RCGA was adamant that the analysis must be more than skin-deep:

Asked why his coalition chose the Battelle, Bill Danforth said:

> We wanted clear benchmarks against other communities, action plans, cost analyses. Porter's recommendations tend to be much more general, such as "work on transportation," etc. Battelle was much more focused than this: they said this is what you can do in life sciences. We in St. Louis know what we have, which institutions we have. We needed to have someone chart a course, not tell us what to do. Battelle provided a road map.[6]

Once the group of civic leaders had a plan, they decided that the best way was to have a coalition to push it forward. It made sense therefore to ask Bill Danforth to spearhead the efforts. From these discussions emerged the "Plant and Life Sciences Coalition." Calcaterra says that what resulted from this foresight and planning – and picking the right community champion to be the flagbearer – was that "everybody [was] raising all boats at the same time." Community leaders were aiming to simultaneously upgrade the region's human resources (from technologists to CEOs) and infrastructure (from transportation to wet-lab space), while at the same time working on national PR.

The activities of the Plant and Life Sciences Coalition are fivefold: research, facilities, networking, workforce, and VC. Among Coalition projects are several seed and VC capital funds including BioGenerator, Preseed, and the Vectis Life Sciences Fund. A central hub of these efforts is Washington University. In 2004 Washington University was the second-ranked medical school in the USA, behind only Harvard and above Johns Hopkins in the popular estimation. In the early 2000s Washington University faculty attracted more NIH money than their colleagues anywhere else. Further, Washington University's endowment is massive, upwards of $5 billion. Some years back they made a goal of raising a billion dollars within five years. They had it raised by the third year of the campaign. Then they raised another half a billion dollars within a year. Most of this money has come from alumni. The university's new chancellor – replacing Bill Danforth, who retired in 1995 after nearly twenty-five years – was recruited from MIT (Mark Wrighton). Soon after joining the university, he hired two people from Johns Hopkins University. Now Washington University has one of the top-notch bio-medical engineering schools in a beautiful new building.

Calcaterra recalls that when he was first interviewing for the NIDUS position he met with local people who were for the first time in their lives thinking of doing VC. They had zero experience and in the late 1990s there simply was no life sciences VC. By 2004, over $450 million of VC was circulating in the region's firms.[7]

Calcaterra has observed that the financial backing for new ventures is all private industry-driven, emanating out of St. Louis, with the state of Missouri government far behind the curve. The McDonnell family, the Danforth Foundation, Monsanto, and Washington University Endowment have got the region's VC community up and running. Two funds in particular are PROLOG and Rivervest. PROLOG was underwritten by the Danforth Foundation and Washington University and had its first close in 2004.

Another example of private industry-initiated change is the leadership at Monsanto. One morning in July 2004, Calcaterra met with Monsanto's CEO about a project NIDUS had initiated. By the end of the same day, Monsanto had kicked in $2 million of support. Calcaterra notes that 60% of his job is fundraising and only 40% management: "Incubators are accustomed to having to go back every year to the same companies to justify their existence. To have company funds for 10 years is incredible – and this is exactly what has happened in St. Louis." This is not enough, though. In order to reach the "critical mass" goal of 70–100 new biotech venture firms Calcaterra estimates that NIDUS will need close to a billion dollars. That means attracting it from other parts of the USA and the world. Things are looking up in this regard, too. NIDUS attracted its first in-house VC fund, from Cincinnati, in the summer of 2004. The Danforth Foundation and Washington University are providing incentive money to draw this and other VCs to the region. These families/organizations – Danforth, McDonnell, Monsanto and Washington University – are also behind the establishment of the Donald Danforth Plant Science Center.

Danforth Plant Science Center

The Donald Danforth Plant Science Center is a non-profit research institute established in 1998, whose mission includes developing and commercializing technologies with applications in human nutrition and human health. In 1999, Roger Beachy joined the Center as its first President. Previously, Beachy had worked for thirteen years in the Department of Biology at Washington University before he was recruited in 1991 to head the division of plant biology at the Scripps Research Institute in La Holla, California. He spent eight years at Scripps and he recalls his time there as vibrant. He also recalls that when he left St. Louis in 1991, there was talk about of creating a "technopolis," an idea aimed at getting faculty at Washington University and elsewhere to be entrepreneurial. At the time the idea was going nowhere. There were no "Angel investors," and St. Louis had no history of successful entrepreneurial projects in the life sciences.[8]

By the late 1990s Beachy noticed a change, the Coalition for Plant and Life Sciences had been formed and was working in tandem with the RCGA. It was obvious that all the key players in the region were communicating – all the time. Beachy noted that what was most impressive in St. Louis was that the region's leaders actually implemented the recommendations of the Battelle Report – the comprehensive study of the region's resources, opportunities and barriers to "cluster" formation. According to Beachy, lots of other places commission similar studies, but few have the gumption to actually do what the reports recommend. Patricia Snyder, president/CEO of the BioGenerator, St. Louis' first seed capital fund for bio-medical ventures, concurs. Having consulted in places like New Orleans and Cincinnati, Snyder finds that St. Louis is unique in that the region's leaders are open to new ideas and new approaches. In contrast, she finds that the recalcitrance of the insular community of civic leaders in New Orleans, for example, has been a major drag on cluster development in that region.[9]

The key in St. Louis has been getting key human rather than financial resources behind the idea of establishing a bio-tech corridor. Of course the money matters, too, but in the beginning what was important was getting the support of the community as a whole. One way the coalition went about this was by convincing the leading local newspaper – the *St. Louis Post Dispatch* – to expand its scientific writing staff and therefore coverage of issues central to the development of a technology and science minded workforce. It also helped that around that time the people at the St. Louis Science Center – perhaps the third or fourth most-attended science center in the USA, stepped up to the plate and said that they wanted the Science Center to become the center for interpretation to the public of the new life sciences in the region.

In other words, Beachy finds that the people behind these initiatives were quite politically astute at how they got the community behind the idea "not with a hammer, but with education." This grassroots education campaign has helped not only raise the general scientific awareness in the local population but also served to get broad groups of people behind the idea of building a regional life science community. This effort has also helped to surmount socio-spatial barriers including the fact that the St. Louis region is dispersed over numerous semi-autonomous municipalities, each with its own distinct identity and way of doing things. According to Beachy, ten years ago when people spoke of the high-tech initiative they would say "oh that's a Creve Coeur thing."[10] Now people think of it in terms of the big picture.

St. Louis is at a crossroads. It needs to get a critical mass of entrepreneurial and technological minded people interacting. It can happen. San Diego in 1980 was not so unlike St. Louis in layout, and transformed a similarly fractious region into an integrated regional system. In the 1980s, when it became advantageous to expand and integrate collar cities, it was done. The school, road, and other infrastructural systems were integrated. Now, according to Beachy, if you walk around places like Pines Road in San Diego, you can find any technological expertise you need.

Civic progress

One major impediment to an integrated city/regional approach is that St. Louis city government is very weak, particularly the mayor's office. Further, the mayor's office is embedded within a local government and wards characterized by an extensive patronage system. A weak city executive means that any new initiative must make its way through a thicket of patron–client relations. One example is that all financial decisions have been made by the "Board of Estimate and Apportionment," with little power resting in the hands of the mayor. Another example is the attempt in the early 2000s by the city to reform the school system, which has met with much resistance from school system stakeholders. The fact that Civic Progress (an organization established in 1952 by then mayor Joseph Darst, which still maintains a closely held membership list of CEOs of large local corporations) is quietly supporting the efforts of the mayor to obtain more autonomy has fueled a backlash in city wards. Civic Progress is seen by some locals as a shadowy corporate cabal, whose civic interest is limited to ensuring greater control over city government and higher profits for member firms.

John Roberts, executive director of Civic Progress in the 2000s, does not dispute the fact that members are interested in benefits to their firms. In fact, when a local group makes a pitch to the organization they are often asked what value-added their projects will bring to the bottom line of local firms. Presenters are inevitably peppered with questions like: Will more people buy our products? Will more people use the airport? At the same time, Civic Progress members, especially of the older generation, want to see regional growth and they know that to make it happen there has to be infrastructure improvements and a major overhaul of the city school system. The latter means improving race relations and closing the gap between white and black students in city schools.[11]

With this in mind, Civic Progress backed the candidacy of a number of people for the School Board, and by 2004 managed to get four of their own on the rolls. Civic Progress also helped to oversee the funding of the Battelle Report, and recently became involved in initiatives at Washington University to develop wet-lab space for growing firms. Roberts notes that Civic Progress is only one of several organizations in a dense overlapping network of organizations and people having a strong civic consciousness. It is this broad-based network that is behind enterprise development in the region. Roberts agrees that now is the time to take St. Louis to the next level. At the helm of these efforts, he sees an aging generation of civic and enterprise leaders – heads of firms and organizations that have been in St. Louis for many generations. In the 2000s the landscape has changed; St. Louis now has more professional managers and absentee ownership. This new generation has no community history, and even assumed successors of the Bill Danforths and others are harder to get involved. Until now, organizations such as Civic Progress have benefited enormously from peer pressure among the top CEOs. In the past, when others saw this high level of CEO community involvement, they got involved, too. For Beachy, Calcaterra, and Roberts, it also helps to have a few leaders with vision, like that of Bill Danforth.

7.6 Innovative coalitions and local visionaries

Bill Danforth is regarded in St. Louis as its top visionary and civic leader. He is also extremely modest and tends to deflect credit for success upon others while leveling blame for mistakes on himself. Asked what got him going on the idea of building a bio-technology corridor in St. Louis, Danforth recounted an experience that he had while Chancellor at Washington University. Before the tech collapse in the mid-1990s several Washington University faculty developed a switch for getting information off of the Internet. After a failed two-year struggle locally to raise VC, they moved the company to San Francisco. In the end, they sold to CISCO Systems for $350 million. For Danforth, this was the catalyst for him to get people together to start discussing what to do to try to keep companies from fleeing the region. Danforth also knew that VC in the Midwest has historically dragged behind that on either coast. Even NIH funds, of which Washington University gets a decent amount, lags behind in the Midwest compared to coastal regions. Lessons learned from lost opportunities like this led to the commissioning of the Battelle Report.

Together with his colleagues John McDonnell and John Dubinsky (a recently retired banker), and others Danforth had set his sights on building the real estate infrastructure needed to house the office and wet-lab space for start-ups who were graduating from the region's two main incubators (NIDUS and CET). This kind of infrastructural development had proved to be the biggest stumbling block so far for St. Louis. Looking at it from the developers' perspective, it you build too late the firms have already left the region; if you build too early, then you lose money. To make it happen, the risk must be distributed across more organizations.

In 2004, Danforth and others were working to raise $24 million from local companies to build the "Cortex" – a wet lab space to be housed near Washington University's campus. By 2004, the coalition had raised $29 million from participating institutions as well as obtaining $12 million in tax credits from the State of Missouri. In his presentations to funding sources and community groups, he says the key is to have a shared vision – to know that we are building the next generation of companies that will help form the economic base of the region. Asked why he is able to get people to help in putting his visions into practice, he replied:

> I am focused on the basics, what you are really trying to accomplish. As a result, I do not micro-manage. I try to work with people who have expertise in their area. I have lived in St. Louis all my life, I know who knows what and how to do things.[12]

Another of Danforth's current initiatives is working in coalition to get some tobacco money into life science capacity. Members of the Plant and Life Sciences Coalition, through lobbying state government, were able to get some tobacco money earmarked for life sciences capacity funding. This has been an uphill battle as the state legislature naturally supports the public University of Missouri foremost and the University's four campuses are spread across the state. At the same time, there is a strong feeling in rural counties and in Jefferson City (the capital) that St. Louis and Kansas City, the other big city in Missouri, should not "get too big for their britches." Danforth and others with experience in research communities understand, however, that limited state money must be used strategically – that is, where there already exists a critical mass of researchers. In Missouri, that place is primarily Washington University. Danforth hopes that by the request for proposals (RFP) process in which funding decisions for this money are made by a panel representing broad groups of state stakeholders and experts, that the money will go where there exists the greatest potential.

Danforth and others in the Coalition are keenly aware that if you are going to have life sciences you need the ongoing support from state government. Specifically, that means supportive, friendly laws (e.g. criminalizing stem cell research is not a viable option), and educational support. For this to happen, they need a well-informed state legislature. One impediment is that in a state with term limits coalition partners find themselves having to re-educate the legislature through its freshmen lawmakers every four years. At the same time, Danforth cautions against depending on government to take care of things. Danforth is clear on the need to take a comprehensive approach to community development, one that is enterprise-initiated, but integrated into scientific research:

> If you wait for the bureaucrats to help you out and tell you what to do – you are not going to make it. You need the entrepreneurs but at the same time, without strong science you cannot do it. When I am trying to explain to people what we are doing, I use the analogy of a child. If you want to grow the life sciences – like a child you have to get the feet, head, digestive system and other parts of the body growing together in tandem. The body of life science is pre-seed capital, incubators, commercial wet-lab space and so forth. All things must grow together – but the food that makes the child of life science grow is the science.[13]

7.7 What it takes to move the region forward

St. Louis is certainly moving forward in a coordinated hit-all-marks way. The region's civic and firm-level leaders are targeting facility upgrading, workforce training, infrastructure development, VC formation, real estate, and image upgrading (via national/international public relations (PR)). At the same time, rapid developments in any one area too far ahead of the others may create a boom/bust situation (e.g. spending limited resources recklessly in underutilized infrastructure and building space and/or a quick fad then loss of confidence in the region on the part of national VC market). Conversely, moving too slow in the development of one or more components creates bottlenecks in overall development (e.g. lagging behind the tax, real estate, and funding initiatives of other states and regions) and loss of opportunities to other regions.

For St. Louis in the early 2000s the most critical element underpinning the level of complex coordination required to move forward is the civic engagement of community leaders. This requires the will and wherewithal of such leaders to support the long-term economic development needs of the community. Further, certain community leaders must provide the vision and leadership in order to get broad groups of community stakeholders behind their efforts. Enterprise-initiated, yes – but with a civic flair.

A strong civic consciousness in St. Louis helps to overcome particularistic interests. In St. Louis, old-money civic leaders are leading the cause (e.g. the Danforths and McDonnells). This strategy poses several long-term challenges. First, this generation of leaders is near retirement (in their 60s and 70s). Will their sons and daughters take up the cause in what certainly will be a multi-generational effort? Second, will the new professional CEO class (many recruited from outside the region) pick up the baton? Even if they do, will the old-money culture (e.g. "where did you go to high school?" social hierarchy) evolve into a more open (in terms of access and thinking) horizontal grouping to attract the best and brightest to the region? A sustained, concerted effort by civic leaders and entrepreneurs, connected to the interests of community stakeholders through innovative coalitions, may be the answer. Comparing St. Louis to Kyoto may offer interesting lessons in this regard.

7.8 St. Louis and Kyoto compared

St. Louis and Kyoto can be compared in terms of the characteristics that they share at three levels: entrepreneur, firm, and region. These characteristics mesh together into integrated wholes – presenting a picture of innovative community building that is strikingly similar despite their differing national contexts. At the same time, a few critical differences remain between the successful Kyoto region and the still-emerging St. Louis region.

High technology entrepreneurs in both St. Louis and Kyoto have strong scientific and technical skills. Washington University and Kyoto University are each top-tier research universities where faculty research ranks among the very top nationally in terms of the creation of new technology. This technology is focused in emerging sectors, particularly bio-pharmaceutical (St. Louis) and nanotech and analytical instruments (Kyoto). Kyoto University has long-standing ties to private industry and a number of enterprise spin-offs have resulted from these synergies. In St. Louis, in contrast, entrepreneurs tend to have worked for decades in one of the local corporate giants such as Monsanto and McDonnell Douglas before venturing into start-ups.

St. Louis' Washington University faculty, faced with commercializable technology, have in the past either not taken the initiative to start independent firms to make marketable products from their technology or, when they have tried, the absence of local start-up capital has driven them

Table 7.1 Entrepreneur characteristics

	Entrepreneur characteristics	
	Kyoto	St. Louis
Scientific and technological knowledge and expertise	Strong (particularly Kyoto University faculty)	Strong (particularly Washington University faculty, Monsanto engineers)
Technology management	OK (founder managers scientists not marketers)	OK (must recruit professional managers from outside)
Entrepreneurial savvy	Maverick	Professional CEOs either (a) recruited from outside or (b) descended from Monsanto, McDonnell Douglas
Political savvy	High (use of regional officials)	High (use of professional lobbyists)

outside the region. In the 2000s faculty developing commercial technology tend to work with professional CEOs. The latter deal with marketing company products and day-to-day firm operations and their posts have often been created as a condition for obtaining VC funds. These professional CEOs have had to be recruited from outside the region.

The separation within start-ups of the scientist-owners from the CEO professional managers (St. Louis) and the managerial inexperience of scientists-turned-entrepreneurs (Kyoto) has posed barriers for both regions in managing and marketing technology. Sales levels in international markets reflect this weakness in both regions, although more so in St. Louis. At the same time, successful firms in both regions, measured by sales and profit margins, are "savvy" at using go-betweens to lobby for favorable government policies, dealing with permissions gatekeepers, and obtaining R&D finance (see table 7.1). St. Louis and Kyoto firms also engage in similar marketing and R&D strategies.

Firms in both regions focus on core competence, niche markets and keeping up with new product R&D. For example, Samco's (Kyoto) emphasis on developing state-of-the-art thin-film technologies has kept

Table 7.2 Firm characteristics

	Kyoto	*St. Louis*
Core competence	Strong	Strong
Niche market	Strong	Strong
International focus	Strong	Moderate (national focus)
Profit/cash flow focus	Strong	VC focus
R&D	Strong	Strong

it out of potentially lucrative large-scale production of the coated bottles as part of its exclusive JV with Kirin Brewery. Working out a licensing deal with a local bottler has helped Samco to maintain its core focus on developing new thin-film technologies.

Chlorogen (St. Louis) may accomplish the same goal by focusing on its best-bet application of its technology in bio-pharmaceuticals. Meanwhile, Chlorogen has established a cash flow through out-licensing its defense and agricultural applications. The USA remains the world's largest market for high technology and Kyoto firms must target their products accordingly. St. Louis firms, on the other hand, can afford a national focus – for now. The absence in the early twenty-first century of a decent VC market in Japan is one explanation why Kyoto firms have tended to grow organically, while depending on pocket-money start-up finance and sales-driven cash flow in the early stages of their firms. The small scale of available finance has made Kyoto firms keenly sensitive to the need for healthy and stable profit margins – margins that they inevitably plow back into new product R&D. St. Louis firms, which in aggregate are at an earlier stage of development than Kyoto firms, in contrast are trying to draw national VC to the region (see table 7.2). Their ability to do so in the early 2000s seems dependent on the efforts of local coalitions of regional stakeholders.

On a regional level, St. Louis and Kyoto share all the basic building blocks for innovative community (or cluster) creation: strong research universities that produce technologists and scientists in a number of fields; communications and other infrastructure (though St. Louis in 2004 has a long way to go in terms of the latter). The strong civic consciousness and civic pride in these regions puts them ahead of other regions – particularly in terms of the ability to build and maintain broad coalitions of regional stakeholders coalesced around a focused developmental vision. This is perhaps what will let these regions stay ahead of their domestic competition.

Kyoto firms are embedded in numerous informal, overlapping socio-political networks. These networks support collaborative manufacturing as well as the region's pocket-money system of finance (that compensates for the lack of VC in the region). The civic culture of Kyoto – respect and even reverence for maverick attitudes and pull-yourself-up-by-your-bootstraps conservativism coupled with a strong sense of a "Kyoto versus outsiders" mentality supports coalition building between broad groups of community stakeholders. The result of these synergies has been the emergence of a self-sustaining core of innovative firms – a critical mass reached by the 1990s.

In St. Louis, a handful of civic leaders and blue-chip firm executives have taken it upon themselves to establish coalitions aimed at building the region's infrastructure and high-tech talent base, in the hope of creating an innovative (and self-sustaining) community of firms. These coordinated activities are a recent phenomenon, starting as late as the mid-1990s. Coalitions in St. Louis, led by visionaries like Bill Danforth, can count on local people to follow their lead. At the same time, the low number of native maverick upstart firms translates into weak inter-firm networks, while provincial attitudes and entrenched social hierarchies undermine efforts to incorporate newcomers into existing human networks. The political system, characterized by a weak local government embedded within a firmly rooted patronage system and fragmented municipalities, exacerbates the impact on innovative potential of these social problems. St. Louis must overcome these socio-political barriers if it is to build a self-sustaining community of innovative firms (see table 7.3). Otherwise, the few entrepreneurial mavericks currently in the region may, as their firms grow, be attracted away from the region to more open communities. Innovative regions in Germany and China exhibit certain patterns reminiscent of St. Louis and Kyoto, perhaps on a larger (geographic) scale.

7.9 Germany

Germany's Baden-Württemberg (BW) region in the southwest is among the highest performing economic regions in Europe. Nearly

Table 7.3 Regional characteristics

	Kyoto	*St. Louis*
Inter-firm networks	Strong	Weak, but transforming
Collaborative manufacturing	Informal	Strategic partnerships and licensing agreements
Innovative coalitions	Many, informal	Few, formal
Civic consciousness	Strong	Strong
Civic culture	Libertarianism, conservatism: *Kyoto-jin* v. outsiders outweighs social hierarchies	Provincialism, conservatism: social hierarchies of equal importance as insider–outsider view Fragmented semi-autonomous communities (fiefdoms)
Self-sustaining community of firms (critical mass)?	Critical mass reached in 1970s and 1980s	On the cusp after late 1990s
Technology/scientific knowledge and expertise	Research Universities (Kyoto, Doshisha) Technical colleges	Research Universities (Washington University, St. Louis University, University of Missouri); technical (community) colleges
VC	Little VC, pocket-money finance as alternative source	Weak, some syndicate VC financing, no critical mass
Patents/university spin-offs	High	Low
Government commitment	Strong local and regional commitment	Strong regional commitment
Government cohesion	Local–regional cooperation	Weak local government, fragmentation/ factionalism, but strong regional coalitions

19% of its workforce is employed in medium-high and high technology industries (Innovation/SMEs Programme 2003). Leading cities within the larger region, such as Stuttgart and Karlsruhe, excel at overall innovation, as measured by a composite of a comprehensive set of indicators generated by the European Commission (EC) (Innovation/SMEs Programme 2003). These indicators include: population with tertiary education, lifelong learning, employment in medium-high manufacturing, employment in high-tech services, public and business R&D expenditures, European Patent Office (EPO) high-tech (and total) patent applications, share of innovative enterprises in both manufacturing and services, innovation expenditures as a percentage of turnover in both manufacturing and services, and the share of sales of new-to-the-firm products in manufacturing. In 2003, Stuttgart (and neighboring Oberbayern, Bavaria) surpassed other German regions in terms of patent performance and manufacturing strength. The top three German cities in terms of overall innovative performance – Stuttgart, Karlsruhe, and Freiburg – are all located in BW.

BW is one of sixteen federal "Länder" (states) and is the third largest state after Bavaria and North-Rhine Westphalia. In 2002, BW's economy centered on manufacturing and its firms occupied a high value-added position in final goods production. Local firms employed the nation's highest concentrations of mechanical engineers and electrical engineers.

Stuttgart, for example, leads Germany in the production of transportation machinery and electronics; 17.7% of Germany's total output of vehicles, ships and aircraft are produced within the region, compared to the national average of 8.8% and 12.4% of German motors, turbines, and transport machinery are produced around Stuttgart, compared to 5.5% nationally. The area even holds a slight edge in electronics, 9.6% v. 8.3% nationally. In terms of economic performance, BW's Stuttgart leads the nation, home to names like DaimlerChrysler, Porsche, and Bosch. The region also is the long-time home to many family-owned innovative SMEs (Strambach 2002).

Stuttgart's export rate surpasses BW's, and Germany's national rate (51.5%, 41.7%, and 36.2%, respectively). It also has low unemployment (4.5% in comparison to the national rate of 9.3%) and high gross value-added (over 58 thousand euro per employee). Table 7.4 summarizes Stuttgart's performance in comparison to the BW region as a whole and Germany nationally.

Table 7.4 Economic performance of Stuttgart, Baden-Württemberg, and Germany

Indicators	*Stuttgart*	*Baden-Württemberg*	*Germany*
Gross value-added (1999) per employee (in euro)	58,201	54,620	50,742
Unemployment rate (%) (2000)	4.5	5.0	9.3
Export rate (%) (2000)	51.5	41.7	36.2

Source: Strambach (2002, table 3).

Historically, BW has been a politically de-centralized, semi-autonomous region, located far from the (autarkic) influences of central government (Herrigel 1996). As a whole, Germany has been described as the archetypical corporatist state. Relatively autonomous regions, a strong SME sector (*Mittelstand*), trade unionism and the like, have a counterbalancing effect on the tendency towards centralization and bureaucratization in governance systems.

In Germany the vast *Mittelstand* is favored by its institutionalized inclusion into regional and national governance systems. It is no surprise, then, that Germany's innovative regions have emerged in more de-centralized regions such as BW where SMEs are important community stakeholders (Bavaria, another innovative region to the east of BW, emerged from an agrarian (un-autarkic) history). BW's regional innovation system has been the subject of research examining the sources of its enduring economic performance (Cooke and Morgan 1994; Herrigel 1996; Simmie *et al.* 2004). The region has all the prerequisite formal institutions, or basic ingredients, underpinning innovative activity. It also has vibrant civic and informal institutions, including inter-firm networks, particularly among SMEs but also including the region's big firms.

Some have argued that local stakeholders have been successful at navigating the institutions of governance at the national level. Political "savvy" on the part of local leaders in this regard has drawn important resources to the region (Scott 1999). BW's innovation system has been found to be firm-based – that is, innovative activity that results in technological product and process innovations (TPP) occurs mainly between firms and their suppliers and customers. Surveys of local firms indicate that regional inter-firm links are the most important to local firms in supporting innovative activity – in contrast to a much weaker role for formal associations and research institutes (Todtling and Kaufmann 1999). The region's firms also have a historical "tradition of cooperation," as measured by collaborative R&D and manufacturing activities (Cooke and Morgan 1994). Innovative regions in China share some of these characteristics.

7.10 China

The Pearl River Delta Economic Zone (PRDEZ) in the southeast of China is one of the country's most economically successful regions (table 7.5). Located within Guangdong Province, the PRDEZ consists of several major cities, including Guangzhou, Shenzhen, Dongguan, Zhongshan, Foshan, and Zhuhai. These cities are located around the mouth of the Pearl River, historically a major export hub. This has been the main appeal of the PRDEZ: rapid capital accumulation, predominantly through FDI. Although the land area of PRDEZ consists only of 23.2% of Guangdong Province and only 0.4% of the entire country, it generates 80% of Guangdong's GDP and 9% of China's GDP (table 7.5). In 2002, the PRDEZ had a total GDP of RMB941.99 billion (US$113.75 billion). The most economically dominant cities in

Table 7.5 The importance of the Pearl River Delta Economic Zone (PRDEZ), Guangdong and China

	PRDEZ % of Guangdong Province	*PRDEZ % of Chinese Mainland*
Land area	23.2	0.4
Registered population (2002)	30.9	1.8
Census population (2000)	47.8	3.2
GDP (2002)	80	9
Total trade (2002)	95	33.8
Exports (2002)	94.2	34.3
Imports (2002)	95.9	33.3
FDI (2002)	88.6	22

Source: *Invest Hong Kong Website* (2004).

Table 7.6 Gross industrial output (GIO), PRDEZ, selected industries, 2002

Industry	*GIO PRDEZ* *Billion RMB*	*Billion US$*	*Value-added % of GIO*
Electronic and telecommunication equipment	410.24	49.55	21.04
Electrical equipment and machinery	147.66	17.83	25.53
Metal products	69.12	8.35	24.44
Raw chemical materials, chemical products	68.07	8.22	27.62
Transport equipment manufacturing	61.12	7.38	26.27
Electric power, steam, hot water	60.49	7.31	62.03
Plastic products	55.94	6.76	25.43
Textiles	53.30	6.44	23.55
Garments and other fiber products	52.97	6.40	24.53
Non-metal mineral products	45.56	5.50	27.50
Sub-total of top 10	**1,024.48**	**123.73**	**25.92**
Other	386.28	46.65	27.29
Total GIO for PRDEZ (*2002*)	**1,410.76**	**170.38**	**26.30**

Source: *Invest Hong Kong Website* (2004).

the PRDEZ are Shenzhen and Guangzhou. Shenzhen, in particular, had industrial output in 2001 of RMB132.14 billion, 37.3% of the output for Guangdong Province. Guangzhou, although second in the province, had industrial output of RMB61.87 billion, 17.5% of the province total (*Guangdong Statistical Yearbook* 2001, 2002; *China Statistical Yearbook* 2001, 2002).

Shenzhen itself is one of three Special Economic Zones (SEZs) in Guangdong, and one of two in the PRDEZ (the other is Zhuhai). SEZs were set up after China's economic reforms in 1979 as part of the new policy to follow a less restrictive economy. Some of the policies within SEZs include tax holidays of up to five years, the ability to repatriate corporate profits and capital investments after a contracted period, duty-free treatment of imports of raw materials and intermediate goods destined for export products, and exemption from export tariffs. In addition, the jurisdiction within the SEZ was given greater economic autonomy by China's national government (*Regulations on Special Economic Zones in Guangdong Province* 1980). In 1988, Guangdong was designated a "comprehensive economic reform area" which allowed some privatization of housing, a land-lease system, and the creation of the Shenzhen Stock Exchange. The area's distance from the political center of China (in Beijing, in the northeast) made Guangdong Province more amicable to market-oriented culture in comparison to other places in China (*Planning Frameworks of Guangzhou, Shenzhen, Zhuhai and Macau* (*Working Paper No: 3*) 2001).

The economic development of the PRDEZ took off after Shenzhen was designated as an SEZ. GDP growth rates from 1980 to 2002 averaged an astonishing 16.1% per year (*Guangdong Statistical Yearbook* 1980, 2002). If looking at 1990–2002, GDP growth rates averaged 17.4% per year (*Guangdong Statistical Yearbook* 1990, 2002). Initially, the PRDEZ was primarily a source of labor-intensive low-technology manufacturing. The region's electronic and telecommunications equipment industry has become a main source of revenue to the region. In 2002, the gross industrial output of the electronic and telecommunications equipment industry within the PRDEZ was RMB410.24 billion (US$49.55 billion). New high-technology start-ups have flourished in Guangdong, and local firms have benefited from financial support from the provincial government. In 1992, there were 1,150 private technology enterprises in Guangdong, whereas in 2001, there were 3,952. High-technology firms with regional financial backing grew from 693 in 1997 to 1,731 in 2002. Meanwhile, the number of patent applications rose by almost 600% (from a mere 1,656 in 1992 to 27,596 in 2001). Overall, the output value of high-tech products grew from RMB14.7 billion in 1992 to RMB430 billion in 2002 with exports of high technology products increasing from US$0.347 billion to US$30.9 billion (*New and Hi-Tech Industries in Pearl River Delta* (*Hong Kong Trade Development Council Website*) 2004).

De-centralization on the part of the national government, coupled with provincial initiatives, have supported the emergence of a high-technology industrial belt in the Pearl River Delta region. A number of China's nationally prominent entrepreneurs hail from Guangdong. As of 2004, Guangdong has remained number one in the country for the fourth year running in terms of its overall strength of science and technology, according to China's Ministry of Science and Technology (*Spiritual Civilization Development of Guangdong (Government's Official Website of Guangdong)* 2004).

There is no doubt that de-centralization prompted by central government reform in the 1990s has had a liberating effect on the region's firms. Other initiatives such as the *Tenth Five Year Plan (2001–2005)*, which pushed for greater focus on information technology (*China: Summary of the Tenth Five-Year Plan (2001–2005) – Information Industry (University of Hong Kong Website)* 2004) have also had an impact. The implementation of the *Five Year Plan* within Guangdong was implemented through the Guangdong Provincial Committee of the Chinese Communist Party (CPC) and the Guangdong Provincial Government.

The Pearl River Delta now has all of the basic (formal) ingredients for innovative community development. For example, by 2003 the region had more than 2,500 R&D institutions and a number of high technology industrial parks. China's national Ministry of Science and Technology (MOST) sponsors a number of these projects, including nine "Sparkle Technology Program" districts, twelve R&D ("863 Program") commercialization centers, and three software production centers (*Spiritual Civilization Development of Guangdong (Government's Official Website of Guangdong)* 2004).[14] Because of the historical prohibition by the CPC-controlled national government of any scholarship that might be critical of the regime, it is impossible to assess whether or not these programs evolved out of regional-level activities or are truly national-level initiatives.[15]

In terms of business innovation, Guangdong is the highest in China, with the number of patent applications in the business sector accounting for about 50% of the national total (*Southcn.Com Website – Pearl River Delta: The Largest Hi-Tech Industry Belt in China* 2002).

The PRDEZ has also benefited from its close proximity to Hong Kong. After the opening of China's economy, Hong Kong businesses quickly moved to invest in the region. The subsequent influx of FDI helped the PRDEZ and Guangdong Province to gain economic prominence within China (*Invest Hong Kong Website* 2004).

It was also Hong Kong's international connections that provided an incentive for other foreign investors to follow suit. Shenzhen, the PRDEZ's most prominent city, is located literally across the border from Hong Kong. In addition, border controls between the two cities have been been opened to twenty-four hours a day, allowing easy and free-flowing access for persons and goods ("24-Hour Border Crossing between Hksar, Mainland" 2003). As the PRDEZ develops more infrastructure to cater to international trade and eventually reaching a self-sustaining critical mass, Hong Kong's fate will be increasingly related to the success of the PRDEZ and the integration of the two regions (*Strategic Thoughts on Integrating the Economies of Guangdong and Hong Kong (Hong Kong Trade Development Council Website)* 2001).

If national de-centralization and political reform continues (the state of civic entrepreneurship remains to be seen), the Pearl River Delta is positioned to emerge as China's most vibrant regional innovation system. With this snapshot comparison of Kyoto, St. Louis (and BW, Germany and the Pearl River Delta, China) in mind, I return to the hypotheses posed at the beginning of this chapter.

7.11 Conclusion: hypotheses in comparative perspective

The hypotheses posed at the beginning of this chapter have only been initially tested here. Nevertheless, in reviewing the hypotheses in context of our findings, we might develop several insights about how certain regions become innovative, and stay innovative.

Hypothesis 1

Civic entrepreneurship enhances innovative outcomes at the community level.

Hypothesis 2

Broad-based coalitions of community stakeholders unified behind community-wide efforts for new product and new business creation (developmental coalitions) facilitate innovative outcomes.

Hypothesis 3

Developmental ideas (or visions) shared by (resonate with the interests of) cross-cutting groups of community stakeholders keep stakeholders "on task" in facilitating innovative activity.

Becoming an innovative region

The findings here indicate that the replicable characteristics of inter-firm networks (and their larger innovative communities) that work (deliver innovative new products that sell, generate new businesses and spin-offs) are twofold: developmental ideas facilitate civic engagement (firm and civic leaders with a larger community) and civic entrepreneurship (not entirely self-serving, civic-minded, yet strategically so, big picture, long term v. firm-specific/short term that provides an attraction for newcomers) transfers firm-level wealth and expertise to community-wide development.

Staying the course

Civic character – or perhaps "cluster culture" – determines the ability of network partners to define common goals and subsequently set up, engage in the right (strategic) interactions, and maintain these coordinating activities over time. In the early 2000s, civic entrepreneurship is far more developed in Kyoto than St. Louis (and seemingly more so in BW, Germany than in the Pearl River Delta, China). This is an interesting finding. Perhaps more importantly, can civic entrepreneurship be fostered, or is it an innate trait (latent) of only certain regions? What aspects of cluster culture make these communities innovative over time? Three features are of note: open mindedness, civic mindedness, and the distribution of risk/benefits across community stakeholders (firms, governments, workers, local residents).

Civic entrepreneurship

The relationships proposed by Hypothesis 1 (civic entrepreneurship) have been observed in Kyoto. Successful entrepreneurial mavericks such as Horiba, Murata, and Tsuji (Samco) have got together to provide seed capital to new local ventures through the Kyoto Venture Forum. In contrast, St. Louis lacks a critical mass of successful entrepreneurs from which to nurture civic minded activity by owner-managers. The prevalence of professional CEOs over traditional owner-managers in St. Louis also raises doubts about the possibility for civic entrepreneurship, at least in the short term.

Broad-based coalitions

The relationships posed in Hypothesis 2 (broad-based coalitions) and 3 (developmental visions) are observed in both regions. The work of the Plant and Life Sciences Coalition, led in part by the foresight and vision of Bill Danforth, is one example in St. Louis. In Kyoto, the work of civic entrepreneurs such as Kyocera's Inamori and ACT's Akita in nurturing younger generations of entrepreneurs (through managerial skills training, collaborative manufacturing arrangements) are evidence of these relationships.

Recent cross-national studies confirm the likelihood that these patterns may provide the basis of a new model for fostering local-level innovation. For example, the OECD in the 1990s conducted a number of cross-national case studies primarily in Finland, Ireland, Japan, and the Netherlands. These studies sought to identify patterns in national innovation systems (NIS), clusters, and regional innovation systems (RIS). One such OECD study, published in 2001, found that the most successful local communities of firms tended to learn through interaction (e.g. firms with suppliers and vendors) while capitalizing on externalities as well as dynamics within civic institutions (OECD 2001).

Another study, by Gonda and Kakizaki (2001), finds that in the most innovative Japanese regions, informal institutions (local enterprise-initiated) matter, not formal (national bureau-political initiated) in producing innovative outcomes. Gonda and Kakizaki conducted a national survey of 5,000 firms (response rate 25%, 1,230 firms) in four sectors: traditional/mature (textiles and apparel), high technology (electronics and machinery), software and services, and other manufacturing. One telling finding of the study was that "*formal* (emphasis added) research and information structure does not function as an institutional framework for knowledge and technology transfer" (Gonda and Kakizaki 2001). In fact, the weakest links supporting tacit knowledge creation and exchange were industry associations and public institutions – the usual conduits for national-level policy targeting regions.

The strongest factors in facilitating this creation and exchange were customers, suppliers, and competitors (i.e. business interactions). The authors conclude their study by noting that national (industrial zone creation) policy in Japan since the 1970s has not strengthened regional innovation through formal institutions because (national policy-created) formal institutions are suited for technology transfer (from outside Japan) of explicit knowledge and not new technology creation and the transfer of implicit knowledge (Gonda and Kakizaki 2001). Further, in the limited cases where NIS-driven policy actually works, we see that these are small, homogeneous countries (e.g. Nordic). Even in Japan, a relatively homogeneous, small island nation, national-style approaches simply do not work (see table 7.7).

Developmental ideas

Keeping stakeholders on task in pursuing innovative outcomes is a shared goal that resonates with notions of a common regional identity. This identity can hark back to the real or imagined glory days of the community. In Kyoto, people speak of protecting and preserving the area's culture (e.g. Nishijin textile) through the application of artisanal ways of doing things in everything from tea ceremonies to developments in nanotechnology. In St. Louis, stakeholders refer to how the region is transforming into a major "hub" of bio- and life sciences in the way that there was a transportation hub in centuries past.

Developmental ideas, sometimes couched in terms of the region surpassing its more powerful domestic rivals, have helped to keep community stakeholders on task in supporting the innovative potential of local firms. In Kyoto, civic entrepreneurs and like-minded civil servants in local government play on the "*Kyoto-jin*" identity and often refer back to the days when Kyoto was Japan's center of political and economic power, though nearly a millennium has passed since then.

Similar ideas circulate in St. Louis, where the region's equivalent of hereditary parliamentarians (or "old money") often mention the days before St. Louis was displaced by Chicago as the Midwest's center of economic activity. Plugging into local identities (real or imagined) help transcend existing firm, district, and even socio-economic boundaries – in pursuit of the goal of supporting the region's "life sciences community."

A new local political economy model of innovation?

A local political economy approach like that employed here in examining innovative communities across national boundaries is useful because

Table 7.7 ***National innovation systems (NIS) and regional innovation systems (RIS) compared to local district clusters***

	NIS	*RIS*	*Local district*
Spatial characteristics	National generality	Geographic specificity	Geographic specificity
Policy characteristics	National policy framework	Distance from national policy framework, use of brokers/ go-betweens	Under the thumb of national policy or neglected – no happy medium
Target/core/main firm characteristics	Large firms engaged in mass production of final (traded) products (Toyota, Sony)	SMEs engaged in specialized production of niche final (traded) products (Samco)	SMEs engaged in production of intermediate goods for local market
Success cases	Japan 1960s–1980s (or so we thought)	Kyoto, St. Louis	Omuta, 1990s, Ota 1960s–1970s
Failure cases	Japan 1990s–2000s	Cleveland	Omuta 1990s, Ota 1990s

it informs us about important local factors leading to innovative outcomes often despite or regardless of national policy. National-level policy aimed at creating innovative communities, upon closer inspection in Japan, seems to be irrelevant or even inimical to sustainable innovative community development. In Japan, national-level efforts, tending to "piggy-back" on existing local-level initiatives, only seem (from the outside) to have positive effects. In the USA, regions situated far from the levers of political power seem to display greater innovative potential over time compared to more closely situated regions.

When targeting cluster development, national governments tend to focus on creating formal institutions (government-sponsored enterprise networks, TLOs) with only a superficial understanding of firm-level needs and local conditions. Consequently, success attributed to national-level initiatives after the fact may actually be (and I would argue are likely to be) the result of locally embedded (and informal) socio-political processes. A nuanced approach, drawing from diverse informal features of the local environment (civic consciousness, networks rich or poor in social capital) is needed to understand causal relationships, if good policy is to be made in the future. St. Louis, an emerging cluster in the early 2000s, is at the crossroads between rising to the next level and falling behind more advanced regions. Examining emerging and/or struggling regions such as St. Louis in contrast to successful regions such as Kyoto may yield more powerful policy prescriptions than relying on national models.

At the same time, national governments, charged with promoting growth and sustainable development, must be responsive to local efforts. This poses yet another challenge. In Japan, for example, peak business associations (the usual conduit for national-level industrial policy targeting individual firm-level behavior) with the greatest links to government are the least tuned into business at the ground level. National governments must provide incentives for greater research, development, and manufacturing collaboration among firms – not merely slap a "national" label on existing initiatives. The question remains as to what such a bundle of policy mechanisms would look like at the national, regional, and local levels. At the very least, the progress made in Kyoto and St. Louis on these fronts provides a template for evaluating other places. The final chapter 8 assesses the potential of this new policy model in light of the findings throughout the book.

Notes

1. Daiwa Securities and a handful of elite private universities in Tokyo including Keio and Waseda have established the "Porter Prize" awarded to (large) firms that demonstrate "innovation" (http://www.porter-prize.org/index.html).
2. David Duncan, Interview July 13, 2004.
3. Susan Bragg, Interview July 13, 2004.
4. Robert Beardsley, Interview July 13, 2004.
5. Robert Calcaterra, Interview July 13, 2004.
6. William Danforth, Interview July 12, 2004.
7. Robert Calcaterra, Interview July 13, 2004.
8. Roger Beachy, Interview July 14, 2004.
9. Patricia Snyder, Interview July 13, 2004.
10. Creve Coeur is a well-to-do city situated within St. Louis County, home to Monsanto's corporate headquarters.
11. John Roberts, Interview July 12, 2004.
12. William Danforth, Interview July 12, 2004.
13. William Danforth, Interview July 12, 2004.
14. The Sparkle Technology Program's name (literally: "Sparkle Technology Program District", *xinghuo jishiu miji qu*) is based on the following proverb: "A single spark can start a prairie fire," wherein "prairie fire" signifies technological innovation. See http://www.most.gov.cn/English/Programs/Spark/menu.htm. The "863 Program" (literally: "863 Program of Technology Transfer", *baliusan jihua chengguo zhuanfa*) is named as such because that was the date of its founding: March 1986. See http://www.most.gov.cn/English/Programs/863/menu.htm.
15. Though since the mid-1990s government censorship has loosened, self-censorship remains.

8 Conclusion

8.1 The socio-political foundations of regional innovation systems

THE aim of this book has been to resolve the puzzle as to why – irrespective of national-level efforts – "clusters" of new product and new business creation persist. Ikeda Manufacturing of Ota Ward in Tokyo and Samco International of Kyoto – the entrepreneurial stories with which this book began – represent the regional variations in Japan's national innovation system (NIS), as the number of other cases throughout the book also illustrate.

Through examining entrepreneurs, firms, and the socio-political characteristics of the regions within which these enterprises are embedded, I have attempted to provide insights into the people and institutions behind the emergence and sustenance of communities of innovative firms in Japan and elsewhere. At the core of these innovative regions are civic entrepreneurs, embedded within certain informal institutional arrangements, including innovative coalitions of local stakeholders.

This book is first and foremost a firm-level case study based analysis of high technology entrepreneurial firms. As such, chapter 2 starts off by laying out the institutional barriers as well as opportunities posed by the so-called "trust-based relational contracting system," or "production pyramid" in Japan. The vertically integrated production system, visualized in the pyramid model in figures 1.1–1.4, came to dominate market interaction in Japan in the last half of the twentieth century.

The impact on business activity, at all levels, of interlocking institutional hierarchies in production, finance, licensing, and so forth are partly to blame for the lackluster performance of the Japanese economy since the early 1990s. Japan's "lost decade" is becoming its "lost generation" in the mid-2000s as the economy as a whole has been slow to come around, despite improved profits for firms such as Nissan and Toyota.[1] Measures such as low ratio of new business start-ups to closures and high unemployment reflect this weak performance.

8.2 Firms

In the face of these macro-level doldrums and national-level institutional barriers, however, a number of entrepreneurial mavericks have survived and prospered. Survival has depended on a number of strategies, including niche market specialization, balance in sales ratios, avoiding technology expropriation, joint R&D, collaborative manufacturing, and tapping into international connections and social networks. Successful use of these strategies has depended in part on entrepreneur (business acumen, political savvy), firm, and regional-level characteristics.

Looking at these strategies alone, one may wonder what distinguishes the experiences of these firms from successful entrepreneurs elsewhere in Japan and the world. In Japan, at least, cross-regional variations in performance cannot be explained by entrepreneur and firm-level characteristics alone. Certain socio-political features of regions such as Kyoto seem to foster performance at the firm level that has outpaced domestic and regional rivals, even after the collapse of the "economic bubble" in Japan. Another way of describing this process is to say that Kyoto has certain synergies between people and institutions that are absent, or weaker, in other regions of this study.

8.3 Regions

Certain synergies between people and institutions emerge from the analyses of firms and regions in chapter 2: Ota in Tokyo, Higashi Osaka, and Kyoto. The picture that emerges from examining the case studies in chapter 2 is one of regional variation in the nature of regional innovative systems. Ota, located closest to the centers of bureaucratic, political, and financial power in Japan, has been under the watchful eye of the central state while at the same time being subject to abuses within the keiretsu-dominated production pyramid. In exclusive relational subcontracting arrangements, suppliers and small firms suffer from the impact of chronic late payments, JIT abuses, and unilateral cost-down measures on the part of their keiretsu buyers. The latter have used their monopsony leverage over captive suppliers – literally squeezing them out of existence in the 1990s as Japan's industrial monoliths struggled to export the costs of excess onto lower tiers of the pyramid and overseas, mainly to China.

Higashi Osaka is a middle case, located far from the bureau–political orbit of Tokyo, but close to Kansai's own keiretsu in Osaka as well as the regional offices of METI and other ministries. Higashi Osaka producers, like Osaka firms in general, have excelled in trading relations with other firms internationally, especially throughout Asia. These international inter-firm relations have helped to shield local firms from the worst abuses of the pyramid system. At the same time, technology levels among firms in the area lag behind their competition to the north in Kyoto.

8.4 Innovation theory

Chapter 3 re-evaluated theories of innovation *vis-à-vis* Japan in the light of firm- and region-level practice. I found that much of the literature comparing the Japanese economy to other advanced industrialized countries has been based on faulty empiricism, and led to misperceptions of how innovation has been – and should be – fostered in Japan.

Misperceptions have led to misunderstanding the historical sources of innovation in Japan. First, the so-called "trust-based exclusive relational contracting" is shown to be a farce. The reality of inter-firm relations within the Japanese production pyramid is that big firms, situated on top, depending on the tacit support (and administrative guidance) of the central state in their assimilation of smaller producers into production hierarchies, have benefited from cost-down, imposition of JIT production and the like. These measures allowed big producers to export the costs of excess (e.g. lifetime employment really existed only for 1% of firms and 25% of workers at the apex of the production pyramid) in the 1970s and 1980s onto their captive suppliers.

The collapse of the system in the 1990s from the weight of its excesses had two impacts on the SMEs that comprised the base of the pyramid. Those suppliers and subcontractors too naïve or weak to avoid exclusive subcontracting went under, while domestic competitors who by design or fiat avoided becoming assimilated into the production pyramid emerged as hyper-innovators.

In sum, explanations based on assumptions of "flexible production" and "flexible specialization" underestimated the innovative capacity of smaller producers, while overestimating the positive role of large assemblers. In standard explanations, smaller producers were nimble in response to the lead of their main (keiretsu buyers) and were content to remain at lower tiers of the pyramid in exchange for guarantees of long-term contracts. Nothing could be further from the truth, as the historical review in chapter 3 and the findings in subsequent chapters confirm. Unfortunately, much of the literature that has compared Japan's national system of innovation to other advanced industrial economies has relied only on the translated works (and public relations materials) centered on big firms and elite ministries in and around Tokyo.

8.5 National Cluster policy

The success of Kyoto notwithstanding, national-level bureaucrats have responded to Japan's economic downturn with a number of policy initiatives. After several fits and starts in the 1990s, METI emerged in the early 2000s with its biggest bet yet: the Cluster Plan. Japan's quest for entrepreneurialism has been a national coordinated effort, at least at the top levels of the central bureaucracy. Seeming to channel the widely popular (in elite circles) Harvard Business School/Michael Porter model, the national METI (and MEXT) initially selected nineteen regions for cluster development. Never-mind that the top-performing regions (clusters) owed their success to long-standing local, organic processes and enterprise-initiated policy.

With much gusto, METI went about implementing a number of Porter-style policy prescriptions, popularized in the scholar/consultant's "diamond model" (of factor, support, and demand conditions) of cluster development. Unfortunately, key elements of the model seem to have been lost in translation. What has been lost are social and cultural factors that reside at the core of Porter's diamond (albeit briefly explained in Porter's own analysis). Inherently *informal* institutional arrangements form the basis of the socio-economy of regions. The informal institutions supporting regional development are what matter in producing innovation in new products and new business creation.

Japan's national bureaucrats have, however, chosen to focus, despite the warnings of METI's own commissioned research in the 1990s, on the formal institutions of clusters. Formal institutions include technology licensing organizations (TLOs) and other state-sponsored "network" links, particularly between universities and firms.

Scratching the surface of national descriptions of the top clusters that METI touts in its Cluster Plan – Hokkaido's Bio, Tama's manufacturing, and Kinki – belies national claims of having facilitated cluster development. Even a superficial examination of the historical–institutional processes behind the emergence of these clusters exposes the organic and fundamentally *informal* origins of existing inter-firm and university–private sector initiatives. The role of civic entrepreneurs – enterprise mavericks with a keen sense of giving back firm-level wealth to the wider community for mutual long-term gain – is evident. These leaders have managed to harness local stores of social capital (reciprocal relations) in nurturing new business and new product ideas across broad groups of local stakeholders. How these socio-political relationships relate to innovation is analyzed in detail at the network, regional, and comparative levels in chapters 5–7.

8.6 Networks

Firms that have managed to de-link from Japan's hierarchies – or have been fortunate by happenstance or effort to avoid them altogether – have been better able at engaging in horizontal networking with other firms in Japan and internationally. The kinds of national policies aimed at establishing formal inter-firm relations are inimical to the development of truly innovative networks. Innovative success is measured, for example, by the increase in sales from often jointly developed new products. In fact, the networks with the fewest historical links to the central state have been the most adept at promoting innovation and growth at the firm level.

Regional location itself, at least until the 1990s, has not been a determining factor behind the ability of firms to access or form networks. Nevertheless, Kyoto networks, though fewer in number than in Higashi Osaka or Ota, produce more tangible firm-level results in the development of new products and increasing member-firm sales. One explanation for this incongruence in number of networks v. output is that the "network" label is often pasted on groups of firms by the national ministries and local governments trying to be responsive to national calls, whether or not they actually have any internal congruence or are even linked at all. Since the 1990s, as other regions continue to falter and massive numbers of SMEs continue to go under, Kyoto has emerged as the most resilient of Japan's manufacturing regions.

The findings in chapters 2 and 3 illustrate how laudatory descriptions over the years of "trusting" relations in Japan have always cloaked the existence of pernicious power asymmetries from the perspective of firms situated at the base of the production pyramid. These firms are the foundation of the Japanese economy, supporting 75% of employment and representing 99% of firms.

The extent that regional location makes a difference, particularly since the 1990s, is explored in chapter 5 in examining representative networks in Ota, Higashi Osaka, and Kyoto. The small manufacturers in Ota Ward owe their very existence to the post-war central state-dictated (and US-backed) industrial build-up. Even before the war, the area was under the close view of the central state and related control associations (*toseikai*). As a result, the kinds of inter-firm networks that have existed in Ota are a microcosm of the Japanese production pyramid. Large assemblers reside at the top and smaller producers have been assimilated below.

An outspoken critic of these practices and champion of small manufacturers, Tomohiro Koseki, observed how firms were discouraged, even forbidden, to forge horizontal ties, lest these efforts undermine the smooth functioning of keiretsu-dominated production (and incremental innovations of Western technologies in automobiles and electronics).

In Ota, "networks" sponsored by local government and backed by METI and keiretsu giants such as Fujitsu have created O-net. Typical of central-state-driven initiatives, O-net has been big on form and small in substance. Many firms report that they were "informed" by local government, never asked, that they would be included in O-net. Though the local government can report to METI bureaucrats that Ota firms are "networked," member firms report that scant, if any, new business has come out of these efforts.

Some Ota firms abandoned by keiretsu producers – as the latter move offshore in pursuit of lower labor costs – have forged survival networks. In these efforts, firms have tried to foster ties with other SMEs inside and-outside of Ota. This has amounted to too little, too late. Innovative firms that managed to break free of the pyramid before the 1990s downturn hit had little sympathy for local firms who were too naïve to do the same before the pyramid collapsed under its own weight. In sum, the future of Ota as a manufacturing center seems bleak, as its strongest firms continue to leave the region.

Higashi Osaka is a middle case, whose broader Osaka region includes keiretsu giants such as Matsushita. Local SMEs have shown themselves to be very adept at making (at least) trading connections outside of the region and Japan. This has helped to insulate local manufacturers somewhat from the underside of the production pyramid (e.g. monopsony leverage) as well as helped local firms bounce back after their sales to keiretsu giants were destroyed in the 1990s.

A number of smaller networks, facilitated by both the local government and the regional Chamber of Commerce, have had some success in fostering new product development. The region suffers from the same top-down style of local government-led network creation as in Tokyo. A number of firms report that they – like their counterparts in Ota – were informed by the local government that they would be included in local champion networks such as TOPS. Enterprise-initiated networks in Higashi Osaka, such as Gyatech, have fared better, although on a smaller scale.

Kyoto, the least linked to either keiretsu production hierarchies or central state overview, has produced world-class high technology firms and spawned enterprise-initiated inter-firm networks, with a civic flair. Kiseiren (or KSR) is one example. Formed in 1982 on the initiative of a local machinery maker, KSR has brought entrepreneurial start-ups together for over three decades to enhance member technology management and marketing skills. From the beginning, KSR leaders wanted to avoid any semblance of the hierarchies ever-present in the larger Japanese economy. With this in mind, KSR instituted a mandatory "graduation" age of forty-five for individual owner-manager members. Graduated members have instead been encouraged to serve the network informally, for example, as consultant/advisors to newcomer firms.

Several spin-off networks have come out of KSR since the 1990s. The track record of KSR in facilitating new product creation and increasing sales of member firms has attracted the attention of Japanese scholars and policymakers alike, as Japan searches for solutions to its problem economy in the 2000s.

How should we reconcile chapter 5, which starts out by saying that regional location itself has – until now – not mattered as much to individual firms? At least until the economic collapse of the 1990s, de-linking from the production pyramid is what appeared to matter most. The findings in chapter 5 demonstrate that regions are varied in the kinds of informal and formal institutions that either support or undermine innovative activity community-wide. While a hyper-innovative firm may do well regardless of regional locale (as have some survivors in Ota), those just starting out or encountering a few stumbling blocks – that is, most new start-ups – are a different matter. As the Ota region as a manufacturing center continues to crumble, the impact on individual firms that choose to stay or are otherwise unable to leave means that regional location is taking on even greater importance.

Characteristics of the Kyoto region – respect for fierce independence, the abundance of networks rich in social capital – have combined to produce more entrepreneurial mavericks that survive the test of time than in other regions. In post-war Kyoto these mavericks were least likely to fall for keiretsu promises for fair treatment in exclusive contracting arrangements.

Kyoto emerged in the early 2000s as a region that seems to have the right alchemy between informal (civic entrepreneurship, social capital) and formal (research universities, transportation infrastructure) institutions from which numerous entrepreneurial maverick-led firms have emerged. So much so, that the area's success is now attributed to the so-called "Kyoto Model" of innovation, entrepreneurship, and technology management. What remains constant between successful regions and unsuccessful regions (which might contain individual survivors) is enterprise-initiated strategies that can count on local stores of social capital for maintaining momentum in translating vision (developmental ideas) into practice (innovative outcomes at the firm level) over the long term.

This means that local and regional governments charged with generating local development policies must identify local champions to act as civic entrepreneurs – if such persons have not self-selected already. Struggling regions must also prepare sober blueprints for the future, based on realistic reflection on regional resources and potential. Not every region can jump on to the high-tech bandwagon.

Chapter 6 showed how leaders in St. Louis, in the American Midwest, took a measured approach to sizing up the region in the 1990s. Community leaders commissioned in-depth analyses of the state of local industry by outsiders without any personal stake in the outcome. From this basis, the region's leaders, in constant communication with key community stakeholders in big and small business alike, were able to chart a course for the nurturing of its emerging bio-tech and life sciences community.

8.7 Comparative lessons

While this book is on the one hand a case study analysis of entrepreneurs, it also addresses the critical role for local and regional governments in responding to enterprise-initiated developmental activities. Involvement of the national government in more than a resource-supporting role may be the kiss of death for local initiatives, as the story of Tama's cluster foreshadows.

Meanwhile, patterns that might transcend national boundaries, certain interactions between formal and informal institutions, are observed in both Kyoto and St. Louis, two regions embedded in quite different national contexts. These regions are rising stars of innovation and competitiveness, measured by rising product sales and new start-ups in growth sectors. At the same time, Kyoto is further along the path to self-sustaining innovative community than St. Louis.

The socio-politics of how these regions produced numerous innovative firms shows the potential of a locally nuanced approach to analyzing regional variations within national innovation systems. For example, examining the success (and failure) of other regions in this light might provide a blueprint for struggling regions to meet the challenges of technology management and frontier innovation. The analytical model presented in chapter 7 brings to the fore the role of individual entrepreneurs in a pseudo-governing capacity in guiding informal resources into start-up firms and network-based R&D and collaborative manufacturing.

The track record of these regions, contrasted with cases in Germany and China, in producing new products and new business is evidence of the growing significance of a locally nuanced approach to studying political economy, development policy, and the creation of innovative communities that can adapt and triumph in the long haul.

Note

1. Toyota's improvement in profits seems to come at the cost of employee morale. See Satoshi (2004).

Appendix 1 Methodology

Measuring innovation at the firm level

Innovation is measured by a composite set of data drawn from patents and R&D figures. Firms were ranked according to their innovative score, which is based upon patents (number and value-added level), value-added level of products and production, and the state of R&D operations. No measure of innovation is problem-free. For example, R&D and patent figures are measures of innovative *capacity* (a firm's ability to create innovative products). Innovative *output* (the successful sale of such products) is measured based on sales resulting from the development of new products. Not all patented products result in significant (or any) sales and subsequently profit for firms (OECD 1997).[1] Firms also reported whether or not they were currently engaged in new product R&D and the state of these operations. The overall innovative score was lowered if the firm was struggling with any of the following: engaging in new product R&D, obtaining new clients, and/or problems obtaining skilled workers for the purpose of new product R&D. The extent of linkage to the production pyramid is measured by factors including keiretsu link: "KL" (stock, capital relationship), keiretsu relation "KR" (employee and/or technology transfers, frequency and nature of interactions, *amakudari* link), and sources of R&D funds (government, private financial institution, in-house).

Data gathering technique

I conducted survey and interview-based case studies of forty-three SMEs in three industrial areas: Tokyo's Ota Ward, the southern technology corridor of Kyoto, and Higashi Osaka.[2] I was able to interview the presidents and technology managers of twenty-two high technology manufacturing SMEs in Tokyo's Ota Ward and of twenty-one firms in Kansai (twelve in Kyoto's southern corridor and nine in Higashi Osaka).[3] In these regions, I also interviewed a variety of local, regional, and central government (e.g. METI) officials; directors and managers of private and semi-public research institutes (e.g. the SME Finance Corporation); and directors of technology parks and industrial promotion centers (e.g. Kanagawa Science Park, Kyoto Research Park, and Gakkentoshi). I also interviewed a number of leading Japanese experts on SME (including Toshio Aida, Hisayoshi Hashimoto, Tomohiro Koseki, and Hirofumi Ueda) to gauge their opinions of my interpretations of the role and position of SMEs in the Japanese political economy.[4] In addition, I obtained survey data on SMEs across industries that seem to indicate that the patterns and trends I identified in high technology manufacturing reflect the overall situation of SMEs in Japan.

Also interviewed were two leading national organizations supporting SMEs: the Chamber of Commerce and the Association of Small and Medium Sized Enterprise Entrepreneurs. I interviewed local-, regional-, and national-level leaders of these organizations. In addition, I obtained survey data on SMEs across industries that indicate that the patterns and trends I have identified in high technology manufacturing reflect the overall situation of SMEs in Japan. The primary method of data collection is a survey-based interview/case study format. Enterprises in Ota Ward, Higashi Osaka, and Kyoto's southern corridor are the central focus of this study. These areas were chosen because the regions of Kanto and Kansai have historically had high concentrations of electrical machinery/computer components (high technology) producers. At the same time, regional variations in the form and function of relations with the state provide the basis for interesting comparisons.

The interview format is based on a survey that I developed that, among other issues, is aimed at assessing the success of government-enacted policies targeting SMEs and evaluating the nature and impact of SME links with the state via various intermediating hierarchies. Briefly, the survey was divided into five questionnaires: production structure, local business networks, locality of innovation, aspects of political economy, and government policies (see the section on Format and content of interview questions). I also created a separate, shorter questionnaire used for material gathering (of other survey results, private research, etc.).

Case selection

To minimize bias in case selection, potential cases were identified randomly. That is, rather than relying on personal introductions (leading to a "snowball" approach to data collection) firms were selected randomly from comprehensive public industry directories (phone books) and subsequently contacted directly via a pro forma letter. Two aspects of this interview process are worth noting. First, the nature of competition in high technology industries, relative to other sectors, places pressure on firms to maintain cutting-edge technologies. That is, we expect to find more innovative leaders than innovative failures, as the latter would have a tendency to go out of business. In fact, innovative leadership can be said to be a prerequisite for survival in high technology industry. Second, when making the initial contacts with target firms, those turning out to be technological leaders were eager to be interviewed, while less innovative firms (as well as those who were found to be highly keiretsified) were often reluctant. While no meetings were obtained with bankrupt firms in 1998, a reasonable balance among all other levels of firm (within SMEs in high technology manufacturing) has been maintained. However, several phone interviews were obtained with bankrupt firms (bankrupted 1997–8). Several firms in the sample went under during the course of this research. Follow-up interviews were obtained with all but one of these bankrupt firms (Table A1.1).

Criteria for selecting firms so that they might serve as the basis for comparative study (across regions/countries) were as follows:

(1) Firm size: 10–300 employees
(2) High technology product base – e.g. computer (IC, semiconductor, etc.) components, electrical machinery and associated precision inspection devices, fiber optic technology, etc. (as the highest levels of innovation and growth should be found in these firms relative to mature/declining sectors)[5]
(3) Capitalization: ¥30 million –¥100 million[6]
(4) Mix of stockholding and privately held firms (with the expectation of finding variation in their dealings with the state)
(5) Mix of exclusive subcontractors and firms with a diversified customer base (in order to assess the variations in the impact of the keiretsu link)
(6) Firms with long histories (allowing for assessment over several decades or more) and more recent start-ups

Table A 1.1 Overview of cases

Innovative position[a]	*Locale*	*Firm*	*Decade Est.*	*# of Empl*	*Industry*	*Keiretsu link*[b]	*Keiretsu relation*[c]	*%Sales top*	*%Sales top 3*	*R&D*
1 Leader	Hosaka	U	1960	> 20	General machinery	Moderate	High[d]	80	100	Y
2 Leader	Hosaka	V	1940	> 80	General machinery	None	None	40	55	Y
3 Leader	Kyoto	DD	1940	> 10	Electrical machinery	High	High[d]	70	Varies	Y
4 Leader	Kyoto	B	1960	> 20	General machinery	None	None	30	75	Y
5 Leader	Kyoto	O	1960	> 70	General machinery	Moderate	High	50	65	Y
6 Leader	Kyoto	F	1950	> 40	General machinery	None	None	20	Varies	Y
7 Leader	Kyoto	Z	1970	> 70	Electrical machinery	None	None	10	Varies	Y
8 Leader	Ota	FF	1970	> 30	Electronics	None	None	20	30	Y
9 Leader	Ota	G	1950	> 10	General machinery	None	None	20	Varies	Y
10 Leader	Ota	D	1930	> 150	General machinery	None	None	Varies	Varies	Y
11 Leader	Ota	H	1950	> 80	Electronics	None	None	30	Varies	Y
12 Leader	Ota	BB	1970	> 40	General machinery	None	None	25	Varies	Y
13 Leader	Ota	P	1950	> 40	Electrical machinery	Moderate	Moderate	43	Varies	Y
14 Leader	Ota	PP	1970	> 30	Electronics	None	None	Varies	40	Y
15 Leader	Ota	HH	1930	> 170	Electronics	None	None	10	Varies	Y
16 Moderate	Hosaka	GG	1970	> 30	Electrical machinery	Moderate	High	38	60	Y
17 Moderate	Hosaka	KK	1930	> 150	Metallic	None	None	1.5	3	Y
18 Moderate	Hosaka	T	1950	> 40	General machinery	Moderate	None	55	Varies	N
19 Moderate	Hosaka	AA	1960	> 220	General machinery	Moderate	None	80	Varies	Y
20 Moderate	Kyoto	QQ	1940	> 50	Engineering design	None	None	10	Varies	N

Table A 1.1 *(cont.)*

Innovative position[a]	*Locale*	*Firm*	*Decade Est.*	*# of Empl*	*Industry*	*Keiretsu link*[b]	*Keiretsu relation*[c]	*%Sales top*	*%Sales top 3*	*R&D*
21 Moderate	Kyoto	M	1950	> 50	Metallic (plating technology)	None	None	25	Varies	Y
22 Moderate	Kyoto	EE	1950	> 10	General machinery	None	None	30	Varies	N
23 Moderate	Kyoto	K	1960	> 10	Precision machinery	None	None	40	85	N
24 Moderate	Ota	N	1930	> 10	General machinery	None	None	50	Varies	N
25 Moderate	Ota	LL	1940	> 20	Electronics	None	None	10	30	Y
26 Moderate	Ota	Y	1970	> 05	Electrical machinery	Moderate	Moderate	33	66	Y
27 Moderate	Ota	CC	1980	> 20	Electronics	None	None	10	Varies	Y
28 Moderate	Ota	A	1960	> 10	Electronics	Moderate	Moderate	80	Varies	Y
29 Moderate	Ota	J	1980	> 10	Electronics	None	None	50	Varies	Y
30 Moderate	Ota	S	1950	> 60	Electrical machinery	High	High	Varies	varies	Y
31 Mixed	Hosaka	I	1960	> 20	Metallic	None	None	12	30	Y
32 Mixed	Hosaka	W	1980	> 30	Electrical machinery	Moderate	Moderate	10	25	Y
33 Mixed	Hosaka	II	1970	> 120	General machinery	None	None	11	25	Y
34 Mixed	Kyoto	OO	1980	> 10	Precision machinery	None	High	Varies	25	Y
35 Mixed	Kyoto	X	1950	> 10	Engineering design	Moderate	Moderate	28	varies	N
36 Mixed	Ota	L	1980	> 05	Electronics	None	None	30	Varies	N
37 Mixed	Ota	R	1950	> 110	Electrical machinery	High	Moderate	30	60	Y
38 Mixed	Ota	Q	1970	> 200	Machinery	High	High	30	Varies	Y

Innovative position[a]	*Locale*	*Firm*	*Decade Est.*	*# of Empl*	*Industry*	*Keiretsu link*[b]	*Keiretsu relation*[c]	*%Sales top*	*%Sales top 3*	*R&D*
39 Mixed	Ota	C	1960	>40	Electronics	High	Moderate	10	65	Y
40 Failure	Kyoto	NN	1960	>05	Metallic	High	None	35	70	N
41 Failure	Kyoto	MM	1960	>20	Precision machinery	High	None	30	90	N
42 Failure	Ota	E	1970	>05	Electronics	High	None	Varies	Varies	N
43 Failure	Ota	JJ	1960	>05	Electronics	High	High	20	Varies	N

Notes:

[a] A firm's innovative position was determined based on its innovative score, which comprised R&D and patent data.

[b] Keiretsu link (KL): (Structural link with keiretsu group through sales, as subcontractor, subsidiary, "parent–child" relation) **none** (no link), **moderate** (one link), **high** (more than one link).

[c] Keiretsu relation (KR): (Accept keiretsu employees, capital, technology transfers, stocks, mutual employee transfers) **none** (no relation), **moderate** (engage in one "parent–child" activity), **high** (engage in more than one "parent–child" activity).

[d] In the two cases of high keiretsu relation, one firm had grown larger than its "parent" while the other possessed a large number of patented proprietary technologies prior to entering into a relationship with its "parent."

Y = Yes.

N = No.

Format and content of interview questions

Questions in the research survey are aimed at assessing the relationship between the *output* of new product innovation and various *inputs*, which include the following:

- Availability and access to capital
- Sources of technological "know how" and creative ideas (attracting skilled employees, technological exchange)
- Degree of exclusive keiretsu (vertically integrated production) ties, parent–child subcontractor links (measured in terms of percentage of stock held by particular client(s), percentage of sales to an exclusive buyer, and so forth)
- Degree of utilization of local business networks, local and central government-sponsored organizations and associations
- Barriers to doing business/investing in new product R&D.

Questions aim to assess the following: What correlations and causal patterns can be identified between various inputs and new product innovation? That is, what factors affect the success of new product innovation and to what degree? What interactions occur among factors?

The interview questionnaire is divided into five sections:

- *Production structure* (of firm) – including assessment of state of new product R&D
- *Local business networks* – how are they utilized, if at all
- *Innovation* – where it occurs, and how
- *Political economy* – opinions on how structure of political economy affects business, and how each firm is positioned structurally *vis-à-vis* the firms and institutions around it
- *Government policies* – utility of government policies and SME institutions over time, access to government policy via what channels.

Notes

1. See the *Frascati* and *Oslo Manuals* for other indicators of innovative activity at the firm level (OECD 1994, 1997).
2. See the section on Case selection for a discussion of selection criteria.
3. Pseudonyms (i.e. "A," "B") are used when referring to some firms and interviewees in the interest of maintaining confidentiality.
4. Including firm representatives, a total of some 200 interviewees participated, not counting multiple interviews with a single source.

5. This definition corresponds to standard OECD classifications of high technology industries. (See OECD 2000).
6. In 1999, the definition of "SME" in Japan was changed to include enterprises with a capitalization of up to ¥300 million. (See SME White Paper 1999) Further, the capitalization of several firms in the sample rose above ¥300 million during the course of the eight-year study.

Appendix 2
Global scope of entrepreneurial activity: top fifteen countries, by number of persons involved in start-ups, 2003

Table A2.1 Global scope of entrepreneurial activity, top fifteen countries, by number of persons involved in start-ups, 2003

Country	Total population: 2003	Total population: 18–64 years old	TEA[a] rate (average 2002–3)	Number of persons involved in start-ups	Number of start-ups	Number of owner-managers of existing firms	Number of existing firms	Number of owner-managers of entrepreneurial firms	Number of entrepreneurial firms
India*	1,049,100,118	598,149,636	17.9	106,930,898	85,380,114	133,730,500	122,102,850	10,047,929	7,972,283
China	1,286,975,468	828,234,620	12.0	99,498,849	56,324,692	202,448,324	141,500,776	28,151,823	19,088,484
USA	290,342,554	181,340,397	11.3	20,502,795	11,067,154	25,864,251	15,026,142	4,987,114	2,436,506
Brazil	182,032,604	111,914,745	13.2	14,782,485	8,590,518	22,023,678	14,321,251	2,222,620	1,308,995
Thailand*	64,265,276	41,142,139	18.9	7,774,876	4,981,277	10,100,884	7,508,979	863,274	413,665
Mexico*	104,907,991	58,634,254	12.4	7,270,079	3,905,636	8,697,117	4,694,624	1,450,761	880,485
Korea*	48,289,037	32,536,775	14.5	4,723,376	2,803,791	7,474,430	5,270,977	1,887,621	1,145,579
Venezuela**	24,654,694	14,338,222	27.3	3,916,163	2,004,250	3,085,137	1,756,080	529,010	311,164
Argentina	38,740,807	22,559,921	17.0	3,827,242	1,991,912	4,791,409	3,144,703	430,820	200,961
Uganda**	25,632,794	10,265,560	29.3	3,003,249	1,718,336	3,549,160	2,351,125	543,320	353,646
Germany	82,398,326	52,646,370	5.2	2,726,907	1,422,563	5,281,607	3,321,691	515,434	304,619
Russia	144,526,278	94,359,896	2.5	2,381,785	1,160,536	3,674,074	1,973,337	174,746	56,161
UK	60,094,648	37,375,347	6.0	2,224,850	1,273,217	4,579,446	2,858,523	727,015	365,376
Japan	127,214,499	81,024,667	2.3	1,836,561	903,858	8,733,699	5,226,273	624,450	464,364
Canada	32,207,113	20,813,726	8.5	1,767,870	931,420	2,642,554	1,481,184	474,904	217,069
Italy	57,998,353	37,263,355	4.6	1,703,261	890,021	3,445,284	1,612,528	383,254	181,912
Spain	40,217,413	26,006,061	6.3	1,646,618	851,139	2,675,659	1,467,425	278,066	131,972
Chile	15,665,216	9,536,646	16.3	1,550,864	732,190	1,501,728	842,345	617,789	319,105

Table A2.1 (cont.)

Country	Total population: 2003	Total population: 18–64 years old	TEA[a] rate (average 2002–3)	Number of persons involved in start-ups	Number of start-ups	Number of owner-managers of existing firms	Number of existing firms	Number of owner-managers of entreprene-urial firms	Number of entreprene-urial firms
South Africa	42,768,678	24,982,327	5.7	1,419,260	864,352	1,152,937	786,768	62,507	35,088
Australia	19,731,984	12,408,149	9.9	1,227,096	726,541	2,251,137	1,338,836	307,980	160,116

[a] Total Entrepreneural Activity (TEA) rate = Number of adults out of every 100 adults that were involved in operating or starting a business less than 3.5 years old.

Source: Global Entrepreneurship Monitor: 2003 Executive Report, http://www.gemconsortium.org/download/1082665152656/FINALExecutiveReport.pdf.

*2002 data.

**2003 data.

All other data averaged for 2002–3.

Appendix 3
Management strategies of semi-Kyoto Model firms

Horiba

Core Technological Competence

R&D Focus

Niche Specialization

Financial Independence and Autonomy

Overseas Market Targeting

Openness

A3.1. Management strategies of Semi-Kyoto Model firms: Horiba

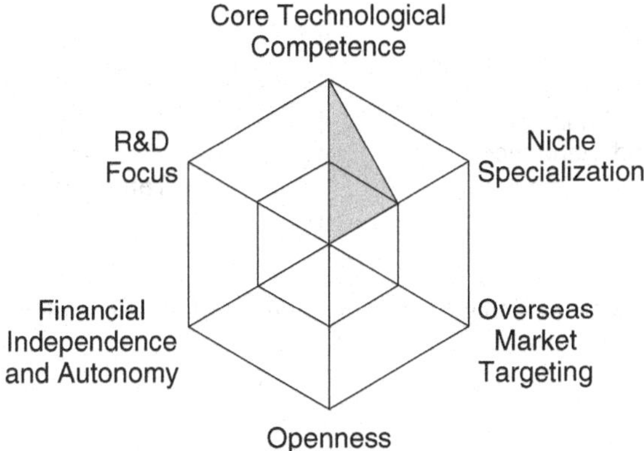

A3.2. Management strategies of Semi-Kyoto Model firms: Japan Battery Storage

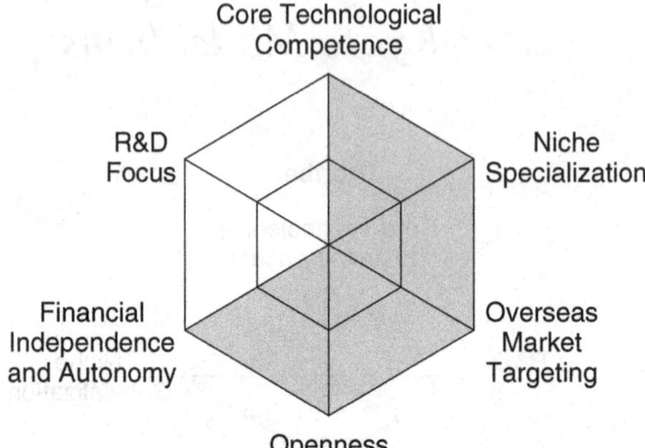

A3.3. Management strategies of Semi-Kyoto Model firms: Nichicon

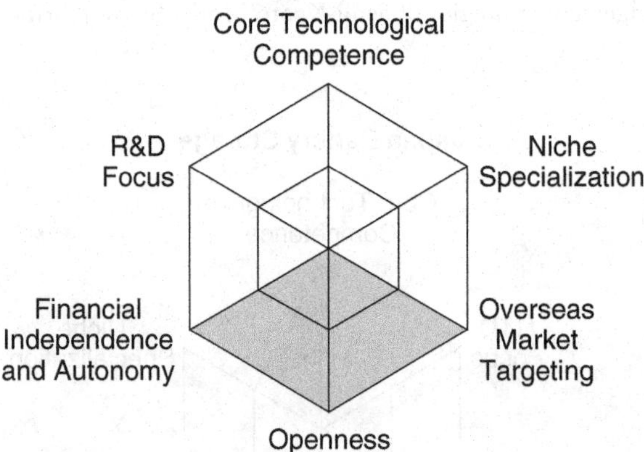

A3.4. Management strategies of Semi-Kyoto Model firms: Nintendo

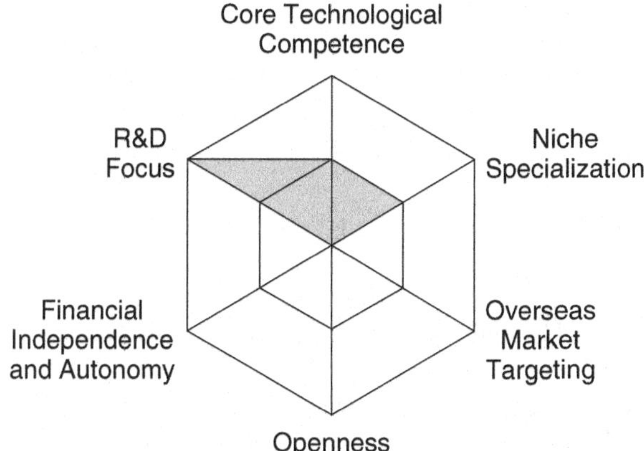

A3.5. Management strategies of Semi-Kyoto Model firms: Shimadzu

References

"24-Hour Border Crossing between Hksar, Mainland," *People's Daily*, January 27

Abdul-Nour, Georges, Jocelyn Drolet, and Serge Lambert (1999). "Mixed Production, Flexibility and SME," *Computers and Industrial Engineering* 37: 429–32

Aida, Toshio (undated). "Small and Medium Sized Companies Problem in Japan," Paper prepared for Japan Cooperation Center for Petroleum Industry Development

Amsden, Alice H. (1989). *Asia's Next Giant: South Korea and Late Industrialization*, New York: Oxford University Press

(1992). *Asia's Next Giant: South Korea and Late Industrialization*, New York: Oxford University Press

Aoki, Masahiko and Nathan Rosenberg (1989). "The Japanese Firm as an Innovating Institution," in Shiraishi Takahashi (ed.), *Economic Institutions in a Dynamic Society: Search for a New Frontier*, New York: St. Martin's Press

Ayuzawa, Takeshi (1995). "Netowaakuka O Tsujita Kei Ei Kaku Shin" (Management Innovation through Networks), *Asakigin Soken Repooto (Asahi Bank Research Institute Report)* 12

Battelle Technology Partnership Practice (2003). "Positioning St. Louis in Advanced Manufacturing Clusters," St. Louis Regional Commerce and Growth Association

Berger, Suzanne and Ronald Philip Dore (1996). *National Diversity and Global Capitalism: Cornell Studies in Political Economy*, Ithaca, NY: Cornell University Press

Bergman, Edward M. and Edward J. Feser (1999). *Industrial and Regional Clusters: Concepts and Comparative Applications*, Regional Research Institute, West Virginia University, Morganstown, WV; available from http://www.rri.wvu.edu/WebBook/Bergman-Feser/contents.htm

Best, Michael (1990). *The New Competition: Institutions of Industrial Restructuring*, Cambridge: Polity Press

Biobelt Website (2004). Available from http://www.biobelt.org

Broad, William J. (2004). "US Is Losing Its Dominance in the Sciences," *The New York Times*, May 3

Burt, Ronald S. (1992). *Structural Holes: The Social Structure of Competition*, Cambridge, MA: Harvard University Press

Callon, Scott (1994). "Unleashing Japan's Venture Business Sector: Problems and Policies for Reform," JDB Discussion Paper Series, Research Institute of Capital Formation, Tokyo: The Japan Development Bank

Chiiki Keizai Repoto (Regional Economic Report) (2001). Tokyo: *Naikakufu Seisaku Tokatsu Kan*

China Statistical Yearbook (2002). Beijing: State Statistical Bureau

(2001). Beijing: State Statistical Bureau

China: Summary of the Tenth Five-Year Plan (2001–2005) – Information Industry (2004). (University of Hong Kong Website) (PDF file), cited November 24; available from http://www.trp.hku.hk/infofile/china/2002/10–5-yr-plan.pdf

Chu, Roderick (1999). "We Have Met the Enemy. And They Is Us," Paper presented at the Cleveland's Path to Regional Economic Advantage: New Findings, Lessons Learned and Some Suggested Strategies, Cleveland, OH: Case Western Research University, January 19

Chushokigyosogokenkyukiko (1995). "*Kigyo Kakushin No Tame No Chushokigyo No Kigyokan Nettowaaku Ni Kan Suru Kenkyu*" (Research on Inter-Firm Networks for the Purpose of Firm-Level Innovation), Japan Small and Medium Sized Enterprise Research Institute: 33–52

Cooke, Philip and Kevin Morgan (1994). "The Regional Innovation System in Baden-Württemberg," *International Journal of Technology Management* 9(3&4): 394–429

Culpepper, Pepper D. (2001). "Employers, Public Policy, and the Politics of Decentralized Cooperation in Germany and France," in Peter A. Hall and David Soskice (eds.), *Varieties of Capitalism: The Institutional Foundations of Comparative Advantage*, Oxford: Oxford University Press

DeBresson, Chris and Fernand Amesse (1991). "Networks of Innovators: A Review and Introduction to the Issue," *Research Policy* 20(5): 363–79

Doane, D. L. (1998). *Cooperation, Technology, and Japanese Development: Indigenous Knowledge, the Power of Networks, and the State*, Boulder, Co: Westview Press

Dore, Ronald (1986). *Flexible Rigidities: Industrial Policy and Structural Adjustment in the Japanese Economy, 1970–80*, Stanford: Stanford University Press

(1987). *Taking Japan Seriously: A Confucian Perspective on Leading Economic Issues*, Stanford: Stanford University Press

(2000). *Stock Market Capitalism: Welfare Capitalism, Japan and Germany versus the Anglo-Saxons*, Oxford: Oxford University Press
(2004). "Innovation for Whom?," *ITEC Research Paper Series*, Kyoto: Doshisha University
Drucker, Peter (1954/1996). The Practice of Management *Gendai no Keiei*, Tokyo: Diamond Publishing
(1993). *Innovation and Entrepreneurship*, New York: Harper Business
Edgington, David W. (1999). "Firms, Governments and Innovation in the Chukyo Region of Japan," *Urban Studies* 36(2): 305–99
Fields, Karl J. (1995). *Enterprise and the State in Korea and Taiwan: Cornell Studies in Political Economy*, Ithaca, NY: Cornell University Press
(1998). "Is Small Beautiful? The Political Economy of Taiwan's Small-Scale Industry," in Eun Kim (ed.), *The Four Asian Tigers: Economic Development in the Global Political Economy*, London: Elsevier Academic Press
"Finding a Way out through Upgrading Technology" (*Gijutsu Saidoka De Katsuro*) (1996). *Mainichi Shinbun*, 5 December
Florida, Richard L. (2002). *The Rise of the Creative Class: And How It's Transforming Work, Leisure, Community and Everyday Life*, New York: Basic Books
Freeman, Christopher (1991). "Networks of Innovators: A Synthesis of Research Issues," *Research Policy* 20(5): 363–79
(1995) "The 'National System of Innovation' in Historical Perspective," *Cambridge Journal of Economics* 19: 5–24
Freeman, Christopher and Luc Soete (1997). *The Economics of Industrial Innovation*, 3rd edn., Cambridge, MA: MIT Press
Friedman, David (1988). *The Misunderstood Miracle: Industrial Development and Political Change in Japan: Cornell Studies in Political Economy*, Ithaca, NY: Cornell University Press
Fumio Hayashi, Edward Prescott (2003). "The 1990s in Japan: A Lost Decade," RECTI, EWC Tokyo Conference, August
Funabashi, Haruo (2002). "*Nihon Keizai Tei Mei No Shinin Wa Nani Ka: Keizaironri No 'Erosion' Moshi Wa 'Deterioration'*" (The Real Reason Behind Japan's Economic Slump: The Erosion and Deterioration of Business Ethics), *Look Japan*, June
Gao, Bai (2001). *Japan's Economic Dilemma: The Institutional Origins of Prosperity and Stagnation*, Cambridge: Cambridge University Press
Gem 2003 Executive Report (2003). Global Entrepreneurship Monitor
Gerlach, Michael L. and James R. Lincoln (1992). "The Organization of Business Networks in the United States and Japan," in Nitin Nohria and Robert G. Eccles (eds.), *Networks and Organizations: Structure, Form, and Action*, Boston, MA: Harvard Business School Press: xvi, 554

Gerlach, Michael L. and University of California Berkeley (1992). *Alliance Capitalism: The Social Organization of Japanese Business*, Center for Japanese Studies, Berkeley: University of California Press

Gilman, Theodore J. (2001). *No Miracles Here: Fighting Urban Decline in Japan and the United States*, Albany: State University of New York Press

The Global Competitiveness Report 2001–2002 (2002). *World Economic Forum, Geneva, Switzerland 2001*, ed. Peter K. Cornelius, New York: Oxford University Press

(2003). *The Global Competitiveness Report 2002–2003*. ed. Peter K. Cornelius, New York and Oxford: World Economic Forum, and Oxford University Press

Gonda, Kinji and Fumihiko Kakizaki (2001). "Knowledge Transfer in Agglomerations: A Regional Approach to Japanese Manufacturing Clusters," in *Innovative Clusters: Drivers of National Innovation Systems*, Paris: OECD

Grabher, Gernot (1993). *The Embedded Firm: On the Socioeconomics of Industrial Networks*, London and New York: Routledge

Granovetter, Mark (1985). "Economic Action and Social Structure: The Problem of Embeddedness," *American Journal of Sociology* 91: 481–510

Grimes, William (2001). *Unmasking the Japanese Miracle*. Ithaca, NY: Cornell University Press, May

Guangdong Statistical Yearbook (1980). Provincial Statistical Bureau

(1990). Provincial Statistical Bureau

(2001). Provincial Statistical Bureau

(2002). Provincial Statistical Bureau

Hall, Peter A. and David Soskice (eds.) (2001). *Varieties of Capitalism: The Institutional Foundations of Comparative Advantage*, Oxford: Oxford University Press

Harrison, Bennett (1994). *Lean and Mean: The Changing Landscape of Corporate Power in the Age of Flexibility*, New York: Basic Books

Hauknes, Johan (2003). *Innovation and Economic Behavior: Need for a New Approach?*, Oslo: STEP (Center for Innovation Research)

Health and Welfare Ministry (2002). *White Paper*

Herrigel, Gary (1996). *Industrial Constructions: The Sources of German Industrial Power, Structural Analysis in the Social Sciences 9*, Cambridge and New York: Cambridge University Press

(1997). "The Limits of German Manufacturing Flexibility," in Lowell Turner (ed.), *Negotiating the New Germany: Can Social Partnership Survive?*, Ithaca, NY and London: ILR Press

(2004). "Emerging Strategies and Forms of Governance in High-Wage Component Manufacturing Regions," *Industry and Innovation* 11(1/2): 45–79

Herrigel, Gary and Friedländer, Wittke (2004). "Varieties of Vertical Disintegration: The Global Trend toward Heterogeneous Supply Relations and the Reproduction of Difference in US and German Manufacturing," in Glenn Morgan, Eli Moen, and Richard Whitley (eds.), *Changing Capitalisms: Internationalisation, Institutional Change and Systems of Economic Organization*, Oxford: Oxford University Press

Herrigel, Gary and Sabel, Charles (1999). "Craft Production in Crisis," in Pepper D. Culpeper and David Finegold (eds.), *The German Skills Machine: Sustaining Comparative Advantage in a Global Economy*, New York and Oxford: Berghahn Books

Hertog, Pim den, Edward Bergman, and David Charles (eds.) (2001) *Innovative Clusters: Drivers of National Innovation Systems, Enterprise, Industry and Services*, Paris: OECD

Higuchi, J. and D. H. Whittaker (2003). *Kyoto Entrepreneurial Business: Course Module*, Doshisha University

Hirst, P. and Jonathan Zeitlin (1991). "Flexible Specialization versus Post-Fordism Theory: Evidence and Policy Implications," *Economy and Society* 20(1): 1–56

Horiuchi, Hiroshi (2001). *Kyoto Dakara Seiko Shita Bencha Kara Sekai Kigyo E* (We Succeeded Because We Were in Kyoto: From Venture Business to Global Company), Kyoto: Yanagihara Shoten

Ibata-Arens, Kathryn (2000). "The Business of Survival: Small and Medium Sized High Tech Firms in Japan," Special Edition on Dysfunctional Japan, *Asian Perspective* 24(4): 217–42

(2001). "*The Politics of Innovation: High Technology Small and Medium Sized Enterprises in Japan*," Dissertation, Northwestern University

(2003). "The Comparative Political Economy of Innovation," *Review of International Political Economy* 10(1), 147–65

(2004). "Alternatives to Hierarchy in Japan: Business Networks and Civic Entrepreneurship," *Asian Business and Management*, 3: 315–35

(2006). "Eschewing Japan's Production Pyramid: The Association of Small and Medium Sized Enterprise Entrepreneurs (SME Doyukai) 1947–1999," *Enterprise and Society*, Oxford: Oxford University Press, forthcoming

Imai, Kenichi (1992). "Japan's Corporate Networks," in Shumpei Kumon and Henry Rosovsky (eds.), *The Political Economy of Japan, 3: Cultural and Social Dynamics*, Stanford: Stanford University Press

(1998a). *Atarashii Nippon Sangyou No Ganban O Sagasu: Mono Dzukuri to Sofuto to Sabisu No Shinketsugou Ga Kagi, Jitsugyou no Nihon*, May

(1998b). *Benchaazu Infura* (The Infrastructure of Venture Companies), Tokyo: NTT Publishing

(1998c) "Chapter Nine: 'Human Networks,'" Conference Discussion at Kansai Silicon Valley Venture Forum (KSVF-KS Benchaa Foramu), with Moderator Shingo Yabuuchi, Managing Director, KS Venture Forum; Participants: Motohiro Okazawa, Administrative Director, Kansai Denryoku Inc.; Junpei Morimoto, Director of Engineering, Corporate Office and Corporate Vice Chairman, Obayashi Co.; Michikazu Murakami, Director, Management Planning Department, Sumitomo Electric Manufacturing, Inc," in *Venchasu Infura,* Tokyo: NTT Publishing

(2004). "*Nihon Wa Shin Kyoto Moderu De Sekai O Rido Subeki*" (Japan Should Lead the World the New Kyoto Model), *Global Communications Platform from Japan*, 5(4).

Imai, Kenichi, Ikujiro Nonaka and Hirotaka Takeuchi (1985). "Managing the New Product Development Process: How Japanese Companies Learn and Unlearn," in Kim B. Clark, Robert H. Hayes, and Christopher Lorenz (eds.), *The Uneasy Alliance: Managing the Productivity–Technology Dilemma*, Boston, MA: Harvard Business School Press

Inaba, Yushi (2002). "Managing New Local Industry Creation: A Japanese Case," Paper presented at the Joint Princeton–Northwestern Junior Scholars' Workshop on the Embedded Enterprise, Princeton, NJ

Inamori, Kazuo (2002). "Talking Business Series: Inamori Kazuo," *Look Japan*, February

Innovation/SMEs Programme (EC) (2003). "2003 European Innovation Scoreboard: Technical Paper No. 1: Indicators and Performance," Brussels: European Commission – Enterprise Directorate-General

Inoue, Hiroyuki (2003). "Activating Industrial Clusters – Rieti Cluster Seminar No. 5," in RIETI Cluster Seminar: Research Institute of Economy, Trade, and Industry

Inoue, Tomokazu and Tsukiji Tsuji (2001). "*Kyoto Shirikon Bare: Kyoto Gata Keiei Ni Okeru Onaa Gabanensu No Atto Teki Na Yasemi*" (Kyoto Silicon Valley: The Incredible Fierceness of Owner Governance in Kyoto-Style Management)," *Japan Economist* July 24

Invest Hong Kong Website (2004) (cited 23 November); available at http://www.investhk.com/gprdmain.aspx?id=607&code=GPRDMAIN

Ishikawa, Akira and Koji Tanaka (1999). *Kyoto Moderu: Gurobaru Sutandado Ni Idomu Nihonteki Keiei Senryaku (Kyoto Model: Management Strategy Challenges the Global Standard)*, Tokyo: Prentice Education

Ishikura, Y., M. Fujita, N. Maeda, K. Kanai, and A. Yamasaki (2003). *Strategy for Cluster Initiatives in Japan*, Tokyo: Yuhikaku Publishing

Japan Association of Small and Medium-Sized Enterprises (1997). "*Chushokigyo Toshi Renraku Kyogikai Kyodo Chosa Hokokusho,*

Daiikai Shuchokigyo Toshi Samitto" (Cooperative Survey Report of Small to Medium-Sized Enterprises), Paper presented at the First Annual SME City Summit

Japan Association of Small and Medium-Sized Enterprises (1998). "*Miryoku Aru Chushokigyo Toshi No Sozo*" (Creating Attractive "SME Cities"), Paper presented at the Chushokigyo Toshi Sumitto (SME City Summit), Japan Association of Small and Medium Sized Enterprises, Tokyo Otaku Sangyo Puraza Pio

Japan. Chusho Kigyo Cho (1990). *90 Nendai No Chusho kigyo Bijon: Sozo no Botai to Shite No Chusho kigyo*, Tokyo: Tsusho Sangyo Chosakai

Japan Industrial Statistics Bulletin (2000)

Japan Industry Revenue Bulletin (1999)

Japan National Census Bulletin (2000)

Japan Small and Medium-Size Enterprise Agency (1998). "*Chusho Kigyo Hakusho*" (SME White Paper), Tokyo: Ministry of Finance

Japan Small and Medium-Size Enterprise Agency (2003). "*Chusho Kigyo Hakusho*" (SME White Paper), Tokyo: Ministry of Finance

Johnson, Chalmers A. (1986). *MITI and the Japanese Miracle: The Growth of Industrial Policy, 1925–1975*, 1st Tuttle edn., Tokyo: Charles E. Tuttle Co.

(1995). *Japan, Who Governs?: The Rise of the Developmental State*, 1st edn., New York: Norton

Johnstone, Bob (1999). *We Were Burning: Japanese Entrepreneurs and the Forging of the Electronic Age*, New York: Basic Books

Katz, Richard (1998). *Japan: The System That Soured, The Rise and Fall of the Japanese Economic Miracle*, Armonk, NY: M. E. Sharpe

(2003). *Japanese Phoenix: The Long Road to Economic Revival*, Armonk, NY: M. E. Sharpe

Keisuke, Nakamura (1996). *Nihon No Shokuba to Seisan Shisutemu* (Tokyo: University of Tokyo Press)

Koike, Kazuo (1995). *Shigoto No Keizaigaku* (Economics of Work in Japan), Long Term Credit Bank Foundation, Tokyo: Toyo Keizai Shinbunsha

Koseki, Tomohiro (2002). *Monodsukuri No Jidai* (The Age of Manufacturing), 155, Tokyo: NHK Library

Krugman, Paul R. (1991). *Geography and Trade*, Gaston Eyskens Lecture Series, Leuven and Cambridge, MA: Leuven University Press and MIT Press

Kumon, Shumpei (1992). "Japan as Network Society," in Shumpei Kumon and Henry Rosovsky (eds.), *The Political Economy of Japan, 3: Cultural and Social Dynamics*, Stanford: Stanford University Press

Kunii, Irene (1999). "Japan's High Tech Hope: Kyoto's Entrepreneurship and Can-Do Exuberance Unmatched by Any Other City in the Country," *Business Week*, May 31

Lamoreaux, N. R. Daniel M. G. Raff, and Peter Temin (1999). *Learning by Doing in Markets, Firms, and Countries* (Chicago, IL: University of Chicago Press)

Lies, Elaine (2003). "Japan Moves to Curb Horrific Suicide Rate," (Tokyo) Reuters, May

Lincoln, Edward J. (2001). *Arthritic Japan: The Slow Pace of Economic Reform*, Washington, DC: Brookings Institution Press

Locke, Richard M. (1995). *Remaking the Italian Economy, Cornell Studies in Political Economy*, Ithaca, NY: Cornell University Press

Lundvall, Bengt-Ake (ed.) (1992). *National Systems of Innovation: Towards a Theory of Innovation and Interactive Learning*, London: Pinter

Marshall, Alfred (1890). *Principles of Economics*, London and New York: Macmillan

Matsumoto, Toshiji (1996). *Monodsukuriniikiru* (Living by Making), Tokyo: Kamata Minsh Maisuta Hakkan Iinkai

METI (2002a). "*Bencha No To: Kyoto No Torikumi*" (Venture City: Kyoto's Challenge), Ministry of Economy, Trade and Industry

(2002b). "*Kinkichiiki Ni Okeru Sangakukanrenkei No Genjoy Ni Tsuite*" (The State of Industry–University Relations in the Kinki Region), Kinki: Office for the Promotion of Industry–University Relations, Ministry of Economy, Trade and Industry

(2002c). "*Sangyo Kurasuta Keikaku Ni Tsuite Purojekuto Gaiyo*" (Regarding the Industrial Cluster Plan: Project Summary), Ministry of Economy, Trade and Industry Regional Economy Industrial Group

(2002d). "*Sangyo Kurasuta Keikaku Ni Tsuite, Chiikisaisei Sangyoshushukeikaku* (Regarding the Industrial Cluster Plan: Project Summary), Ministry of Economy, Trade and Industry Regional Economy Industrial Group

(2002e). *METI White Paper* (Tokyo: Gyosei Press)

(2003a). *METI White Paper* (Tokyo: Gyosei Press)

METI Kinki Region (2003a). "*Kaurasuta Coa Jittai Chosa*" (Cluster Core Survey on Actual Conditions), in *2002 Annual Survey on the Actual Conditions Among SMEs*, Kinki: Ministry of Economy, Trade and Industry

METI Kinki Region (2003b). "*Kaurasuta Coa Jittai Chosa*" (Cluster Core Survey on Actual Conditions), in *2002 Annual Survey on the Actual Conditions Among SMEs*, Kinki: METI

Mitsubishi Research Institute (MRI) (1996). "*Shuseki Jibasangyo Shinnettwaaku Kochiku, Jireichosa*" (Comprehensive Report on the

Structure of Local New Business Networks: Case Study Report), Tokyo: Mitsubishi Research Institute, March 29

Miyashita, Kenichi and David Russell (1994). *Keiretsu: Inside the Hidden Japanese Conglomerates*, New York: McGraw-Hill

Morales, Rebecca (1994). *Flexible Production: Restructuring of the International Automobile Industry*, Cambridge: Polity Press

Murakami, Michikazu (1998). "Chapter Nine Human Networks: Panel Discussion," in *Benchazu Infura*, Tokyo: NTT Publishing

Naikakucho (2001). *Regional Economic Report*

Nakagawa, Takeo (2003). "The Creation of Intellectual Clusters in Japan – Rieti Cluster Seminar No. 3," Paper presented at the RIETI Cluster Seminar, May 16

Nelson, Richard R. (ed.) (1993). *National Innovation Systems: A Comparative Analysis*, New York: Oxford University Press

New and Hi-Tech Industries in Pearl River Delta (Hong Kong Trade Development Council Website), 2004 (cited 24 November 2004); available at http://www.tdctrade.com/econforum/tdc/tdc030802.htm

NHK (1997) "*Koba no Kaigai Iteno Minaose*" (Re-Considering the Move of Manufacturing Plants Overseas), *NHK Kurosappu Gendai*, NHK

Nonami, Masaki (1998). "*Chousakekka, Higashi Osaka Nikan Kougyou Shinbun*" (Investigation Notes Prepared by Masaki Nonami, Higashi Osaka Bureau Reporter, Business and Technology News, November 9, 1998 Interview), Higashi Osaka

Odagiri, Hiroyuki and Akira Goto (1993). "The Japanese System of Innovation, Past, Present and Future," in Richard R. Nelson (ed.) *National Innovation Systems: A Comparative Analysis*, New York: Oxford University Press: x, 541

OECD (1994). *The Measurement of Scientific and Technological Activities: Proposed Standard Practice for Surveys of Research and Experimental Development* (Frascati Manual), 5th edn., Paris and Washington, DC: OECD

(1996). SMEs: *Employment, Innovation and Growth*, Paris: OECD

(1997). *Oslo Manual: Proposed Guidelines for Collecting and Interpreting Technological Innovation Data*, Paris: OECD and European Commission, Eurostat

(1999). *Scoreboard of Indicators*, Paris: OECD

(2000). *Indicators of Industrial Activity, Main Industrial Indicators Database* (Paris: OECD)

(2001). *Innovative Clusters: Drivers of National Innovation Systems*, Paris: OECD

Oguri, S (1998). "*Chiiki Keizai No Saisei to Chushokigyou Nettowaaku*" (Networks and the Revitalization of Regional Economies), Unpublished paper presented to the Tokyo Chapter of the Association for Small and Medium Size Enterprises, Tokyo

Okamura, Nobukatsu (2003). *Chosen Suru Kyoto No Kosei Ha Kigyo 70 Sha (The Kyoto Challenge: 70 Unique Companies)*, Tokyo: Nikan Kogyo Shinbun

Okazawa, Motohiro (1998). *Benchaazu Infura* (The Infrastructure of Venture Companies), Tokyo: NTT Publishing

Omae, Kenichi (1995). *The End of the Nation State: The Rise of Regional Economies*, New York: Harper Collins

Osaka Small and Medium Sized Enterprise Information Center (OSBIC) (1997). "*Higashi Osaka Ni Okeru Chushokigyo No Shuseki to Kigyo Nettowaaku No Henbo*" (Industrial Concentration of Small and Medium Size Firms in Higashi Osaka and Changes in Network Formation among Higashi Osaka Firms), Osaka: OSBIC

Pages, Erik, Doris Freedman, and Patrick Von Baren (2003). "Entrepreneurship as a State and Local Economic Development Strategy," in David M. Hart (ed.), *The Emergence of Entrepreneurship Policy*, Cambridge: Cambridge University Press

Pempel, T. J. (1979). "Corporatism without Labor? The Japanese Anomaly," in Philippe Lembruch and Gerhard Schmitter (eds.), *Trends toward Corporatist Intermediation*, London: Sage

Perrow, Charles (1992). "Small Firm Networks," in Nitin Nohria and Robert Eccles (eds.), *Networks and Organizations: Structure, Form, and Action*, Cambridge, MA: Harvard Business School Press

Piore, Michael J. and Charles F. Sabel (1984). *The Second Industrial Divide: Possibilities for Prosperity*, New York: Basic Books

"Planning Frameworks of Guangzhou, Shenzhen, Zhuhai and Macau," (Working Paper No: 3), Hong Kong: Hong Kong SAR Planning Department

Porter, Michael E. (1990). *The Competitive Advantage of Nations*, London: Macmillan

(1998). *On Competition, Harvard Business Review Book Series*, Boston: Harvard Business School Publishing

(1999). *Clusters and Competition* (Cambridge, MA: Harvard University Press)

Porter, Michael E., Hirotaka Takeuchi, and Mariko Sakakibara (2000). *Can Japan Compete?* Cambridge, MA: Perseus Publishing

Porter, Michael E. and Scott Stern (2002). "The Impact of Location on Global Innovation: Findings from the National Innovative Capacity Index" (*The Global Competitiveness Report 2002*)

Powell, Walter W. (1990). "Neither Market nor Hierarchy: Network Forms of Organization," in B. M. Staw and L. L. Cummings (eds.), *Research in*

Organizational Behavior: An Annual Series of Analytical Essays and Critical Reviews, Greenwich and London: JAI Press: 295–336

Regulations on Special Economic Zones in Guangdong Province (1980) (cited 24 November 2004); available at http://www.novexcn.com/guangdong_regs_on_sez.html

Ritchev, Dimitry and Robert E. Cole (1999). "The Role of Organizational Discontinuity in High Technology: Insights from a US–Japan Comparison," Unpublished paper, February

Roelandt, T. J. A. and Pim den Hertog (1998). "Cluster Analyses & Cluster-Based Policy in OECD Countries," Paris: OECD

Sakaguchi, Syunichi, Yuji Uenishi, and Hitoshi Mashimo (2003). *New Wave in Supporting Baby Companies: Activities of Kyoto Business Model Empowerment Center*, Kyoto Chamber of Commerce and Industry (PDF file) (cited May 9, 2004); available at http://www.mtc.pref.kyoto.jp/shien-kenkyu/2003/

Sakai, Kuniyasu (1990). "The Feudal World of Japanese Manufacturing," *Harvard Business Review* 68(6)

Sako, Mari (1994). "Neither Markets nor Hierarchies," in P. C. Schmitter, W. Streeck, and J. R. Hollingsworth (eds.), *Governing Capitalist Economies: Performance and Control of Economic Sectors*, New York: Oxford University Press

Satoshi, Kamata (2004). "Toyota: Suicide and Worker Depression at the World's Most Profitable Manufacturer," *Japan Focus*, 1 November

Sawai, Minoru (1999). "Noda Shouichi and Roku-Roku Shouten, a Machine Tool Manufacturer: A Case Study of a Competent Small-to-Medium Sized Enterprise in Pre-War and Wartime Japan," *Institute of Social Science* 2(1): 107–22

Saxenian, AnnaLee (1990). "Regional Networks and the Resurgence of Silicon Valley," *California Management Review* 33(1): 89–112

(1994a). "Lessons from Silicon Valley," *Technology Review*, July: 42–51.

(1994b). *Regional Advantage: Culture and Competition in Silicon Valley and Route 128*, Cambridge, MA: Harvard University Press, 2nd edn. (1998)

Schumpeter, Joseph Alois (1934). *The Theory of Economic Development*, Cambridge, MA: Harvard University Press

Scott, Allen John (1999). "The Geographic Foundations of Industrial Performance," in Alfred Dupont Chandler, Peter Hagstrom, and Örjan Sölvell (eds.), *The Dynamic Firm: The Role of Technology, Strategy, Organization, and Regions*, Oxford: Oxford University Press

Sellers, Jefferey M. (2002). *Governing from Below: Urban Regions and the Global Economy, Cambridge Studies in Comparative Politics*, Cambridge and New York: Cambridge University Press

Sengenberger, Werner, G. Loveman, and Michael J. Piore (1990). *The Re-Emergence of Small Enterprises: Industrial Restructuring in Industrialised Countries*, Geneva: International Institute for Labour Studies

Shinoya, Yuuichi and Mark Perlman (eds.) (1994). *Innovation in Technology, Industries and Institutions: Studies in Schumpeterian Perspectives*, Ann Arbor: University of Michigan Press

Simmie, James (1997). *Innovation, Networks, and Learning Regions? (Regional Policy and Development, 18)*, London: Jessica Kingsley

Simmie, James, Corinne Siino, Jean-Mark Zuliana, Guy Jalabert, and Simone Strambach (2004). "Local Innovation System Governance and Performance: A Comparative Analysis of Oxfordshire, Stuttgart and Toulouse," *International Journal of Technology Management* 28(3–6)

SME, Agency (1999). *SME White Paper*

(2002). SME *White Paper*

Smitka, Michael (1991). *Competitive Ties: Subcontracting in the Japanese Automotive Industry*, New York: Columbia University Press

(1996). *The Decline of the Japanese Automotive Industry: Causes and Implications*, Cambridge, MA: Center for International Studies MIT Japan Program

Southcn.Com Website – Pearl River Delta: The Largest Hi-Tech Industry Belt in China (2002) (cited November 24); available at http://www.southcn.com/english/features/pearlbelt/analysis/200205151213.htm

Spiritual Civilization Development of Guangdong (Government's Official Website of Guangdong) (2004) (cited November 24); available at http://www.gd.gov.cn/GD_Info/GD_3_3_e.asp

STLRCGA (St. Louis Regional Chamber and Growth Association) (2004) (cited September 1); available at http://www.econdev.stlrcga.org

Storper, Michael (1997). *The Regional World: Territorial Development in a Global Economy, Perspectives on Economic Change*, New York: Guilford Press

Strambach, Simone (2002). "Change in the Innovation Process: New Knowledge Production and Competitive Cities – the Case of Stuttgart," *European Planning Studies* 10(2): 215–31

Strategic Thoughts on Integrating the Economies of Guangdong and Hong Kong (Hong Kong Trade Development Council Website) (2001) (cited November 24); available at http://www.tdctrade.com/econforum/boc/boc010101.htm

Streeck, Wolfgang and Kozo Yamamura (eds.) (2001). *The Origins of Nonliberal Capitalism*, ed. Peter J. Katzenstein, *Cornell Studies in Political Economy*, Ithaca, NY: Cornell University Press

Suematsu, Chihiro (2002). *Kyoto Yoshiki Mojuruka Senryaku* (Kyoto System of Modulization Strategy), Tokyo: Nihon Keizai Shinbun

Takeda, Shuzaburo (2002). *Demingu No Soshiki Ron* (Beyond Bureaucracy), Tokyo: Toyo Keizai Shinpousha

(2003a). "Japanese Challenges to Change her Culture," Paper presented at the Conference on Institutional Responses to the Changing Research Environment, Bonn

(2003b). "Japanese Innovation Policy: From Phenotype to Genotype," Paper presented at the International Conference on Technology Clusters, Montreal

Talking Business Series (2002). "Talking Business Series: Inamori Kazuo," *Look Japan* February

Tanaka, Toshio (2003). *Kyoto Genki Kigyo Dokuso No Kiseki* (Healthy Kyoto Firms: The Original Wonder), Kyoto: Kyoto Shinbun Publishing Center

Taneda, Ryuji (2003). "*Dento Kara Sentangijutsu O Unda Kyoto Kigyo*" (Advanced Technology Kyoto Firms Born from Tradition), *Look Japan* December

Todtling, Franz and Alexander Kaufmann (1999). "Innovation Systems in Regions of Europe: A Comparative Perspective," *European Planning Studies* 7(6)

Tokyo Manufacturing (2001). *Summer Report of Comprehensive Survey Results (Tokyo No Kogyo Hensen 13 Kogyo Sukeichosa Sokuho Yori)*, Tokyo to sumukyoku sokeibu (Tokyo City Management Agency Statistics Division)

Ueda, Hirofumi (1997). "The Subcontracting System and Business Groups: The Case of the Japanese Automotive Industry," in Takao Shiba and Masahiro Shimotani (eds.), *Beyond the Firm: Business Groups in International and Historical Perspective*, Oxford: Oxford University Press

US Economic Census (1997). Available from http://www.census.gov/epid/www/guide.html

Uzzi, Brian (1996). "The Sources and Consequences of Embeddedness for the Economic Performance of Organizations: The Network Effect," *American Sociological Review* 61: 674–98

(1997). "Social Structure and Competition in Interfirm Networks: The Paradox of Embeddedness," *Administrative Science Quarterly*, 42: 35–67

Verbeek, Hessel (1999). "Innovative Clusters: Identification of Value-Adding Production Chains and Their Networks of Innovation, an International Study," Erasmus University, Rotterdam

Wada, Koji (2003). "Developmment of Policies to Support Industrial Agglomerations in Japan and Future Issues," in H. Fukushima (ed.), *Globalization, Regional Concentration and Clustering of Industry*,

Tokyo: Research Institute of Economic Science, College of Economics, Nihon University

Walsh, Mary Williams (2004). "Tyco Unit Loses Patent-Infringement Case," *The New York Times*, March 27

Wang, H. (1998). *Technology, Economic Security, State, and the Political Economy of Economic Networks: A Historical and Comparative Research on the Evolution of Economic Networks in Taiwan and Japan*, Lanham, MD: University Press of America

Whittaker, D. H. (1997). *Small Firms in the Japanese Economy*, Cambridge: Cambridge University Press

Worldwide Agriculture and Forestry Bulletin (2000). Ministry of Agriculture, Forestries and Fishing; available at http://www.maff.go.jp/esokuhou/index.html

Wright, Gavin (1999). "Can a Nation Learn? American Technology as a Network Phenomenon," in Naomi R. Lamoreaux, Daniel M. G. Raff, and Peter Temin (eds.), *Learning by Doing in Markets, Firms, and Countries* (Chicago, IL: University of Chicago Press, 1999)

Yamamura, Kozo and Wolfgang Streeck (2003). *The End of Diversity?: Prospects for German and Japanese Capitalism. Cornell Studies in Political Economy*, Ithaca, NY: Cornell University Press

Yamashita, Shoichi (1995). "Japan's Role as Regional Technological Integrator and the Black Box Phenomenon in the Process of Technology Transfer," in Denis Fred Simon (ed.), *The Emerging Technological Trajectory of the Pacific Rim* (Armonk, NY: M. E. Sharpe, 1995)

Yano, Hiroshi (2001). "Armed with User Know-How, Providing Tailored Information Systems" (Yuzaa Nohau O Buki Ni Saiteki Na Joho Shisutemu O Tei Kyo: Araki Takehiko), *Management and Technology*, October

Index